I ORDER YOU TO HOPE
Memories of Youth in the Time of the Nazis

I ORDER YOU TO HOPE
Memories of Youth in the Time of the Nazis

Gisèle Rey-Roberts

The Book Guild Ltd.
Sussex, England

This book is sold subject to the condition that it shall not, by way of trade or otherwise, be lent, re-sold, hired out, photocopied or held in any retrieval system or otherwise circulated without the publisher's prior consent in any form of binding or cover other than that in which this is published and without a similar condition including this condition being imposed on the subsequent purchaser.

The Book Guild Ltd.
25 High Street,
Lewes, Sussex

First published 1993
© Gisèle Roberts 1993

Set in Baskerville
Typesetting by Kudos Graphics,
Slinfold, West Sussex

Printed in Great Britain by
Antony Rowe Ltd.
Chippenham, Wiltshire.

A catalogue record for this book is
available from the British Library

ISBN 0 86332 772 9

CONTENTS

Map		7
Foreword		9

Part One: In The Unoccupied Zone

Chapter 1	*The Last Day*	13
Chapter 2	*By the River*	15
Chapter 3	*Refugees*	19
Chapter 4	*Opinions and Attitudes*	25
Chapter 5	*The Mysterious Caller*	29
Chapter 6	*Delayed Departure*	32
Chapter 7	*The Return of the News-bearer*	35
Chapter 8	*The Beginning of Term*	41
Chapter 9	*Life with Father*	45
Chapter 10	*Thoughts of England*	49
Chapter 11	*School-Days Under the New Regime*	52
Chapter 12	*A Studious Summer*	59
Chapter 13	*What Now?*	65
Chapter 14	*Guests on Their Way*	69
Chapter 15	*The Opportunist and Others*	73
Chapter 16	*New Horizons*	80
Chapter 17	*Visit to Grand'mère*	85
Chapter 18	*Exodus*	90
Chapter 19	*Keeping Us Guessing*	97
Chapter 20	*Destination: the North*	102

Part Two: Under the New Order

Chapter 21	*Home-Coming*	109
Chapter 22	*The Sorrows of Others*	112

Chapter 23	*Friends and Foes*	117
Chapter 24	*Into Another Year*	122
Chapter 25	*Correspondence*	129
Chapter 26	*The Old Gentleman*	132
Chapter 27	*The Star of David*	136
Chapter 28	*My Spell in Paris*	138
Chapter 29	*Hospitality*	142
Chapter 30	*Vive le Roi Albert!*	147
Chapter 31	*The Easter Break*	151
Chapter 32	*The 'Zone Libre' Revisited*	158
Chapter 33	*Wagon-lit*	165
Chapter 34	*The City of Beauty and Sadness*	169
Chapter 35	*Life With My Friends*	173
Chapter 36	*Mein Onkel*	177
Chapter 37	*Farewells*	182
Chapter 38	*Working For Father*	189
Chapter 39	*Freedom of the Press*	193
Chapter 40	*The Rugby Match*	197
Chapter 41	*The Challenge of the Curfew*	202
Chapter 42	*Heavy Seas*	207
Chapter 43	*Confidential Matters*	212
Chapter 44	*High Risk Activity*	215
Chapter 45	*The Dawn of Hope*	218
Chapter 46	*Bad News*	222
Chapter 47	*Early Morning Call*	226
Chapter 48	*The Crime of Carlos Bonar*	231
Chapter 49	*While We Wait*	234
Chapter 50	*The Third of September . . .*	239
Chapter 51	*. . . And the Days that Followed*	246

Part Three: . . . And Beyond

Chapter 52	*The Town and the Tommies*	255
Chapter 53	*Not Such A Happy New Year*	262
Chapter 54	*Happy Moments*	271
Chapter 55	*Legacy of the Occupation*	275
Chapter 56	*The Railway Bride*	284
Chapter 57	*Dénouements*	292

Postscript 300

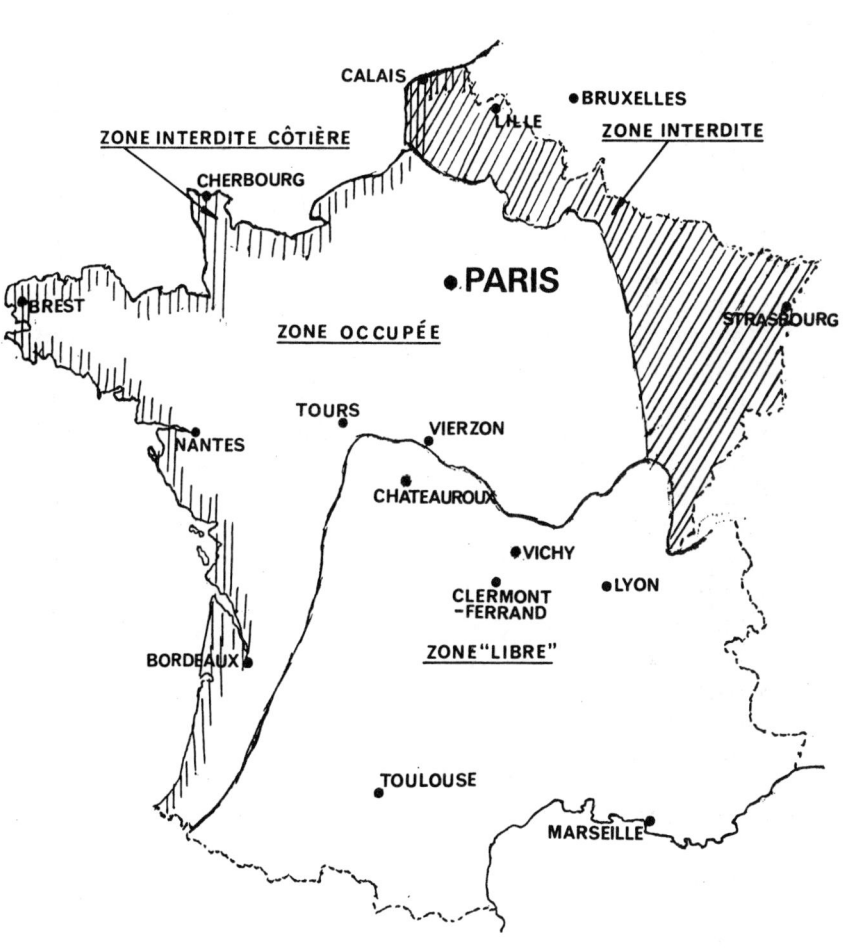

FOREWORD

This narrative attempts to look back over the years of Vichy government and German occupation and to recapture the impressions of that grim era before they fade from my memory. I was seventeen at the outbreak of war, patriotic, idealistic, and I had faith in humanity. The shock inflicted to these candid sentiments by the events that followed, not least by the conduct of some of my own countrymen, has ensured that those impressions remain with great clarity. The memory of my experiences and observations has been assisted by the fact that my father was a hoarder of documents and correspondence, much of which has added evidence to my recollections.

I have tried to chronicle the atmosphere of the war years through everyday events, school, family life, contacts with people I knew or encountered, and to select from amongst so many vivid memories those which reflect the time most truthfully. These are of course personal reminiscences – my own experience is not necessarily typical – just a record of a period of history as it affected me as a young person. Because the years of Nazi tyranny seemed endless, life had to go on and we adapted to the circumstances. They became the norm of our existence. Yet most of us knew in the depth of our hearts that this way of life was transitory, that one day we would return to the way we had known. The unwavering feeling of hope which never left me and which I shared with many others kept us going. Writing these pages, I came once more to realize how lucky our family was to emerge unscathed from the war years when so many we knew have not survived to tell their tale – although our luck sometimes held by a thread.

In my story I have preferred to give people fictitious names, but the people themselves were real enough. The only true names are those of my immediate family.

How gratified I would have been, had my parents and my brother Gilbert been able to share in these recollections. Sadly they all died too soon even to know of my intention to put them down on paper. But I thought that a period of our life when our closeness as a family, our support for each other, our involvement, kept our morale high, deserved to be recorded, if only for my children and grandchildren.

PART ONE

IN THE UNOCCUPIED ZONE

1

The Last Day

It was the last day of the exams. They took place at the local *Collège de garçons* instead of the nearest university town where in normal times they would have been held. The authorities had quickly set up an emergency scheme because of the chaotic war situation and the complete disorganization in the country, with millions of refugees and retreating troops pouring into every town south of the Loire. The news was bad, yet we were still hoping against hope. I walked into the exam room feeling, like the other candidates, in a state of gloom; we had felt like that during the four days of the examinations, but somehow we had not experienced the usual exam fright, that sensation which paralyses your mind when you need it most. On the contrary, the extreme concentration had been beneficial and had helped to alleviate the universal heart-ache.

Today we were sitting the English exam, my best subject, for I had spent two enjoyable holidays in England when I had been able to master the language. I found the paper easy, even satisfying and I had finished before everybody else. So I left the class-room and went outside to wait in the sunshine.

Little by little I was joined by the others and by the staff and someone broke the news. It was really over! France had capitulated to the victorious armies of Hitler's Reich. The very word capitulation sounded like doom. We had expected it, yet when it came it was a great shock. Suddenly life had lost its meaning, had come to an end. It was not just the last day of the exams, it was the last day of our country, our last day. We did not yet know the details of the terms but it meant disaster and shame and many of us cried. I could not conceive a world without France, the future did not exist anymore and the pain was unbearable.

Now we had to go home, to our families, and nobody asked me if I had done well in the exam. My mother and two young brothers, who were not at school because it had been taken over for the exams, had been listening to the radio all the morning, and here I found renewed despair, all the more because my father was somewhere in the mêlée and we had received no news from him since the hostilities had started in earnest. You could not just stand there and cry. Somehow the sheer material necessities of life would take over and claim your attention, then the feeling of anguish would return and you remembered why.

2

By the River

The sun shone endlessly in a cloudless sky. It was a beautiful summer that seemed to invite all the world to leisure, to joy, to laze in the sunshine and to be merry. It was like a cruel irony. My brothers were finishing their term at school but I had broken up and I was expected to revise for the oral exams which were usually held two or three weeks after the written papers. The oral accounted for a large part of the Baccalauréat at both levels and included most subjects, some difficult like physics and chemistry. I tried to revise but I felt quite incapable of fixing my attention. As I sat on the bench in the garden with my book, I could only think of the situation or doze in the sunshine. My mother sat with me, disconsolate and anxious; always a pessimist, she was quite sure that my father had been killed. I tried to reason with her, pointing out that there had been little resistance and that there could not be many casualties, not like in the First World War. There were so many soldiers arriving in the region, he might just turn up, especially as he was not in a fighting unit, but she persisted in her gloom.

Her task was not easy, having the responsiblity of three teenage children still at school, in the middle of this disastrous and uncertain situation. We were ourselves like refugees here; our home was in Brussels where we had lived for many years but when war was declared, my father, who had heard many dreadful stories from Belgian people about the invasion of Belgium in 1914, had insisted that we took refuge with his relations in southern France. Then he had himself been immediately called up. His family lived in a village not well served by transport, so when the term started in our new collèges, we had to move to the town and rent a house. It was a pleasant enough house to look at. The size was adequate, but it was completely devoid of modern comforts. No running water, we had to collect it from a pump in a shed outside, and for cooking, we had an old-fashioned coal cooking stove and a primitive two-ring gas plate. No bathroom, of course, We bought a tub and had to do our ablutions in the kitchen. Sparsely furnished and with no heating appliances, it had obviously been meant as a summer house. The first winter of the war, which had been very cold, we purchased a wood-burning stove which was installed with a long flue pipe running right across the living room.

We made the place quite cosy and in spite of the lack of comfort, we managed. Now that the débâcle had arrived, how thankful we were to be settled here and to be spared the fate of the refugees pouring in from the north. The large garden was very pleasant; one entered it by a grand gate, rather out of keeping with the modest house, and it contained some fine established trees and a variety of bushes. There was a bench where we were now sitting, under a lime tree, by a small pond. We returned to the burning theme and discussed the news once more, expressing some relief that the cessation of hostilities meant that the German troops would advance no further, at least for the time being, for who could trust the pledge of a power which had committed so many violations?

The son and daughter of our neighbours came in and had a little chat with us, commiserating for a while, and they asked me if I would join them for a swim in the river. Why not? The feel of the water would be soothing.

A group of us would often meet after school in a thicket on the bank where the water was easily accessible. I found the others already there, sitting in the shade. Instead of swimming, they were engaged in conversation. We joined the party and entered the discussion, but my neighbour Jojo had little to say. He made a long face, brooding over his lost dream of joining the airforce and training as a pilot. Someone retorted that perhaps all was not lost for ever, that the colonies might serve as a springboard to carry on the struggle, that Britain was still in the war. Jojo's sister

Hélène, who was in the second year of her English degree at Toulouse university, echoed her brother's mood. She feared that English would hardly be a subject encouraged by our new masters. We all aired our anxiety about our own futures within the new dimension caused by these events.

Only Gérard Marchand was saying nothing. He was sitting with his arms crossed on his chest, his chin thrust forward, the only one of us not in his swimming gear because he did not like water. He looked as though he was about to pounce. Then without hesitating, he launched into a diatribe against our past governments, our politicians and democracy in particular and he pursued his line with great determination in spite of the occasional calls of 'you are mad' or 'you have been indoctrinated by "le traître de Stuttgart".'[1]

'This military defeat is not a catastrophe,' he said, 'it serves us right for being so decadent, it is going to open our eyes and bring a new order!'

There was no stopping Marchand. It was not a debate. It was a monologue, so outrageous to our ears that we could not find the words to engage in controversy. I knew there were Fascists in France, even a Fascist party, the PSF, but in my innocence, I would never have believed that a friend could deliver such a speech the day after the collapse of our country. I felt so uneasy, I had to escape and I slipped into the water, hoping that it would heal my wounded emotions. I swam across to the other side and the cool water acted like a balm on my body. The river was wide and when I reached the other side, quite exhausted, I had calmed down. When I returned, more composed, nobody had yet gone in for a swim and some of the boys were now lashing out at Marchand. There was a newcomer to our swimming group, a boy called Jean-Paul, newly arrived from Paris as a refugee. Although he looked very young he seemed more mature than his seventeen years and he was finding the right words to deride Marchand's opinions and at the same time trying to reason with him. Marchand had somewhat run out of steam, but the others, in spite of their disapproval, were not averse to blaming and condemning

---

[1] The French equivalent of the British Lord Haw-Haw.

our leaders for our present predicament. I sided with Jean-Paul in their defence, with the argument that whatever their failure to be ready for a war they had not wanted, the crime lay only with Hitler and his henchmen, with the nation which sent its hordes to crush other peaceful lands, sowing destruction and death in its wake.

I was intrigued by Jean-Paul. His pleasing features crowned by unruly locks of fair hair, his eyes of an unusual dark amber that smiled amiably and tended to drift away in a world of their own, awoke in me a certain romantic fascination.

I learnt from the others who had befriended him at the Collège that his father was a professor at the Sorbonne who had chosen to stay in Paris, yet had sent his family to safety. Jean-Paul's mother and sister were in another town, but he himself resided here in the refugee-centre, opting for complete independence. I also learnt that he was a gifted pianist and that he had befriended a family who owned a grand piano, so that he could indulge in his favourite pastime.

Decades later, when those afternoons by the riverside had faded from memory, I heard a radio programme about French academics who had been victims of the Nazis and the surname of one professor who had been executed sounded familiar, an unusual surname. Then I remembered it was the same as Jean-Paul's whom I used to meet by the river – very likely it had been his father.

3

Refugees

The sun shone brighter than ever and life had to go on.

The political scene was beginning to take shape. France was to be divided into two zones. The northern half would be under the administration of the German army, while in the south, we were to have a self-appointed government, residing in Vichy of all places. It would dissolve all our political institutions and replace the Republic by *l'Etat Français*. But in Britain the war went on and Churchill was galvanizing his country in a fight to the finish.

The BBC became our frequent source of news since in London resided also that young French General who had not accepted defeat and wanted to fight on to preserve the Republic. Many listened to his appeal at the end of June 1940 and a little ray of confidence and hope returned to some hearts.

When the military situation had looked totally desperate, we had indeed met a person amongst those fleeing from Paris, who had mentioned a young general of her acquaintance. She had declared that he was so dedicated, so capable, that he could not fail to do something, even in this last hour, to redress the situation.

'We shall hear of him,' she concluded.

But the young general had only just been promoted from the rank of colonel and his name was unknown to the French public. Where were all the others? The well known politicians, the service chiefs, the personalities whose names would appeal to the population? The whole nation seemed stunned, paralysed, it must be suffering from concussion.

In the climate of these early days it did not help people's

confusion and soul-searching that the name of Charles de Gaulle, who wanted to continue the struggle from London, was obscure whilst the name of Marshal Pétain, who was capitulating, had been and still was a famous and respected name.

Our senile old 'Maréchal' made many speeches, usually live on the radio and usually disapproving of 'Monsieur Churchill'. On one occasion, when he had said in a quavering voice:

'Monsieur Churchill – est juge – des intérêts de son pays, – il ne l'est pas – des intérêts – du nôtre!' He added for himself and certainly not for public consumption: 'this place is full of draughts'!

It gave us the chance of a good laugh but to our disappointment, it was cut off from the later recorded version.

The refugees were still crowding into the town; some came by train and the small station was constantly swarming with new arrivals. The streets were packed with overloaded cars. These families who had left everything behind to flee the invaders were a distressing sight; some did not know where to go next and others were unable to find accommodation for the hotels were bursting at the seams. We were constantly on the lookout for somebody we might know. I did recognize a girl from my school in Brussels one day, but her family was going on south and there was no help we could offer them.

The sudden increase in population posed considerable problems for the small towns in the region. They had to improvise reception centres and provide large quantities of food.

The Boy Scouts had been immediately mobilized to attend to the needs of this mass of people. My brothers, who were only aged thirteen and fourteen, were members of this organization and it gave them a great sense of achievement to take part in the relief operation. In spite of adversity, there were some comical incidents. My brother Gilbert came home one evening with the story of the fat Belgian lady, obviously dissatisfied with her rations, who thought that by changing her clothes several times, she could pretend to be several people and obtain several servings. Gilbert had noticed her little game and he unmasked her with a few words in her own priceless accent that he could well imitate. After all there had to be fair distribution to ensure that nobody went hungry.

There was a run on provisions which had not yet been rationed, and one day, on returning from a difficult shopping expedition, I saw a car with a Belgian number parked in our drive. I hurried towards the house, curious to see who had arrived. It was the Bonar family, old friends from Brussels with two young children. I greeted them with open arms, for in those unfortunate circumstances, we were longing to have people we could help and comfort.

The strenuous journey and the sleepless nights in the refugee centres had taken its toll of the children's health. The little boy was ill on arrival and our first task was to fetch a doctor.

The house was not really suitable for so many people. We did not have enough beds, so my brothers happily pitched a tent in the garden and I slept with my mother. Our refugee friends settled down very well and shared in the household tasks.

When we first moved to the house, my mother had insisted that we rear some poultry and that we cultivate a small vegetable garden, for she had remembered rationing during the First World War. Now this mini-farming came to the rescue when there were so many mouths to feed.

The little two year old boy had a high fever for several days and he felt very sorry for himself. Only when I brought one of our new-born chicks to his bed, did we see his first real smile for days.

The Bonars had relations in Spain and they planned to go and live with them until the situation was stabilized, but the time they spent with us was to seal a friendship that became invaluable in later years.

Now I simply gave up revising for my oral, come what may. I had neither the time nor the inclination and I was quite prepared to fail. It was possible to try again in October anyway.

It was during the Bonar's visit that we received official news that my father had been taken prisoner – like most of the French Army. It was not good news, but it was news and he was alive. Above all it was the end of uncertainty and not a day too soon for my mother.

Then the results of the written examination were published and I still found enough spirit to rejoice in the fact that I had succeeded.

The greatest surprise of all however was that there would be no oral exams this session. Successful candidates could just proceed to the final level.

It was for me a tremendous relief and I could relax until the start of the new school year. I have wondered later if the satisfaction I felt at the time was not moderated by some doubt, some unconscious feeling of guilt, as if I had stolen my laurels. Does it explain the dream that recurred from time to time in my life, in which I would face an examiner, completely unprepared and unable to answer the questions?

Later in the summer, we began to receive news from my father, sometimes on officially printed POW cards, but other times the letters originated from a post office in Laval, the town where he was being held. He obviously had a means to have them smuggled out of the camp. He mentioned amongst other things that he was very hungry, could we send him some parcels? So we did our best to obtain and make things that could be despatched by post.

The financial difficulties that we experienced in the chaos that followed the military defeat were not the least of the problems my mother had to face. The families of officers and men ceased to receive their allowance and for a while we had no income at all. Any money we might have received from my father's firm in Brussels had stopped altogether and I remember my mother going to a jeweller in town to sell a few articles. It helped us to survive until the monetary situation was restored.

The next refugee to call at our door was very welcome indeed. It was our Uncle Henri, my mother's young brother, whose artillery unit had miraculously avoided capture. He was now demobilized and was waiting to hear about his job with the official French News Agency which was apparently moving to Vichy. So in the meantime, he was seeking refuge with his older sister. He would be great company for us young ones, for he was just thirty and a very good swimmer.

While the Bonar family had been with us, I had interrupted meeting my friends by the riverside since I was too busy. I had met Jean-Paul a couple of times in town and he had sweetly complained that I was not seen any more and that he was missing my company. I explained the reason for my absence and he informed me that the swimmers had migrated down river to the old lock and the weir.

That was nearer to our house for our road led into the tow-path and it was also a beautiful site which was now becoming the fashionable beach, with water bathers and sunbathers. And the swimming was good in the lock, it was more like a swimming pool.

We had no problems persuading Uncle Henri to join us. Jean-Paul himself unexpectedly vanished, nobody knew where or why. Maybe he needed his family after all.

The Scouts were no more needed for refugee work and my brother Gilbert could now join the swimming party, but my younger brother Georges disliked water and enjoyed more practical activities such as fishing. When we fried some of his catch, it gave him much satisfaction.

He was also engaged, with an older boy, in a second-hand bicycle enterprise when he found out that my mother had money problems.

With his 'colleague' he would visit neighbouring farms to purchase for a paltry sum old, sometimes antiquated cycles, which the farmers had in their barns and were pleased to get rid of. When the cycles were renovated, they found that there was a good market for them, due to the shortage of petrol. How proud Georges was to buy himself and his brother a new jacket with his earnings before the start of term. I must add that he liked working with his hands and he had always preferred to hang about the local garage than to do his Latin homework.

During our swimming afternoons with Uncle Henri, Gilbert and I made progress and we greatly improved our confidence and also our endurance. The river was wider here and presented a certain danger due to the proximity of the weir and of the swift waterfall in the middle. But with Henri, we felt safe and after his departure we were able to swim across safely on our own.

When my brothers were at a well deserved Scout camp, my mother had to go away to the préfecture – the county town – about some documents. It meant a fairly long train journey and she would not be back until very late that day or perhaps the next morning. Before leaving, she told Henri and I that we could eat one of the chickens for our lunch, for they had now reached the right size.

But the chicken was running about in the hen-house. We did not know how to catch it and we created a terrible commotion amongst the poultry community. But when we had captured our lunch, it was still alive and we had recourse to our neighbour, M. Desforges, who as usual, performed the gruesome task. We townsfolk were hypocrits, we enjoyed eating the fowls but we left the killing to others.

The dead chicken was returned to us but it still had all its feathers and its inside, a new challenge! Displeased with my mother who had not given us any instructions, we started to pluck the beast in a very inexpert way, in a flurry of feathers. It was not yet ready to roast however, how did one draw a chicken? In despair I consulted *Tante Marie*, the staple cookery book of French families, and sure enough, the instructions were there, not very clear to the uninitiated, but helpful all the same. The chicken was delicious; we fed them with maize and they had an incomparable taste, but never had we worked so hard for a meal.

Soon Henri had to rejoin his post and start a new life in Vichy. He was only employed in a clerical capacity and would not be involved in manipulating the news, a business in which our new government was already adept. We hoped he would write to us about the rumours and scandals of the new capital and pass on any unofficial information that came his way.

4

Opinions and Attitudes

In the aftermath of June 1940 and the political upheaval that followed, people formed opinions that would affect their attitude or their conduct for the duration of the war. Although some would change their views with the turn of events, for many it was clear-cut. Others would be influenced by the opportunities that the new situation offered them.

The positions taken in those days would sometimes lead to tragic consequences during the years of occupation or after the country was liberated. The issues were so grave, they transcended the normal political arguments that take place between people of opposite views in a democratic country in peace time.

There were to be tragic divisions in families, life-long friends would quarrel and already in those early days, some embarked upon the path that was to lead them to heroism or treachery or simply to be victims.

Even before the armistice, we had a taste of some people's lack of concern for their compatriots. Our landlord, M. Martin, had a daughter who sometimes came to gather the produce of their large vegetable garden, adjacent to ours, and tended with great skill by their gardener. On such an occasion, Mlle Martin, in conversation with us had expressed her exasperation with the war by declaring:

'Why on earth don't we give them Alsace and Lorraine and the North of France if that's what they want?'

'So, it's all right,' I replied, 'as long as we don't give them your town!' And now her father extolled the virtues of our great Maréchal for having ensured that the Martin's half of France remained intact. Fortunately the Martin's parochial preoccupations were not representative of attitudes in our little town, however provincial its inhabitants might be. We had many acquaintances in the district since my father was a native of a nearby village and in his youth he had played rugby for this town. In our conversations with the locals it soon became clear that people's grasp of the situation was very similar to ours. It felt good to have a chat, to show our support for each other, and when on shopping expeditions – the centre of the town was only fifteen minutes walk from our house – we spent far more time discussing the situation with the tradespeople than we spent on our purchases.

On the main square there was an exclusive gift-shop called *Simone* kept by a lady of the same name, a friend of my father from his youth. She was always neat and well made up, as elegant as her display window which contained Dresden figurines, Limoges bonbon-dishes and semi-precious jewellery. Soon there also appeared some brooches in the shape of a cross of Lorraine – the new emblem of de Gaulle's *France Libre* in exile in London. I had hardly any pocket money but Simone made me a special price and I purchased a cross of Lorraine which I pinned proudly on my blouse.

It was not to everybody's taste, for one day, adorned with this trinket, I met Madame Marchand, the mother of Gérard whose words had so shocked me the day after the capitulation of France. She displayed the same opinions as her son's and expressing disapproval at my badge, she concluded:

'Ma petite fille, quand on est vaincu, on baisse la tête.'

I replied defiantly that I would keep my head high.

Vichy's propaganda was now directing its fire against the British and, especially because of the Dunkirk episode, people were encouraged to believe that our allies were cowardly traitors. It did alas find an echo in some hearts, as Gilbert was to find out when he met in the bread queue the evacuee from Alsace my mother had employed to help with the housework until our financial difficulties arose. He returned all het up and red in the face to tell us that, seeing him in the queue, the lady had greeted him with these words:

'Have you seen these English? Have you seen how they

ran at Dunkirk? Dirty race! What a pity they were not all drowned in the Channel!'

Fortunately people like that were in the minority.

M. Boisseguin, the Martin's gardener who had worked the odd hours for us in better times did not share his employer's opinions. He now willingly gave us free advice on how to grow vegetables but mostly he enjoyed discussing the latest news we had all gleaned from London, a friendly little exchange of views that gave one heart to start the day. But with Boisseguin, the conversation would always return to the same topic, the great disappointment in his life. He had twenty-two children and yet had failed to reap the *Prix Cognac*, the outcome, he thought, of an unjust decision.

This prize, perenially awarded to the largest family in France, was a relic of the time when the country was suffering gross depopulation. It had been given instead to the de Barcy de Risle, whose twenty-second child was born at the same time as the Boisseguins' and the gardener contended that the jury had been impressed by their noble name. There were some de Barcys in my school and I knew that in spite of their prize money, the family had been forced by hardship to let their manor house and to live in a somewhat dilapidated outbuilding. Whenever Boisseguin mentioned the subject, I thought with sorrow about the plight of the two mothers.

In the countryside, we also found much antagonism towards Vichy. The farmers, with their simple peasant logic and basic patriotism saw the German invaders as their enemies and condemned the present rulers for collaborating with them.

In the days when petrol had been plentiful, we had enjoyed visiting farms to buy our supply of grain for the poultry and small barrels of wine at a price that made mineral water a real luxury. Now we had to cycle to the farms with hampers fixed on the carrier. The rides on country roads were delightful and the farms themselves, primitive but picturesque. We were always welcome because of our local connections and while we chatted and voiced our concern and hope, we were usually invited to a glass of wine.

The one dissenting voice in this harmony of opinions, I

found in the house of M. Demaruel, a Belgian farmer who had settled in the region after the First World War. We had been invited to visit his farm and sample his produce. It was so different from the other farms in the district, the Demaruels had brought their own style of agriculture. They kept a different breed of cattle and the place even smelt different. The Demaruel daughters had a local accent, but the parents had retained their Belgian-Walloon way of speaking.

I was buying milk and butter there one day and I had already paid for it, but it still stood on the kitchen table, when old Demaruel started to talk about the war. It soon became clear that he favoured the Germans and their regime and he suddenly launched into a tirade of hatred against the British, so violent that I could not find the words to counter his onslaught. As he went on, he related a story from the First World War to illustrate his view point and show that his loathing was not new.

'Do you know,' he said, 'during the Great War, there was a British officer lying wounded in the ditch outside my farmhouse in Belgium, and do you think I helped him? No, I let him die there like a dog! That's how I feel about them.'

Those last words rooted me to the ground, speechless. Not even enemy armies treated a wounded man like that! In the next instant I picked up my butter and milk, ran out of the house, and once on my bike, I pedalled with all my might until the horrible picture had faded away from my mind. Needless to say we never went there again. But when in later years we returned to Belgium, we made enquiries in the village where the Demaruels came from. We discovered that Demaruel had not only been a collaborator during the First World War, but he was also an informer and he had to flee the country in great haste when the allied victory came. Even his brothers had turned their back on him.

The Demaruel farm was situated in the vicinity of a small airfield, quite close to our town. At the very end of the war, this airfield was bombed. One of the bombs fell on a house, the house of the Demaruels. Nobody was hurt but the house was blown to bits, the only house in the region to be destroyed by a bomb. It was purely coincidental of course, but one would love to read in these events a just retribution.

5

The Mysterious Caller

At the end of the summer, a young man, perhaps in his late twenties, called at our house. As my mother opened the door to him, he enquired politely:

'Madame Rey?' Then he said in a quiet voice: 'I have some news for you.' He was invited in and said a few more words in an even quieter voice; I could hardly hear him from where I stood, but I could see him. He was tall and slim and was wearing two ill-matched halves of a suit, the jacket too short for him. I sensed that the news he bore was from my father and I came closer.

After the first moment of surprise, we listened eagerly to what he had to say. He spoke in a courteous but guarded way and seemed to avoid some of our questions. He never said who he was. We heard that my father had been held in a vast seminary transformed into a makeshift POW camp, but that following a violent attack of sciatica which had completely immobilized him, he had been moved to the hospital. How did this young man know so many details? Gradually we grasped the meaning of his discretion and his evasiveness. He had undoubtedly escaped from the camp where he had known my father. From now on, we avoided any questions that might have embarrassed him and my mother displayed a calm that belied her real emotions. On seeing my brothers cycle past the house, I ran out to put them in the picture.

Lunchtime was approaching and the visitor accepted our invitation to lunch. I was despatched to the kitchen to make an 'omelette aux cèpes' – a country relation had been canning some of these delicious wild mushrooms for us – and my mother took out some 'confit d'oie'[1] from the earthenware jar, another delicacy prepared for us in a little farm. One brother was sent to the garden to find the biggest lettuce and amidst all this culinary agitation, the guest followed us to the kitchen, telling us more of what we wanted to know.

Yes, they had been terribly hungry in the early days; the logistics of the German army had not allowed for such a vast number of prisoners, and at first it had been impossible to organize enough food supplies. Later the German authorities had enlisted the help of the inhabitants of the town, who were allowed to adopt some prisoners and bring them food parcels; they also smuggled letters out of the camp for them. That was the explanation of the few letters we had received, mailed from the local post-office.

The guest was clearly enjoying his lunch, his first good meal for months, he said. He had been justly cautious in his conversation yet now he seemed a little more relaxed.

Point blank he said to my mother:

'Your husband is recovering very well from his sciatica, but he is going to have a small operation – nothing at all serious – and he wants you to go and see him.'

My mother looked at him as though she had not heard properly.

'See him?' she asked.

'Yes, it is perfectly feasible, I shall tell you his location and give you all the instructions you need. You see, half the civilian hospital has been taken over by the German military but of course it is still the same building. The nurses who are nuns will help you to have access to him. I was in the hospital myself, I cannot tell you more, but I'll tell you how to get there and where to stay.'

The whole thing seemed to be properly organized already! As a chorus, we three children told my mother:

'You must go!'

She enquired about crossing the demarcation line between the 'Zone Libre' and the 'Zone Occupée'. He said that was quite easy. In a certain town, on market days, there was a bus that took you to the other side without any check.

---

[1] In Gascon cookery, portions of goose cooked in goose fat and preserved in stoneware pots, completely immersed and covered in the same fat.

'Just pretend to be one of the locals.'

We agreed that my mother had better make the trip soon in case the circumstances changed. Already mail between the two zones was no longer permitted.

After lunch they sat down to discuss the details while we cleared the table. We all felt immense gratitude towards this escaped prisoner who had delayed his return to his own family in order to deliver his message to us. We were a little puzzled by the operation he mentioned, although he had insisted that there was nothing to worry about.

Having concluded his mission, he went on his way. My mother accompanied him to the garden gate and as he walked away in his ill-fitting, inelegant clothes I thought how smart he must have looked in his uniform. We did not know where he was going; we did not even know his name.

6

Delayed Departure

Planning the journey, organizing the children, it was all done speedily and efficiently. It was impossible of course to make a detailed time-table because the journey on the other side of the line was to some extent a journey into the unknown and we would not be able to communicate.

So everything being in order, my mother could probably leave tomorrow. The weather is still glorious and later that afternoon I decide to go for a short swim in the river.

I find Hélène Desforges there, sunbathing, and as she joins me in the water she tells me that her secret ambition is to swim across to the other side but that she does not dare do it alone. Could we do it together? I often do it on my own, so it is no problem for me and we set off at a leisurely pace.

Halfway across the river, I realize that her swimming skill is not what it seems. She swims so slowly now and nearly comes to a standstill. As I keep close to her, she says:

'I am sinking.'

She seems to be struggling to stay above water and I have not a clue what to do. I have never found myself in such a situation, know nothing about lifesaving and in any case I am not a first class swimmer. I tell her I will give her a tug if she will co-operate and I try to grab the strap of her bathing costume but she is wearing an elegant two-piece and the strap around her neck proves to be the flimsiest little cord. I try to pull her by her chin, but it is exhausting and I go back to the strap. She for her part is very helpful, she does not try to grab me or struggle, she is just limp. While all this is happening, we are slowly moving towards the waterfall, the current is drawing us closer and closer and suddenly I realize that we are only a few yards away. I redouble my efforts but swimming for two is slowing my pace. With some relief I see the concrete curb that edges the fall, I am sure that I will reach it, and yes, I do reach it.

I try to put my hand on the piece of concrete to anchor us against the swift current, but alas, it is covered in a slimy, slippery growth and my hand just slides on it. I am hurled into the waterfall, Hélène on top of me.

The descent is very rapid. At the base there are large rocky stones on which we bounce, then I plunge deep into the whirlpools and I am tossed up and down like a cork.

In the dark green world at the bottom of the river, my mind stays clear and works fast – I remember that one must not struggle in such a situation, just let the currents carry you up and down. I think it is the end for me, although I breathe when I am tossed briefly to the surface. But finally, I come up for good and I am carried a little down river, incredibly in one piece.

Then it becomes possible to swim towards the bank, although it is a big effort. Soon, I perceive Hélène, floating just under the surface, inanimate, but I have no more feelings. I can only just manage to pull myself along. I can see some men swimming towards us and a boat is pushed into the water. I have not lost sight of Hélène and I can show the men where she is. They pull her into the boat but I refuse all help. I just want to go ashore, alone and unseen.

As I stand up in the shallow water, I see that my bathing costume is in shreds. I gather the bits and try to hold them together as I emerge. The current has not carried me too far away from the area used as a beach and people come to meet me, but I assure them that I am all right. When I get to my things, I put on my wrap and I just want to walk home, but I must find out what happened to Hélène.

She has come to, without the help of artificial respiration. She had just fainted, so I don't bother to dress. I walk home on the tow-path in my wrap.

There is nobody at home. I dress myself and collapse in one of the uncomfortable wicker armchairs. My back hurts, but I reckon that I have had a narrow escape.

Soon my mother comes in and seeing me so dishevelled enquires:

'What is the matter?'
'I fell in the weir!'
'You careless girl, I told you it was a dangerous place to swim!'

She is very angry because she is preoccupied by her departure and she has of course no idea of what I have been through. I break down, for I am still very shaken by the experience. Now my mother becomes sweet and wants to know everything. No, it was not pure recklessness on my part but I admit that I had not even thought of the risk of escorting somebody and that I should never have been talked into it. A few more tears and a big hug. Mummy looks at my back which is covered in bruises and she wants me to see the doctor. She also wants to postpone her departure for a day or two which makes me feel very guilty and upset. I insist that she can leave, that if I could swim back to the bank, it proves that I am all right, I just need a good rest.

A night's sleep puts things in perspective. Of course, the incident is talked about in the district, and in our local daily appear a title and a few lines about two foolish girls who nearly drowned after falling in the weir. It describes us as completely incompetent swimmers and says a few things about Hélène. Of course she is known round here and someone from the press talked to her last night. She could have mentioned my efforts at helping her, but perhaps she did not even realize what was happening. The story makes us both equally bad swimmers and equally foolish, and I certainly feel very foolish when I read it.

My mother, now that she knows the details, is angry about the press story and she has also decided to leave two days later, when she is sure that I am all right. Now everything is in order, we wish her a very successful journey, give her messages for Papa and above all, I promise not to go swimming while she is away.

7

The Return of the News-bearer

Life on our own was less regulated, mealtimes tended to be lax and friends were more often asked in. Although we missed our mother and worried about her hazardous venture, we enjoyed the temporary absence of parental authority. We all had our tasks of course and were kept busy looking after the poultry and caring for ourselves. I had to see to my ducklings who were now getting bigger and looking a little squat but still downy. When I appeared with the bowl of bran and chopped nettles which I had prepared for them, they would crowd around me, stretching their necks to tug at my cotton skirt with their funny little flat beaks and turning me into a half opened umbrella.

A farmer of our acquaintance had persuaded me to breed these Barbary ducks which were supposed to grow fast and to be economic to raise. But they were so sweet and so tame, I hoped they would not grow too fast and I tried to repress any thought of the time when they would be ready for the pot.

The three of us got along quite well on the whole. Being the eldest by a few years gave me a certain authority, but it was of no avail on the day my dear little brothers had one of their Boy Scout arguments.

They were both 'Patrol Leaders' and because they kept the equipment of their respective patrols here at home in an outhouse, there were occasional arguments about who owned what. This was a particularly heated argument about the claim to a large frying pan. First I heard a commotion, then I saw them chase each other out of the house, one carrying the pan and threatening the other with it. They were both shouting with a voice I did not know they had and using words I did not know they knew and my concern was that the pan might be used as a weapon. I was powerless in my efforts to end the hostilities but fortunately the unarmed combatant was able to escape, only to return when the situation was cooler. I could then try to mediate and help to sort things out.

Of one thing I was certain, the neighbours would never again compliment my mother on her charming boys.

The start of the new term was drawing near and this being my final year at school, I had to decide whether to register with the 'classe de Mathématiques' or the 'classe de Philosophie' which led to different branches of learning.

My father had always assumed that I would choose maths because he wanted me to take a diploma in chemistry and become an assayer in the small bullion smelting company he had founded a few years back. It was a foregone conclusion for a French father who owned a business that his children would continue in his footsteps. But what did it matter now? What did the future hold in store for us? We may never return home, there may not be a future.

Why should I pursue this line rather than follow my own inclination? I had not been particularly good at maths since a change of master in a lower form had stemmed my interest in a subject in which I had shown early promise. If I had passed my maths paper in the first part of my Baccalauréat, it was much more owing to a sense of exam tactics than to an understanding of the subject.

Besides, the teaching of science in our College was enough to drive one mad. The maths and physics mistresses were bitter old spinsters who carried on with the syllabus regardless of whether we understood or not.

Something in their life must have made them embittered, but I did not fancy having the bulk of my subjects taught by them. I realized that my father would be disappointed and that I was taking advantage of his unfortunate absence, but in spite of a twinge of conscience I registered for the 'classe de Philo'. If the subject appealed to me I would no doubt work better after the break of this long, sunny and distressing summer.

As the days went by after my mother's departure, our initial carefree feeling slowly gave place to apprehension.

Her trip was only intended to last a few days, but the journey itself was long and difficult due to the unauthorized crossing of the demarcation line. We were in contact with aunts and uncles in a village only a few miles away and they would be our last resort if something went wrong but that was a prospect we would rather not contemplate.

Yet, late one afternoon, as we were sitting in the garden, the garden gate opened unexpectedly and our mother appeared, looking tired but cheerful. Her only luggage was her shopping basket, so as not to awake suspicion. We were overjoyed at her return and were at once given messages and news from our father. That night, we went to bed very late for there was much we wanted to know.

The kind person who had adopted my father's little group of prisoners in the early days, Madame Potier, had now acted as a go-between. She had procured my mother a room in the town and introduced her to the nuns in the hospital. They in turn had shown her the clandestine way to the prisoner's bedroom and instructed her on how to circumvent the greatest hazard, the German guard patrolling up and down the corridor.

So one morning, my father, who was just recovering from an operation, had a very special visitor. It was quite an emotional experience for both of them. He had of course engineered it all himself via the young escapee who had visited us, and this wonderful person, Madame Potier.

I was puzzled about the operation he had undergone for nobody had yet mentioned its cause. So in great confidence, we were told about it.

As he was recovering from the worst attack of sciatica he had ever suffered, it became clear to my father that he would soon be sent back to the POW camp in the seminary. He was receiving news secretly from other prisoners there and from his men in another camp and he knew that trainloads of them were leaving daily for Germany. There were some spectacular escapes but he was not in a physical condition to take such a risk, so he wondered on what grounds he could possibly stay longer in the hospital. Perhaps if there were just a few lame men left behind, the Germans would not run a train just for them and would send them home on compassionate grounds.

He discussed it with the Medical Officer in charge, a young surgeon who was also a POW and who happened to be my father's namesake. Unfortunately there was no medical excuse to retain him there much longer.

'Isn't there a remote reason that could justify an operation?'

A further examination revealed nothing operable.

'Can't you invent something?' asked my father, a rather improper question to put to a doctor. After a further and very thorough examination, the MO ventured:

'I suppose one could say you have a weak hernial point, but it does not require surgery.'

After much soul-searching, for it really posed an ethical problem, it was agreed that in this particular case, it would require surgery.

The risks involved in any operation were pointed out and also the risk that the subterfuge might not work.

'What if they send you to a camp in Germany, regardless of your medical condition?'

But my father had insisted on taking the risk and that is why, he was now in the early stages of a long convalescence. It was the fear of being sent to Germany for goodness knows how long that had prompted him to plan his wife's visit, for my parents had now been separated since August 1939, apart from one short leave.

He was completely dispirited about the war situation and saw nothing but gloom in the future; he did not even feel the little spark of hope that we, at home, had gleaned from London through the BBC.

That was the mood that prevailed in the defeated French army. But in the little group of seven that had shared a small bedroom with one single bed – in which they slept in turn – in the seminary, there was a Scottish lieutenant. His grief was extreme but he had not lost hope, but then he had not lost his country.

In that late summer of 1940, numerous German bombers were taking off daily from the neighbouring airfields and it was a known fact that they were going over London which was being subjected to a merciless aerial attack.

The Scottish officer soon noted with great satisfaction that the number of planes returning from their ominous missions was significantly smaller than the number that had taken off, so he began a detailed observation of the aircraft, noting their types and the number taking off and returning.

The others envied his enthusiasm but could not share his optimism. He was able to pass this information outside – where he said he had a contact – probably via Madame Potier who used to smuggle letters for the little group when she was allowed to visit the camp to bring them food parcels.

I found much comfort in that story which strengthened my resolve to hope.

It was getting late, yet we wanted to hear more. Now we learnt about the escape of the mysterious messenger who had visited us. He was helped by the nuns, who had procured him some civilian clothes and shown him how to enter the hospital chapel by a secret door when a civilian funeral service was in progress; he was then able to leave the church unsuspected by joining the mourners.

The nuns were extremely brave to help prisoners to escape, for it was well known that twenty-three years previously, Nurse Edith Cavell had faced a German firing squad for similar activities.

My mother visited the hospital every day for they had much to tell each other; she talked about our life, how we coped, and she listened to the heart-breaking account of the retreat, of the fateful moment of the surrender. But they always talked quietly in order to hear the steps of the German guard. When they came close, my mother would swiftly spring to a position beside the door, which screened her when it was open.

This little comedy occurred a couple of times. But one morning, the guard came to see my father, and with the help of a few French words and some sign language, he conveyed the following message: a lady comes to this room – that is forbidden – it's all right with me – this afternoon the 'Offizier' is making an inspection and you'll be in trouble if he finds her here – now you are warned. My father could not understand how they had been detected but he was moved by so much concern on the part of one of his captors and on that day, the lady stayed away.

When we had been told everything that mattered, we had to go to bed, we would hear the other details tomorrow. That night, I found it difficult to sleep.

8

The Beginning of Term

In those days the summer holidays lasted nearly three months and by the end of such a long break, even the most indolent pupils looked forward to returning to school. This year though, it was different. The eagerness was dampened by circumstances and the joy of writing the first title on the white page of a new exercise book was not evident.

There was no formal address from our 'Directrice' on the first day. We were simply given our timetables and in my year, because of the weight of the syllabus, there was no time to lose before the exam so we launched immediately into serious work. At break, there was much exchange of views between the pupils and generally much agreement.

Cycling home for lunch, I caught up with my brothers and saw one of them carrying a long thin roll of paper. Their school year had started differently: their Principal had gathered all the pupils in the playground and had made an impassioned pro-Vichy speech. Later everyone was given a large poster with an outsize portrait of Maréchal Pétain, with the explicit demand that it should be displayed in their homes. We felt nothing but contempt for such a request and we had certainly no intention to adorn our home in that manner.

'Let's put it behind the kitchen door,' said someone – that door was permanently opened onto the hall – 'so we shall never see it, but we can't be accused of not putting it up.'

And there it stayed until we moved from the town.

During the first few days of term, my classmates and I reviewed the situation over and over, searching for a scrap of hope. The most vociferous girl amongst us – not necessarily the one with the best arguments – Marie-Louise Salice, was trying to stir with glowing rhetoric those whose support for De Gaulle in London was only lukewarm.

There was now a noticeable shift in the way people were associating. Last year, there had been two clear groups, the local girls and the newly arrived girls from Paris and the northern towns – the so-called refugees. The northerners were more sophisticated, they dressed better, and to the annoyance of Madame Pélissier, the member of staff in charge of discipline, they wore make-up.

'Who do you think you are?' she would say, 'Hollywood stars?'

She was particularly incensed because we objected to the wearing of the regulation pink overalls and we kept them blatantly unbuttoned. But now it was opinions rather than style that attracted people together.

I made a new friend, Marianne Delambre. She was extremely fat but had a pleasant face framed by curly blonde hair. She was not particularly talkative in public but was always ready for a laugh. It was our common concern about the events and our need to discuss them that started our friendship. Her family came from the very north of France, from a town near the Belgian frontier, but she was not a refugee. Her father was an agronomist who worked for the Ministry of Agriculture and he had recently been posted to this region.

Marianne shared my Anglophilia, only hers was not due to some wonderful holidays in England, it came from the historical links that families from that part of France had formed with the Tommies during the First World War and that bond had survived in the younger generation.

I had been looking forward to studying my new subject. I had bought my text-books before the term started and I had been able to glance through the course. It seemed an awful lot to absorb in one year and we would need a good teacher to liven up the subject and guide us through its complexities.

Unfortunately, Mademoiselle Chardonnet, the 'Prof de Philo', proved a disappointment from the start. A mouse-like figure in her fifties, she was a kinder person than the disagreeable spinsters who taught us maths and the science subjects, but she gave her course in the same uninspiring way. It was so obviously a repetitive task that she had performed year after year. Somehow we did not take to her style of teaching and when it transpired through some of her pronouncements that she favoured a collaboration with the occupying power, we began to resent her.

I would have to make the best of it, however, for I wanted to pass my exam next summer. As regards discipline, Madame Pélissier had once told us in her thundering voice that we were not to be met by boys outside the school, not even by our brothers. So I was puzzled some three weeks after the start of term when I found my brother Georges waiting for me outside the school gate. Upon inquiring about his unexpected presence, he answered in the calmest of manners:

'Papa has returned.'

My heart missed a beat and for a while emotion numbed my senses. I let my bicycle fall on the pavement and it took me a few seconds to recover from the shock. Then we both cycled home as fast as we could. I still hardly believed it to be true when I entered the house, yet there he was, standing in the kitchen next to Maman and Gilbert. They still had tears in their eyes.

I was at once struck by his appearance, for he had lost much weight and his uniform looked shabby and too big for him. He was unshaven and part of his hair had turned grey. He no longer fitted the familiar image I had of him. Seeing him again after so long and seeing him so changed was like looking at him through the eyes of a stranger.

Overcome by emotion, I hugged him and I joined in the general tears of joy. It was a moment of blissful togetherness in our family.

So the strategem had worked! He had been taken to hospital in Rennes when the remaining prisoners, including the doctor, were sent to Germany, and there he had been found so unfit by the German military authorities, that he had been sent home. The unnecessary operation had not been in vain.

His release document was there to prove it; on it, it stated that he suffered from Traumatischer Lumbago – Wirbel Kompression – Doppelter Leistenbruch – Schwaches

Bauchfell – Asthenie – Allgemein schlechtgesundheitlicher Zustand. It really sounded terrible. But he did look poorly and weak and now we would nurse him back to health.

There had not been an instant of real joy since May 1940, but now we could forget the rest for a while and just live for the happiness of the moment.

9

Life with Father

We would now have to readjust to being a family of five. It was not difficult for we were overjoyed that my father's captivity had ended in this way. My parents' happiness was very evident. My mother was not yet forty and my father only forty-two – this must have been a second honeymoon.

My father's health soon improved but his morale was also in need of a convalescence. He had lived these last few months in depressing circumstances, had suffered some humiliation to his national pride, and he saw no ray of hope on the horizon. It seemed that the battle for opinion had started already in the POW camps where propagandists had been dispatched to give lectures.

From early childhood, we had always discussed things freely with my father and now I used my powers of persuasion to cheer him and to make him see the events in a broader perspective. Listening to the BBC broadcasts of the Free French revived his spirits and before long he was as convinced as we were.

He had tried to keep a diary from the time of the collapse of the front but it had been lost with other possessions at the time of his capture; however having once written things down helped him to reminisce more clearly.

His most painful memories were of the pounding of refugees by the German Stukas. The refugees had got mixed up with columns of retreating soldiers during the débâcle and the bombers dived on these human caravans, sounding their terrifying sirens and causing casualties at random.

He talked much about the nuns who were nursing in the hospital, of their devotion to the patients, of their readiness to help those who tried to escape. But being nuns, of course, they did not forget the spiritual salvation of their patients and attempted whenever possible to steer the conversation towards a pious subject.

My father had been somewhat alienated from the blind simple faith of his childhood by several years in the trenches of the First World War. He had witnessed the horrific waste of innocent young lives from the age of sixteen, when he ran away from home and lied about his age to join a regiment. The experience had raised doubts in his mind and Sister Marie-Jésus spared no efforts to reconvert him. She had given him a book as a parting present, Thomas à Kempis's *Imitation of Christ*, which he found very beautiful and from which he would occasionally read us a passage.

He seemed to have made some kind of vow to become a better person. Although he was a kind man and a man of principles he was impulsive and was inclined to lose his temper. This trait in his character improved greatly for many years and never reverted to its early phases.

Our financial situation was now much better, for he received his full pay and allowances. Those servicemen who were not allowed to return to the northern and eastern parts of France, now declared 'Zone Interdite' by the Germans, were kept temporarily in a unit run by the Ministry of Defence, but to do civilian jobs. My father who was posted in it, lived at home with us, but most of the men who did not have their family with them lived in wooden huts erected by the unit. They did menial jobs and some were employed in producing charcoal in the local woods, a fuel which now served to propel many vehicles. Many of these poor fellows felt demoralized and despaired of ever returning home, so it provided my father with a chance to show his spirit of enterprise. He organized activities and sports that greatly improved their morale.

He founded Basket-ball teams that sometimes played teams of the neighbouring villages on Sundays. Because of his job, he obtained permission to use his car again, but not with petrol, which had become an extremely rare commodity – no, he had to purchase a gas-generating charcoal trailer which made our American car look very undignified.

But what a joy to ride in a car again, even if we had to stop every few miles to stoke the fire in the trailer.

We accompanied the teams to some of the village events and I liked to talk to the players about their families and their homes. I remember a young steel-worker from Longwy, the steel town of Lorraine, who was telling me of his longing for his home-town as we walked through a picturesque village. Not for him the lyric beauty of our countryside, or the tranquility of those ancient villages. His ideal landscape was one of steel-works, high chimneys and blast-furnaces whose flames lit up the sky at night. He was pleased that I listened to him and he must have had some love of nature for he picked a cluster of climbing roses from the wall of a little house and gave it to me; the old lady of the house saw him, but she smiled and told him to pick some more.

With my gregarious father back home, the family enjoyed more social life. One of the young officers in my father's unit lived in our road with his wife and baby. They were from Lorraine and like us could not return home. The two families played bridge together, but I preferred to look after their sweet little baby, Jean-Luc. I often minded him when his parents went out and I saw him through his first steps and witnessed his first words: a tender occupation that gratified my nascent maternal instinct.

1940 came to a close without bringing any cheer in the war situation, but Britain remained undefeated. All we could count on was hope; all the same, since we were now a happy family, we decided to celebrate the new year with a festive lunch. We invited our young neighbours who pooled the resources of their larder with ours and together, we produced a wonderful meal. One of my poor ducks, alas, had to be the main dish. My brother Georges enjoyed making rhymes, so before the guests arrived, he jotted down the menu:

> *Pour commencer nous mangerons*
> *Un bon potage de soissons,*
> *Des huîtres et du vin blanc doré*
> *Et un beau foie gras truffé,*
> *Un très gros canard farci,*

La spécialité du pays,
Des petits pois à la française
Et une salade pas à l'anglaise,*
Enfin pour corser le menu,
Un joli fromage qui pue,
Des meringues Chantilly
Comme dessert seront servies,
Des ananas de la Martinique,
C'est ça qu'est chic!
Et pour terminer le dîner,
Une excellente tasse de café.
J'espère que vous allez tous bien déjeuner
Et il me reste à vous souhaiter
Une bonne et heureuse année.

---

*Because I had told my family that people in England ate their salad without oil and vinegar.

10

Thoughts of England

I felt a great nostalgia for England, now so remote. I enjoyed reminiscing and day-dreaming about my happy holidays there. I recalled the people I had liked, the family who were my hosts, and all the fun I had had.

My father's friend, who had organized my visits to England, had seen to it that I was well entertained. He was a schoolmaster and not only had he arranged tennis partners for me, but some of his boys would escort me to London to see the sights and visit museums. And there were also the Saturday dances at the Old Boys Club – such a dizzy life for an adolescent girl who had never known such freedom or such a full social life. No wonder I had learnt the language so quickly.

For someone who lived in an urban flat, typical of a continental city, that suburb of London had seemed like a vast garden. Everywhere was so green, so full of flowers, and the lawns looked like soft carpets!

Letting my mind wander in this recent past, I longed to be back in the summer of 1939 rather than in the spring of 1941. We felt so isolated nowadays, if only I could be in touch with someone I knew across the Channel.

The Vichy press printed nothing but accusations and criticism of Britain. But it occurred to me that, since we were not officially at war with our former ally, it had never been declared that communications were interrupted. So, in a moment of inspiration, I sat down at my desk and wrote a long letter in my best English to our friend, the schoolmaster, giving all my family news and trying to express my views in a veiled manner. Even if by a miraculous chance the letter was dispatched, it would most probably be censored.

Then, I walked to the main post office and with my tongue in my cheek, I asked the clerk how much was a letter for England. She was puzzled by my request and she did not know whether the letter would go through, but there were no instructions to refuse them. So with a feeling of mischievous satisfaction, I dropped the letter in the posting box.

Returning from school, one lunch-time in mid-April, I found the table laid and on my plate was a letter, a letter with an English stamp. I picked it up as though I had found a treasure. It had been opened and examined by French and English examiners, but it had reached me.

Could I really be reading those words in April 1941? In the so-called free half of France where in every town a German *Commission d'Armistice* in uniform made sure that we toed the line?

> My dearest Gisèle,
>
> What a pleasant surprise it was to receive your letter this morning! We are all terribly delighted with the fact that we have had a *letter* from you, not to mention the good news it contained and reading between the lines it is not difficult to realize that 'our' Gisèle has not changed except that she is perhaps even 'tougher' than ever and does not easily allow herself to be demoralized.
>
> Yes, my love, I give you full marks! You certainly can go on hoping, nay, I *order* you to hope.
>
> Oh, our district has been considerably knocked about by bombs and in one place by a shot-down bomber. The school itself has had a bomb on it, but like you, there is no sign of demoralization here, far otherwise in fact. The ruins are cleared up almost immediately and life goes on just the same as ever. I am not quite sure that the local inhabitants are not a little proud that theirs was the first London district to be bombed.
>
> And what good news to hear that your father and all your family are safe! Incidentally you are the

first French person amongst all the thousands I have known, to communicate with me since the armistice.

Our school has not lost many of its sons – the only one I am positive you must know was Ben F. whom you first met in Brussels. He was killed somewhere near the Franco-Belgian frontier about the time your own father was taken prisoner. We have also lost two school-boys in night raids.

Life at the Old Boys Club is brighter than ever, particularly on Sundays when all the different branches of the Service come in to play Rugby and are well and truly entertained. We have frequently entertained de G's men and even the 'Corps Féminin'. You would like it very much and now we know you are all right, we'll know that you are with us, at any rate, in the spirit.

My wife is very well. She goes up to town as usual every day, kicking live bombs out of her way, as she pursues her distinguished course along the streets of London town.

All our love to you and your family,
Yours jusqu'à la mort.
N. E.

I translated the letter to my family and I showed it to my friend Marianne at school.

Oh yes, it was wonderful to receive a letter which made England a reality again, but what sad news it contained behind the cheerful tone. Yes, I remembered Ben very well, he was good at French, and was pleased at the chance to practise with me; and those school-boys killed in the raid; our friends were experiencing the real terror of war. But they still had their freedom.

I felt nearer to them, now. Emboldened by this epistolary success, I wrote more letters to more people, but they did not get through.

11

School-Days Under the New Regime

When she entered the classroom, Mademoiselle Chardonnet would sometimes find slogans chalked on the blackboard, suggesting that her pro-Vichy views were not generally shared by her pupils.

She wiped them off swiftly, as one would drive away a troublesome insect and sat at her desk as though nothing had happened. At a time when the British forces were suffering many reverses and our biased press was exulting over it, the following message appeared on the blackboard:

> *Les anglais perdent toutes les batailles sauf la dernière!*
> *Signé: NAPOLEON.*

We knew immediately who had written it. Marie-Louise Salice had not even disguised her hand-writing. The daughter of a retired colonel, she idolized Napoléon and she loved anything military. She had even infused some enthusiasm into the Latin class last year, when we were translating Caesar's *Gallic Wars*.

Mademoiselle Chardonnet wiped off the offending words in her usual manner, but this time she added a comment:

'Of course we cannot like the Germans, but we must hate the British even more!'

It was received in cold silence and on that day, the atmosphere in the class was not one of studious concentration. We began to taunt her and to make fun of the particular habit she had of calling the Philosopher Henri Bergson 'Monsieur' Bergson – an honour not granted to any other philosopher or author still living. Voices were heard saying: what about 'Monsieur' Freud? . . . or: according to

'Monsieur' Epicure . . . She went on giving her course in her banal, unexciting way, but there was anger on her face and sharpness in her voice, and we felt we had scored a point.

We knew that the Directrice, Mlle Renaud, held different views. How could she possibly come to terms with the instructions of the Government? It had now been decreed that every morning, schools should assemble in their playgrounds, hoist the Tricolore and break into song with a soapy, sycophantic hymn to the Head of State:

Maréchal, nous voilà!
Devant toi le sauveur de la France . . .

The poor Directrice kept a blank expression as she sang or pretended to sing near the flag-mast. At first, Marianne and I remained mute and later, we sang any silly thing that came to our heads, trying not to laugh conspicuously if one heard the other say anything funny.

What an interesting year this could have been, in another time, in another place. Our brief incursion into the history of psychology, the description and the study of mental processes, the many different theories and philosophical speculations, it should have been absorbing and should have stimulated lively discussion, had we had the right guidance. But in the prevailing atmosphere, I found no enthusiasm; I wrote my essays and tried to memorize what was necessary for the examination, that was all.

I enjoyed the English lessons with Madame Duteil, our English teacher. She was knowledgeable and always made interesting comments on the texts that we translated. Her English accent was still reasonably good, although she had only known England as a girl, before the First World War, and we found great delight in her descriptions and anecdotes about the England of those days. But she was a quiet person, with a sad, resigned face. She had had too many children; her philandering husband had never earned enough to keep the family, so Madame Duteil had to go on working in spite of bad health. She had two daughters, still in our school – one in our form, called Alice, a sweet, meek person like her mother, and Bobette in the form below. A complete contrast to her sister, Bobette was noisy, cheeky, totally uninhibited and very funny. She was often in trouble with teachers for answering back, and, because she preferred the company of our form to hers, she would often come into our classroom before the teacher arrived, having to tear away at the last moment. Unfortunately, Madame Duteil became ill and we were not to finish the school year with her.

Our temporary replacement had obviously never heard a real English sound; she pronounced English as French and complained that she could not understand me when I read. She said that I spoke in a 'funny way' – so much for the good accent I had acquired in England!

Our Government was obviously keen to show interest in educating the young, for the '*Ministre de la Jeunesse*' was going to visit our town. We heard the news one day, in the playground, after having sung our hymn of glory to the Maréchal.

The Minister's idea of being acquainted with the school population was to have us all assembled on the main square where he would review us, military fashion. Madame Pélissier, who made the announcement, said that the Directrice had received her orders: we were to wear a uniform – although no uniforms were ever worn in French state-schools.

Our outfit for the great day was to consist of a navy blue skirt, a white shirt, a tie, a navy blue cardigan and a navy blue béret! Those who did not have those things would have to borrow them.

There was nothing to find in the shops and it was preposterous that we should invent a uniform in a few days, just for the Minister. But there was no point in resisting and getting Mademoiselle Renaud into trouble – we were now living under a dictatorship. So I gathered my different garments, although the blue of my pleated skirt was far from navy and I borrowed a shirt from Gilbert. Then I remembered that I had a tie, yes, just the tie to wear on such an occasion.

It was a tie worn by English school boys for the coronation of George VI and given to me as a souvenir, and I had brought it here with me, together with other mementoes of my holidays in England; on it, were all the insignia of the British Monarchy. I also found I had some brooches with the Arms and names of towns I had visited, like Windsor and Brighton and I would wear those pinned on my cardigan, and my cross of Lorraine too. It would be my silent protest.

I did not reveal my armoury of ornaments until we departed for the parade; as Bobette Duteil saw me pin them on, she laughed her irrepressible laugh all the way to the square and Madame Pélissier had a field day marching us through the streets. As we were lined up like soldiers, the Minister alighted from his black limousine and started to walk amongst the rows of young people, stopping here and there to exchange a word.

He was a tall young fellow, smartly dressed, he had a Clark Gable moustache and looked more like a film star than a minister. He came into our row, walking briskly, and to my stupefaction, he stopped just opposite me, turned, and began to address me. My heart started to beat, as I became conscious of my paraphernalia and I looked at him intently to deflect his gaze away from them. He asked me in what class I was.

'So you are a Philosopher,' he said, and walked away. I don't suppose he noticed anything, he was only eager to create an impression.

A friend is a precious asset in troubled times. Marianne and I spent a lot of time in each other's houses, chatting and discussing; she lent me her books for she owned many and she was an avid reader. Deprived of our belongings, as we were in my family, it was good to be able to use the Delambres as a lending library. If my knowledge improved at all that year, it was more from reading Marianne's books than from my work at school. I was introduced to some recent English novels, some from the past, to German books written when their authors were allowed to think and speak, and to other works of interest. In our free time, we explored the countryside and we might discover an old church that was a gem of romanesque architecture and ascend the hidden staircase that led to the top of the fortified tower.

Marianne's father, through his occupation, had much contact with the country people and he knew about the local flora. He could always tell us where something interesting was growing, like that day in spring, when on his advice, we walked through a rather swampy wood and came upon a clearing where myriads of strange flowers were growing. They resembled small tulips, of a purple colour, and the petals had a fine, scale-like pattern. I had only seen them portrayed in old Dutch paintings of flowers. We brought a bunch back to decorate our homes, but the sight of that enchanting wood was unforgettable.

It was when we met at school in the morning that we usually discussed the news we had heard the night before on the BBC. One particular morning in May, we were grieving over the sinking of the battle-cruiser *Hood*, the saddest piece of news for a long time. When would we hear something cheerful?

It was disheartening that the British Navy could suffer such a disaster. Yet we kept up our spirits and thought that the *Hood* would not remain unavenged. It was only three days later that Marianne arrived at school, wearing a bow of black crepe pinned onto her jacket.

'What is that ornament for?' I asked.

'I am wearing mourning for the Bismark, haven't you heard?'

No, I had not heard, it was incredible, so soon, and we jumped for joy. We spread the news round the school that embattled Britain was holding her own. It was just the sort of thing we wanted to hear, it meant that there was a will, a capacity to fight back, that one day the Nazis would be defeated. Our friend from England had written 'I order you to hope': his advice would be heeded.

There was now something invidious happening in the school. It is difficult to tell when we first became aware of the conversations between Marie-Louise Salice and her friend Armande Restout. They seemed to be always together and soon they began to ignore the rest of the class.

Armande Restout, recently arrived from Paris, had joined the class mid-way through the school year. A tall girl, with eyes heavily made up, and a frizzy half-fringe falling at a cocky angle on her forehead, she looked much older than the rest of us. Her clothes seemed of another age, the way women dressed in the early thirties. One could somehow imagine her, waiting by a lamp-post in some seedy district of Paris. She did not communicate with anybody except Marie-Louise Salice, with whom she lunched every day at the Hotel Bristol. As they both lived some miles away, they came to school by rural bus and were unable to go home for lunch. The Hotel Bristol was the smartest hotel in the town and one had to be very well off to eat there every day. It was obvious that the girls' private conversations, which were whispers at first and became increasingly louder, were about men – men they had met at the Hotel Bristol. In that hotel resided the German Officers of the 'Commission d'Armistice', a reminder that our half of France was not strictly 'unoccupied'.

It is the names that Salice and Restout gave their men which started to intrigue us. They were names of German romantic heroes, like Werther or Siegfried. Soon they were to talk quite openly about them, even trying to attract our attention:

'Did you see how the trick of dropping my lace handkerchief worked wonders!'

Any remark directed at their conduct would be received with a snub. They hinted that we were a lot of juveniles who knew nothing about men and they were not prepared to discuss such matters with us. There was no doubt any more that they were going out with those German Officers. It caused great shock and disapproval amongst the other pupils. How could Marie-Louise Salice, of all people, behave like that? Where were all her patriotic noises, her exhortations? What kind of double standard was that? Her love of things military, the lure of the uniform, it was now sheer treachery.

Many of our former statesmen were behind bars and we knew what was happening in occupied France: arrests, persecution of Jews, the Gestapo firmly in control. Resentment at the two girls mounted and the atmosphere in the class became tense. Exam time was approaching and the affair was creating too much perturbation. I agreed with a group of others that something had to be done about it. To make sure that the girls were not bluffing, we sent our spies to follow them after school and obtained the assurance that they met their Germans, dressed as civilians, in a little café in the old town.

Our plan was to send a delegation to the Directrice, tell her what we knew, and say that we were not prepared to remain at school with those girls – they would have to go, or we would go. After all, it was quite legal to sit the Baccalauréat without attending a learning establishment. But Alice and Bobette Duteil, who knew more about the ways of the school, thought we would have more weight if we involved our parents. Bobette, with her frank approach, had several times given Salice and Restout a piece of her mind, but it had no effect; they seemed to enjoy the outrage they were causing. So we organized a meeting with the parents who were prepared to support us and sent a delegation backed by many signatures to Mademoiselle Renaud.

The affair posed a difficult problem for her; she was very distressed by the incident, but unfortunately she could not openly mention 'Germans' in any disciplinary action she might take. But first she would see for herself, and sure enough she found the group at their meeting place; there was even another girl, from the form below, whom they had persuaded to join in the venture on that day.

Mademoiselle Renaud had gone into the café, ostensibly to buy a packet of cigarettes. She must have been somewhat out of place, a respectable spinster, in a back street tavern. But she saw what she had come to see and Salice, Restout and the other girl were expelled for misconduct.

Marie-Louise Salice, always a master of oratory, tried to tell a cock and bull story in their defence: how they had met 'those Englishmen', left behind at Dunkirk, who were trying to rejoin their country. A thought came to mind: they could not really believe that they were being chastised just because of meeting men, or could they? It was the tale they could tell for ever after.

12

A Studious Summer

Before the end of term, Madame Duteil died. All her pupils attended her funeral and we felt great sorrow for Alice and Bobette who loved their mother. They would miss her very much, being at an age between childhood and adulthood when one still needs a shoulder to lean on. And her pupils would miss her, having lost an understanding and kindly teacher. It was a premature but timely death, for she would never know the fate that was awaiting Bobette; she would be spared the torment of seeing her daughter deported to a concentration camp and the distress of her death through inhuman ill-treatment.

Candidates were now informed of the date of the second Baccalauréat and of the town where it would take place, a fifty kilometre journey. This was again a makeshift arrangement for the university town on which our establishment depended was now in the occupied zone and the regional structure of the Education System had to be reorganized.

The exam started at 8.30 in the morning, which meant leaving the evening before; and transport was not easy, with no direct train and few buses. Marianne and I, my neighbour Jojo Desforges and one of his friends booked ourselves in a gas-propelled taxi that ran a shuttle service between the two towns. Jojo decided it was time he did some revision and he buried himself in his text-book, avidly reading a chapter which he thought could be the subject of a question. Some people are lucky, for it turned out to be one of the options. But I don't know how he could read, let alone study, in that noisy car, on those endlessly winding roads, which were enough to make one car-sick.

I shared a room with Marianne in a modest hotel and just

after eight o'clock, we were sitting in our improvised exam-hall, a horse parade and training arena under a glass roof. It was a lovely warm summer's day, but not a day for sitting under that glass roof. The heat soon became unbearable, yet we had to sit for four hours in this stifling discomfort. The invigilators became worried about some of the candidates, who seemed overcome by the heat and they ordered buckets of cold water to be placed at intervals between the desks where we could dip our hands and arms and splash our faces when the conditions became too uncomfortable.

Heat may well stimulate the mind for I wrote my four hour essay stopping only once to immerse my arms in the cool water. I have long forgotten the wording of the question, but it had to do with aspects of memory, such as committing to memory, retention and recall and the theories of 'Monsieur' Bergson on the subject could be expanded at will. When it was all over, I could never remember what I wrote, but it must have made some sense, for I was soon informed that I had passed the written exam and I was invited to attend the oral.

So Marianne and I stayed again at the same little hotel. I did not sleep very well partly because of the temperature and I did not feel too good when I arrived to face my first examiner. I was very nervous for I had never taken an oral before, and it did not help that the 'Philo' Examiner, a woman about fifty, had the expression of a judge about to pass sentence.

In an icy voice, she asked me a question on Descartes' *Discourse on Method*, one of our set books. I had revised it – yesterday I knew the answer, but just at that moment, I could not think of it.

I was forced to admit that I was suffering a mental block and I begged for a word of guidance or a phrase that would trigger my recollections.

'It is not my job to help the candidates' was the reply and she obviously gave me a nought. That meant that I could not pass, whatever mark I obtained in the other subjects. It was a painful experience and one that shook my confidence for ever more. I could of course think of the answer soon after leaving the room.

I was in no hurry to arrive home and admit to my father

that I had made a fool of myself. Marianne who had passed without difficulty came with me to soften the blow, and sure enough, my father was displeased; Marianne, seeing my misery, invited me to spend the night in her house.

I would have to try again in October and it meant a working holiday; fortunately, all the spade work had already been done and it would be a question of keeping things fresh in my memory. As for Marianne, she was now free to start her medical studies in Toulouse in October.

It was a frustrating summer; any activity I undertook, I could never enjoy wholeheartedly because I had to think of getting back to my books. I was uneasy lest the same circumstances occurred again.

I was not so keen on swimming in the river after last year's accident but I played more tennis. Gilbert and I belonged to the local club; it was rather cliquish and not too welcoming to 'refugees'. But Gilbert had grown into a good looking young man who looked older than his years and he found plenty of partners and admirers among the girls of his age group. We occasionally played doubles with one of Gilbert's girlfriends and Alain Dubois, not quite a refugee, for his parents had bought a country house at the start of the war, close to the village where my father's family lived. Alain Dubois, who was only about sixteen, would curse in fluent English every time he hit a ball into the net. One day, after such an incident, I addressed him in English and it made him blush, for he had thought nobody else knew that language. It turned out that he had just spent a year in an English school, just before war was declared. Now, whenever we met, we practised our English as well as our tennis, until one day, a very hot day, we played in the midday sun and we both got sun-stroke. I was quite ill for a day or two and I heard that he suffered the same fate. Alain Dubois was another of our young friends we would not meet again when war was over, for he was later deported to Dachau concentration camp, together with his father, and they were both to die in a gas chamber for no known reason, for there had been no trial, no charge. Probably a denunciation.

My brothers went to their Scouts' summer camp in a lovely region, some sixty kilometres away, and my parents and I cycled all the way there to pay them a visit. We stayed in a little hotel nearby, and one evening were invited to the camp fire, where we joined in the singing. The ride had been tiring, up and down hill, but it had been enchanting, for there was no traffic on the roads apart from the occasional charcoal-propelled car, or a horse and cart and, unexpectedly, a large green open car full of Germans, going at such tremendous speed that we were nearly blown into the ditch.

I also spent time with Marianne during the holiday and she sometimes brought interesting friends to my house: a young Greek refugee, Menios, who had been a student in France when that country was overrun and a Polish girl, Anna, who with her family had arrived literally destitute after fleeing from a Warsaw in flames. Anna's father, who was an agronomist and spoke fluent French, had been found a job in M. Delambre's department, a humbler job than he had had in Poland, but the tragedy had a fortunate ending for them for the whole family was together. Anna's mother, however, could not accept the situation. She was disconsolate in the tiny house where the family of four had to live, ill-furnished, lacking in comfort, and she yearned for the big house she had abandoned and for the leisurely social life of a Polish lady of her standing. She spent much time languishing and chain-smoking on the worn out sofa of their room, which was a kitchen, a living room and, at night, a bedroom. Anna, on the other hand, was full of high spirits and made the best of the situation; she soon adjusted and coped where her mother had given up. She had a fiancé who was an officer in the Polish army but she was never to have news from him again. I learnt after the war that Menios and Anna who had both been active in the resistance, were joined in marriage and went to live in Greece.

So the summer slipped by and the time came when I would have to face an examining jury once more. An old acquaintance, Juliette Helmond, offered to accompany me to the examination town 'to bring me luck', she said. The offer was not as candid as it seemed for she knew a young man there, on whom she had some design and she hoped to meet him. Juliette had failed her first 'Bac' with no hope of ever passing it, so she had left the College and was now involved in the running of her parents' estate. I had known her for many years, since her family had at one time lived in Brussels, and I had always visited her during the holidays, in their enchanting small manor house. Juliette was a pretty blonde girl, tall and slim. She constantly had new friends because she was rather superficial and fickle in her relationships and I don't know why our friendship had lasted so long, but she was good company for she liked to enjoy herself and since she was uninvolved in the turmoil of exams she would help to lower my tension.

With Juliette, I shared a room in a more classy hotel and during dinner I did not even think of the exam. Breakfast was also an entertaining experience, for at the table facing us was a good-looking young fellow whom we presumed was also a candidate. We noticed that he had a camera on a shoulder-strap and wondered if he was going to take pictures of the examiners.

The oral of the 'Bac' is a public examination, anybody can go and watch. So Juliette followed me to the Lycée where it was held.

One could choose the order in which one faced the different subjects and I wanted to start with English, for I thought it would boost my confidence. Feeling our way about the place, we glanced in one or two classrooms and as we peeped into the room marked 'Physics' I was bewildered to find, sitting at the desk and looking important, the young man who had sat facing us at breakfast and who can't have failed to notice that he intrigued us.

He laughed and invited us in and I could not possibly retreat. His question was easy, he did not want me to elaborate on it. Then he wanted to test Juliette and was disappointed that she was only a spectator. What a lucky start.

The young man who tested me for English was also very pleasant. Because I read my page of literature with fluency, he asked me if I had visited England and we entered into a congenial discussion in English, about the war and our hope and belief in the final victory. That was instead of questions on literature, and I knew he gave me good marks.

Whilst things were going so well, I might as well face 'Philo', although I had some apprehension, remembering my previous experience. The examiner had white hair and a white beard. He looked like an ancient philosopher – a kind philosopher. He called me 'my child' and said a few words to put me at ease. His questions were not particularly easy, but I felt no panic and I answered as well as I could. As I left the room, I reflected on the part that luck plays in such examinations, how different this 'Jury' was to the previous one.

The other subjects must also have gone well but I cannot recall much about them, only that in Natural Science, I was asked a question about the structure of leaves and also about the phenomenon of osmosis and its role in animals' bodies; the fellow in Cosmography who had a round face, like a moon, said: 'talk to me about the moon' and I nearly laughed.

The results were pinned on the notice board, in the lunch-hour, and a very anxious group of candidates rushed forward to see if their names appeared on it. Juliette got to the list before me and she turned with a look of triumph when she saw my name – I experienced the most glorious feeling.

We saw two boys we knew back home and decided to have lunch together; unfortunately one of them had failed but he was magnanimous enough to pretend to be cheerful – he did not want to spoil our joy. The other one was an attractive young man, popular with girls and fond of them. He had lost the use of his right hand in an accident in childhood and he was not beyond using his disability to ingratiate himself with the fair sex. I was sitting next to him and he asked me to cut his meat – quite in character and a move I had expected. It was a jolly lunch, we drank too much wine, we laughed and we talked too loudly and in the end we were the only people left in the restaurant.

The others were all staying another night, Juliette because she was going to meet her young man, and I had to say goodbye to the party to make my way to the bus terminal. I was no sooner installed in my seat, than the group turned up and begged me to stay another night, we all deserved to have a good time after our effort!

I was truly reluctant to refuse, but I had no way of warning my parents, and no money to stay another night and to have a good time. So, I went home, like a good girl, but bearing some good news.

13

What Now?

I was now in possession of my first academic grade – but where did I go from there? I had an entry to any of the universities in France but because we lived in such an unsettled situation, there were now no plans for my future. The nearest university lay hundreds of miles away from where we lived and with my father's modest income, there was no question of maintaining me in another town. Besides, my father's employment situation was becoming precarious; there was talk of winding up the unit where he worked, as men were gradually finding employment in the unoccupied zone and others were slowly allowed to return home. Decisions about the family future would soon have to be taken – should we try to return to our home in Brussels, what were the chances of being granted permission? Or should we settle down here for the time being? – But how?

My father proposed that I attend a shorthand typing course, the only tuition available in our small town, until things were sorted out. The very suggestion offended me, puffed up as I was with my title of 'Bachelière' – what a come down after my years of scholarly studies! It was pointed out to me that such a skill could come in handy in a variety of circumstances but I argued doggedly against the idea.

My real fear was to end up doing a tedious job in some mouldy provincial office, quite apart from my conceit of the moment. It was in any case an occupation that I always regarded as second-rate, because one just copied other people's words like a mere machine – better be a shop assistant, I thought. My father gave up trying to persuade me and my problems remained the same. I was secretly very envious of Marianne who had set herself a clear path and had the means to pursue it.

As my parents were pondering over what was best or most practicable for the future of the family, a change occurred in our situation that directed our thoughts towards a new aim. My father suddenly found that he had some capital available because of some provision he had made at the onset of war, in case Belgium became a battlefield again.

He had instructed a firm in Paris to keep in their care some precious metal ingots that he had deposited with them until the time he would be demobilized. With Paris overrun by the Nazis, he had no more access to this nest-egg. But now, he discovered that the firm in question had been evacuated to Lyon just in time with all its assets and he only needed to go there to recover his possessions.

With this new windfall, my parents favoured the idea of buying a property in the vicinity that would provide the family with some income and a home. My father reckoned that he had a good knowledge of the local husbandry, acquired in his childhood when he spent his holidays at his grandparents' farm. Besides, he had the capacity to run an enterprise efficiently and managing a small farm would at least ensure that his growing family was properly fed.

I joined wholeheartedly in the venture, ready to play my part in discovering the ideal place and later in doing my share of the work. The novelty was invigorating. Something happening at last, when life was becoming very boring, with no end to the war in sight and nothing to do in this dull little town.

Our searches meant many a ride in the surrounding countryside, on our bicycles or with the car and charcoal trailer and many social chats with farmers and villagers. I found these errands very enjoyable. We visited a number of places for sale, some in a dilapidated condition, their soil left fallow for years, and others too grand for our means. There may be many properties on the market but there never seems to be the one that fulfills your requirements. The quest took a long time, until one day, we came across a house and land that were both the ideal size.

The house was inviting and the outbuildings and the land

afforded just the kind of smallholding that my father thought we could manage with a small amount of outside help – and we could always have it as a holiday place when the war was over. One great advantage was the manageable distance to my brothers' school.

The house itself was a well-proportioned one-storey building with a tall roof and arched windows and shutters that gave it character. A few elegant stone steps led to the main entrance door and the setting at the foot of a hill was most pleasant. It was called Tertrebas.

There were now no bounds to my home-creating imagination, I was furnishing the rooms, choosing one for myself that I would make into a study-bedroom. I would decorate it with shelves full of books, I would scan the countryside in the hope of finding a rustic oak table in some farm, to use as a desk, and I would make the room cosy, my very own retreat after a hard day's work. The house actually had a bathroom and a proper flush lavatory. What incredible modern comfort after the Saturday tubs in the kitchen and the pails of water we had to carry to the toilet.

The present owners of Tertrebas had teenage children and they had installed a table tennis table in one of the outhouses which they were willing to leave behind. That pleased my brothers, and all of us, for it was a game we had enjoyed playing in the past. Everything about the place seemed just right. Whilst the necessary transactions were being initiated, we began to collect jumble from friends and relations, we made enquiries about auction sales and discussed our choice of furniture and decoration, hoping to acquire some antique oak dressers and cupboards in the local style. We were already in our minds the inhabitants of Tertrebas.

I got to know the owners' daughter, who showed me how she produced some delectable cream cheese in heart-shaped moulds from the milk of their three cows and for which there was much demand. I was certainly willing to carry on this trade.

The negotiations were not going fast enough for my parents' taste. We could detect a certain procrastination on the part of the vendor; then he asked for some delay while he was winding up some other business. The delay expired and he finally decided that he could not sell for the moment, next year perhaps.

The shock was hard to bear, a real anticlimax to our great expectations. Tertrebas was the only property on the market that had suited us and that we had really liked. We were back to square one.

We went on looking half-heartedly, without success. In fact my father had made a very unsatisfactory transaction; he had sold his bullion that had been unexpectedly saved and the value of his paper money declined rapidly whilst the value of properties and everything else went up sharply.

My parents would have to choose another course of action – perhaps investigate the chance of going back to Brussels. After having explored the local business scene, my father found that the only thing on offer was the tenancy of a large café-brasserie in the centre of the town. My mother and I felt no inclination towards such an occupation and the matter, which had never been considered really seriously, was dropped.

The question now was, do we implore the Germans to allow us to return to our place of residence, or do we cross the line without their permission? In any case, my father would want to go first and find out for himself what the conditions of life were like on the other side of the line.

14

Guests on Their Way

Soon after losing Tertrebas, we had returned from an unsuccessful search for another property, to find a Belgian gentleman waiting by our front door. It proved a real tonic to our morale when we discovered the purpose of his journey, for on our way, we had paid a visit to an elderly relative of my father and we had come back rather upset by the event.

He was an army officer, many years retired, and had settled with his family in a house down the hill from my father's village. In our past holidays, we had always enjoyed visiting this friendly household. There were two married daughters whose husbands were unfortunately prisoners of war in Germany and two sons in their early twenties whose hope of an army career had been thwarted by the occupation. This time, the friendly atmosphere had turned sour, when the conversation had broached the subject of the war. It appeared that the Major had been completely won over to the views, not only of the government, but of that sinister character Pierre Laval and also of Admiral Darlan, who both wanted nothing less than to declare war on England. The Major favoured complete collaboration with the Germans in order to help them fight the British.

'Why should we fight the British?' asked my mother, incredulous.

'They are our natural enemies,' said he, 'they burnt Joan of Arc, they imprisoned Napoleon on that dreadful island, and now, look at what they have done to our ships!' – referring to the action taken by the British Navy to prevent the French fleet from falling into German hands.

For once my father was very close to recant in his vow not

to lose his temper any more. There was no possible reply to such stupid arguments. Our relative's wife was visibly distressed because she did not share his views and she would have liked us to persuade him that he was wrong. But he was very much in charge of opinion in his family and his two sons took his side. One of them, encouraged by his father was later to join the infamous *Milice*, a force that fought their own compatriots in the Resistance; he was arrested at the liberation, condemned to death and was lucky to have his sentence commuted. His poor mother died soon after – was it of sorrow?

Such confrontations made one despair of what was happening to some of our countrymen. This is why meeting Captain Janson, himself a regular officer of the Belgian army, proved to be so uplifting. He had escaped from a POW camp in Germany, gone into hiding for a while, crossed one frontier and two demarcation lines secretly to arrive at our door. Some old acquaintance in Brussels had given him our address in France and we were to be a halting-place on his way to Marseilles. He had a contact that would help him on his journey to England. As a career officer, he saw it as his duty to try to rejoin the Belgian forces in England that carried on fighting for freedom.

I felt ashamed, remembering the words of my father's relative. Of course, the Belgian government, like most governments of occupied countries, had gone into exile in Britain; it was able to speak to its people and guide them via the BBC. Our so-called government was the only one who had accepted defeat and consented to being a Nazi stooge; this was bound to cause perplexity in some minds.

Captain Janson talked openly about his venture. He was a bachelor and such a decision was certainly easier for him than for a family man. We questioned him about Belgium, the morale of the people, the conditions of life, but his knowledge was limited since he had been in hiding. We told him that on reaching Britain, he should contact our friend in London who would surely give him any assistance he required, and with our help, he learned the address by heart. We were to learn several years later that Captain Janson had succeeded in his perilous enterprise.

Some weeks later, we were to have another visitor. This

time, we were to be a halting-place for someone travelling in the opposite direction. He had been a POW with my father in Laval, had escaped from the camp in the seminary, and when my father had been freed, they had kept in touch. He was at the present time living in a little town near the Pyrenees, and since he wanted to go to Paris, we were more conveniently placed to reach the demarcation line. My father had also let him know that we had a good tip about crossing the line.

Our guest, Monsieur du Plessis de la Chesnaie, was an archaeologist and a university teacher and his visit on the other side of the line was purely to settle personal affairs. In earlier years, it had been my dream to become an archaeologist, when I had discovered the ancient world through the lessons of a keen and interesting history master. Now I looked forward to meeting our erudite guest with a noble name that sounded like mediaeval poetry.

He was a discreet and charming man, very willing to satisfy my curiosity about his profession and to tell me about the excavations in the Middle-East in which he had been engaged just before the war. He also liked his food and wine and a convivial evening was enjoyed by all.

I joined the expedition to the crossing point that started early the next morning and we cycled to the station, having lent our guest a bicycle. We booked ourselves and our bikes on a train that took us to the last little station in the 'zone libre' and from there we cycled to a farm that would be the base for the operation. Monsieur du Plessis de la Chesnaie was obviously not used to cycling, and looked ill at ease on his mount – a far cry, I thought, from the bearing his ancestors in armour must have shown on their palfreys.

My father had been in touch with the Bousqueyrolles and we were expected for lunch. Their farm was conveniently situated near the back gate of the churchyard which was still in the unoccupied zone, but the main entrance of which, beyond the church, opened into a small road that lay in the occupied zone.

We were warmly welcomed at the little farm where a most delicious smell of food exhaled from the open hearth. A large chicken was roasting on a spit, and close by, keeping warm in a three-legged cast iron pot, was the traditional soup – the staple food of Gascony peasants for generations. There is more to this soup than the chunks of vegetables in season, the thin slices of country bread and the mixture of minced parsley, garlic and fat bacon that give it its savour; its delight comes at the end, when, having kept some of the broth in your plate, you add to it plenty of the local red wine and drink this 'mélange' from the plate which is specially shaped for the purpose.

It is called *chabrol*, and is guaranteed to keep you warm in the winter as well as being a cure for a number of ailments. It certainly had a warming effect on us. The conversation became lively, my father showed off his fluency in the local 'Patois' and we nearly forgot what we had come for.

But the serious business had to start. We walked to the churchyard, accompanied by Madame Bousqueyrolles who was carrying some small garden tools, and while my parents and their guest walked on towards the church, she and I ostensibly tended the family tombs.

We could not see the trio any more once they were beyond the church and I became a little nervous when nobody reappeared after a reasonable time. But my parents eventually came back, smiling, and my mother, seeing my puzzled look, explained the delay.

'We were nearly at the churchyard gate when Papa and I found ourselves walking alone! We wondered where M. du Plessis had got to, so we retraced our steps and found our archaeologist entranced by some stone carvings in the porch of the church, in complete oblivion. He began to lecture us on his find, how unusual it was, how remarkable for such a small church . . . I told him that we must get on, but it was like talking to a sleep-walker. Only when I reminded him that it was dangerous to linger here did he come out of his trance to follow us to the gate.'

So eventually the genteel professor was on his way, on the other side of the line. He had previously rewarded the Bousqueyrolles generously although they did not help people for gain, they did it as a good turn to their acquaintances and as a protest against the occupation. On the way back, my father had the problem of an extra bicycle to ferry to the station.

15

The Opportunist and Others

It always hurt when one's friends and acquaintances started to diverge from the honourable path and began to preach the objectionable ideas emanating from Vichy – particularly at a time when it was necessary to remain united to maintain our morale. One of the last times I saw Juliette Helmond, she exclaimed as we were passing a life-size poster to Admiral Darlan: 'I love that man, I think he is a fine leader!' She knew my views about the war and she had probably said it to provoke me, but it showed the complete reversal of opinion that had taken place in her family.

I had been acquainted with Juliette in my early school-days in Brussels and I had always visited her when on holiday at my grandmother's. Our parents had also met and my family had occasionally been invited to Gleygeolle.

During the first year of the war, when we still lived with our relations in the village, Juliette would call for me every morning in a 1920 two-seater Renault – for she was old enough to drive – and we would arrive at the collège in a flourish of noise. She sometimes let me drive on the open road, which was strictly illegal and could have got us both into serious trouble. In those days I was a frequent visitor to Gleygeolle where Juliette and her mother felt a little lonely, since her father had also been called up in the forces. I often stayed the night and I felt content in what I considered the most perfect of homes. It was an ancient building of pale limestone, with a picturesque turret in one corner. The rooms were not lofty, so one could admire the dark oak beams of the ceilings which contrasted with the walls, where the stone had been left bare. The floors were of large flagstones smoothed and polished by centuries of wear. It was furnished with the best of taste, but without studied refinement; every antique piece of furniture, mostly regional, falling rightly into place and just enough of it to make the rooms feel 'lived in'. In the library and in one of the bedrooms, where according to legend, Rabelais had spent a night, the ceiling beams retained some faded paintings of the renaissance. I loved to sit by the vast fireplace in the dining room and contemplate everything around me in the light of a glowing log fire.

Juliette was a very different friend from Marianne. Although the walls of Gleygeolle's library were lined with venerable leather-bound books, she did not read much. But she always bought the latest literary prize that one ought to be seen with. Our conversations were light-hearted, usually about the latest films or fashions and about boys; we washed our hair and tried new hairstyles and we practised dance steps with the latest records. Juliette's mother had perfect manners, perhaps too perfect for it was difficult to discover the person behind them. Her father, Alfred Helmond, who was a naturalized Frenchman, was said to be an academic, but in recent years he did not seem to have any particular occupation except to run the farm attached to Gleygeolle. He had in the past, taught ancient history in a Belgian university and in France, but he had also been engaged in promoting further education for factory workers – a very laudable task and in the mood of the time. Although he had fought with the Belgian army in the First World War, he had managed to obtain a commission in the French army as a reserve officer.

He was demobilized immediately after the armistice was signed and when he arrived at Gleygeolle, he found a number of refugee friends from Brussels and Paris. He resumed his life as a country gentleman in their midst.

When the Helmonds heard that my father had been released from captivity, they invited us to spend a weekend at Gleygeolle. There were other guests there as well as the refugees and Alfred Helmond obviously enjoyed presiding over this large assembly. He had a fine presence, somewhat blunted by a certain stiffness and if he was friendly, it was not without effort. One had the impression that he was always playing a role.

During dinner, on the Saturday evening, Alfred Helmond, striking in his captain's uniform – although he had been demobilized – was seated at the head of the long refectory table, full of guests, when he suddenly addressed my father.

'Rey,' he said, 'let's go to England and join de Gaulle's forces.'

My father was taken aback by such a dramatic suggestion in the middle of a pleasant social evening and for a while, did not know what to say. He was still weak physically and certainly not ready to embark upon some heroic venture. Besides, as there was no known way of getting to England, the thing sounded like pure fancy.

My father replied that for the moment, he was not in a state to take such a risk and that he would need time to ponder over the matter. But Helmond never alluded to it again; perhaps it had been meant to impress the audience at a time when de Gaulle was beginning to attract attention and Britain was proving capable of holding her own; or perhaps he meant it at that moment and circumstances changed his mind.

After Juliette had left the college, I still saw her occasionally; she usually had lunch with us if she came to town and many months after the above incident, we were again invited to Gleygeolle. We found the same company that had been there before and the dinner had hardly started when we felt a chilly atmosphere prevailing in the party. Helmond was not talking any more about joining de Gaulle, on the contrary, he was speaking of him with derision and pouring scorn on the British:

'They are running like rabbits in North Africa, the Germans will be in Cairo in no time. And the Russians won't last, they are useless in a modern war.'

Fortunately, his views were not shared by anybody else, except his wife and daughter. After dinner, there were hushed conversations between guests, so great was the disappointment to see Alfred Helmond turning his coat in such a blatant manner. Soon the people who visited Gleygeolle were no more those we had known. The old friends kept away and the new visitors were influential people in the Vichy machine. The very nice couple employed by the Helmonds – the husband assisting with the farm work and the wife an excellent cook – could not stand any longer the company kept at Gleygeolle and they gave in their notice.

The scandal of Alfred Helmond's behaviour was not so much that he jumped on the pro-German bandwagon when things were going badly for the allies, but that he became a propagandist, always making sure not to get too deeply implicated himself. He went on to give talks in towns and villages, encouraging the young to join the *Milice* and with his fine oratory and his poise, he made recruits.

And what happened to those recruits in the years that followed? Maybe they were sent to fight against their own people in the Maquis, maybe they were later arrested as traitors and condemned to death. And what happened to Helmond, who was never himself a member of the *Milice*?

When de Gaulle advanced at the head of the Free French to liberate Paris, many of the resistance groups were enrolling in this victorious army, and amongst the leaders was a certain Major Helmond. By the strangest coincidence, someone who had known of his activities down south and who was on a mission to the headquarters in Paris saw this name on a list of duty officers. He could not believe his eyes and went straight to the highest authorities to enquire if they were satisfied with the credentials of that officer. A couple of telephone calls sufficed to unmask the self-promoted Helmond and he was arrested on the spot.

He did not suffer the fate of the young men who enlisted in the *Milice*. He found the right lawyer who found some willing witnesses and he got away with a few months in jail.

Alfred Helmond had nobody to blame but himself for his behaviour but others, more vulnerable, more susceptible to influence, gave in easily to a new form of propaganda. It came from those elements in Vichy, who, having failed to persuade Pétain to declare war on England, could now see another chance of involving France more closely in the Axis: they tried to recruit Frenchmen to fight on the Russian front, as part of the German army. The scourge of the human race were no more the British, they were now the Russian communists – let's help those valiant Germans destroy the common enemy!

In spite of meeting general contempt, those responsible did alas raise a small contingent of Frenchmen who were to serve in Hitler's war machine. It was called the LVF – *Légion des Volontaires Français*. The propaganda was particularly strong in what remained of the military establishment and even the unit where my father was employed was not immune from it. We did once come face to face with someone who contemplated joining the LVF.

That old dare-devil Captain Lapie, who came from the northernmost part of France, was, like my father, a veteran of the Great War. He detested the 'Boches' for what they had done to his homeland in 1914 and the suffering they had caused to its people. In fact, he detested them so much, that one evening, on seeing a drunken German soldier come out of the hotel Bristol, he provoked him and punched him so hard that the soldier fell into a trench recently dug by road workers. Those who were with Lapie were very frightened and they led him away from the scene in great haste. The affair had fortunately no consequences but those in the know thought his action reckless.

My parents and I met him one day, as we were walking across the market square, and we stopped to have a chat. He was in one of his dramatic moods and told us that he was in despair at just about everything. Soon he would have no employment, France was finished, he had nobody to return to in his hometown – he was a widower – and he only had one thing left to do, to enrol to fight the communists.

'To enrol where?' asked my father.

'In the only contingent that is going to the Russian front, the LVF.'

'Do you mean with the German army?'

'There is no other way.'

'You are crazy Lapie! We should be thankful that the Russians are helping to pin down the German Army.'

I could not believe my ears. Captain Lapie had sometimes been invited to our house, because he was a lonely man, but we all thought him a little crazy – an eccentric who liked to perorate in a melodramatic way. He had never expressed any political opinions except for high-sounding patriotism; surely, he did not know what he was doing?

I could not just stand there and let a French officer join

the Nazi army. Trying to find the words that would hit hard at his pride, I said:

'You will look nice in one of those Boche helmets. Presumably you will greet your superiors with a Nazi salute and say heil Hitler! Anyway, what have the Russians done to you? Who is it that is enslaving our country?'

Words rushed to my mind, generated by my indignation, until I saw that he was near to tears. My father said:

'Come on Lapie, let's all go and have a drink and discuss this thing quietly.'

And it did not prove difficult to dissuade him from his course; it may be that the last one to speak was always right. Anyway, Captain Lapie did not join the German Army, he even worked for the Resistance in later years.

I felt I had scored a point against our invaders; I had denied them the services of a crazy, but brave man. A negative achievement, perhaps, but an achievement all the same.

I was to hear about another volunteer on the same trail, but unfortunately, I could not intervene with that one. He was a comrade of Alain Duvivier, the soldier we had invited for Christmas after an appeal from the local authorities to welcome one of those lonely boys into our homes at a time of family gatherings. The diminutive French Army allowed by the armistice treaties, was composed mainly of young men whose homes were in the occupied zone and who had signed on because there was nothing better to do. Alain Duvivier missed his family and he had been very grateful for our invitation and he continued to visit us from time to time. He was an old-fashioned young man, conventional in his tastes and formal in his politeness, and although well educated, he had no definite plans for a career. We did not see eye to eye about 'the Maréchal' and we had serious discussions on this subject, but always in a civilized manner.

He called on us, late one afternoon, looking a little flushed and more relaxed than usual, saying that he had been to a lunchtime party in the mess and that he had the rest of the afternoon off. He had obviously had plenty to drink.

As we enquired about his party, he said:

'You won't like it – it was a goodbye party for a friend of mine who is going to fight on the Russian front. I would not do it myself, but we all have our opinions.'

I replied that this kind of opinion made me so angry, I preferred not to discuss it and he agreed to change the subject. I understood however that only a small number of soldiers had attended the party.

From talking to Alain Duvivier, it was clear that many soldiers had different views: those for example who had mounted such a successful review at the local theatre, enjoyed by many people in a town deprived of entertainments. The band had had a definitely Anglo-American flavour and the leader, himself a good saxophonist, had charmed the audience with melodious tunes . . . 'There's a Chapel in the Moonlight' . . . while the whole orchestra had livened everybody up with jazzy numbers like 'Tiger Rag'. The local press had been perforce muted in its praise of the Anglo-Saxon style. Alain Duvivier, who liked me, although I could never really take to him, was irritated by my praise of the review. He did not like 'this modern trash'. His tastes were only for the serious. He admired German romantic literature and German romantic music and he saw it as an excuse to come to terms with a German *entente*. It was an attitude that I met occasionally in genuine admirers of German culture and my argument was always the same: that I understood their admiration and that one day, when Hitler had been defeated, I would want myself to explore it in greater depth. But this admiration cannot provide a reason to accept the present regime, which is a negation of that very culture.

Alain Duvivier thought that such a talented nation was invincible. He could not see that the might of Britain, the USA and the USSR together could break down their forces.

One afternoon, shortly before my final departure from the town, Marianne and I joined forces to try to persuade him that he was wrong – unsuccessfully, of course – so we had a bet. He that Germany would win, we, that the Allies would. We were going to meet somewhere after the war to see who had been right. But we never did; other things were more important then.

16

New Horizons

The time had come to test our chances of returning to Brussels, which was after all our place of residence and where my father had his affairs. The possibilities of settling in this area had been exhausted and it was obvious that we were in for a long war, that no miracle would suddenly change the situation. A friend from Paris who had permission to come to the 'Zone libre' had pointed out to us that being occupied was no worse than living under the pseudo-freedom that reigned here; at least, in the north, people knew where they stood.

But Brussels was not just the 'Zone Occupée', where a good many people had been allowed to return. It was, like the industrial north of France and the provinces of Alsace and Lorraine, a 'Zone Interdite', and it had not been easy to obtain our permit. When it came, my father went alone for he did not want to take the family back until he had tested the situation for himself. Something was happening at last; some movement could be felt that enlivened our dull existence, although we did not know where it would lead.

Since leaving the Collège, I had experienced a certain amount of frustration, feeling insecure about the future, being busy yet aimless. I often looked after little Jean-Luc, my neighbours' baby, who could now walk and talk, and maybe it awoke in me a longing for motherhood. Maybe I was suffering some emotional deprivation that caused me to lose my heart when a young man came to stay for a few days with our neighbours, although I knew I would never meet him again. Now that there was the prospect of a journey, of seeing different people, however far off, I felt much happier.

To our astonishment, we received the occasional letter from my father, posted just inside the unoccupied zone. He obviously had a tip from someone on the other other side and some people obviously took the great risk of conveying the mail across the line. We had heard on good authority, but in great secret, that some railwaymen whose trains had to cross the line were involved in this kind of clandestine transit.

The news was quite encouraging; my father said that he had found the situation in the firm chaotic but capable of improvement. He spoke warmly of the welcome he had received from people at work, from old friends and acquaintances and said that someone invited him to dinner practically every day. When the situation was a little clearer, he would come back and talk things over with us. And it was not long before he returned, via the churchyard near the farm of the Bousqueyrolles.

We had been so long settled in our sleepy little southern town, that he sounded like someone arriving from another world. We heard with joy that all was safe, our home, the firm and its employees. Those two aspects of the life of the family had always been closely linked because our private dwelling consisted of the two upper floors of a building, the lower storey and the ground floor of which formed the business premises. At the rear was the workshop which occupied most of the large courtyard and there was more workshop space in the basement floor.

So as children, we had always called first into the office on returning from school, to greet our parents and the other people, before going 'home' upstairs. Now we wanted Papa to recreate the picture for us and give us all possible details. We inquired about Pompon, our tabby cat, who had been as much an office as a family pet. Every day, he would grace some desk by his presence and when the accountant opened a new page of his big ledger, Pompon would make his way towards it, relaxed and elegant and sit himself on the clean white sheet. After work, he would follow my parents upstairs.

Alas poor Pompon had to be put down during the chaotic days that followed the fall of Brussels. People who had not taken to the road with the flood of refugees had more urgent worries than the office cat and had no means of feeding him.

My father had been struck on his return by a certain transformation in the appearance of his firm; it looked more like a provision store than the premises of a bullion merchant. On the shelves under the counter were a basket of eggs, packets of butter, loaves of white bread and miscellaneous other foodstuffs. It appeared that some of the employees were running their own little trade of a different kind when they dealt with the customers of the firm. They did this in order to exist, for the firm was only just ticking over under the Chief Clerk, and their wages were totally insufficient to live on.

It had taken a few weeks for my father to assess the situation, by visiting all his former customers, by talking to his friends, and the picture that emerged was that of a parallel life being lived behind the officialdom and bureaucracy of the occupying power. Commerce flourished behind the scenes and one could find – at a price – things that were scarce or unfindable in France, such as real coffee, sugar and even chocolate. Few people ate the ration bread, which felt like lead on one's stomach, they made their own with real flour bought from a *smokkeleer*; an occupation now very widespread, if only as a second job.

A tentative explanation amongst the Belgians for this state of affairs was that their country had always been at the crossroads of invasion and right through their history, they had been occupied by this or that great power; they had learnt to survive in such conditions and had foreseen the present situation. Enormous stocks of merchandise must have been stockpiled during the 'phoney war' that were to last till peace returned.

Behind this preoccupation with material things, my father had also discovered a very high morale. The Belgians hated the 'Boche', for they had never forgotten their sufferings at the hands of the Kaiser's army during the First World War.

These first few weeks in Brussels had not been without suspense. On returning home one afternoon, after lunching with some friends, my father had found all the yale keyholes in the apartment sealed with little red labels that had eagles and swastikas on them. There was a letter pinned to a door, asking him to contact the Military Authorities, so that they could search the apartment.

He found out from one of the employees that there had been a search downstairs during the lunch hour. He became frightened because he had in his bedroom a bundle of *Libre Belgiques*, a clandestine newspaper, that someone had lent to him, and they were not even concealed. Then he remembered that he had not locked any of the doors; he turned one handle and the door opened. They had sealed unlocked doors and he was able to hide the offending newspapers before going to the military authorities to say that he was ready for the search. We always kept one of the little labels on the keyhole as a souvenir! The German soldiers appeared to be looking for metal, they had some kind of detector and maybe they thought the place was full of gold. But there was none to be found and they left empty-handed. It taught my father to be careful if nothing else.

The Germans had put an embargo on the precious metal trade and only barter was allowed; they had made a careful inventory of our stock, alloys and supplies, down to the tiniest chain-link. But luckily, they had labelled as 'base metal' something very precious: a number of heavy, rough looking, unpolished bracelet watches sold to us in 1939 by some unfortunate Jews fleeing Germany – they were made of pure platinum and could now legally be removed from the stock. Hearing that story reminded me of the odd collection of precious metal objects smuggled out of Germany by Jews in the pre-war years; my father had once been presented with a motor car bumper made of platinum but it had been too costly for the firm to buy.

Now that we had a picture of the situation, it was time to take decisions about the family's future. It was all right for my mother and me to return; my father had indeed enquired about the possibilities of training and studying for an assayer's diploma which had been my intended career. But he had reservations about my brothers. There were all sorts of dangers for young men on the other side of the line; the boys were still very young, but Gilbert was already sixteen and how long would the war last? Their education posed a problem since our former Lycée, that had catered for the education of French expatriate children and prepared them for official French exams, had been closed by the Occupation Authorities. My parents thought it desirable that their sons should carry on with their French education, so one of the options was to send them to a boarding school near here, which a cousin of ours was attending and they would spend the weekends with his family.

Friends of ours, also refugees from Brussels, had been anxious to hear a first hand account of the situation from my father, and they had taken part in some of our discussions. The husband, Jacques Bailly, although a Brussels resident of many years, was actually of Swiss nationality and he proposed a solution that sounded like pure fancy – why not send the boys to Switzerland which seemed, thank heaven, sheltered from the war? He had relations who ran a small school where the boys could continue with their present studies, and like himself, his relations were so distressed by the fate of France that they would no doubt be willing to consider this as a special case. The Baillys had no children, they were fond of my brothers and me, and they sincerely wanted to help us, but we thought their idea could only be an illusion. How does one get a visa from Vichy? From the Swiss government? What about money matters?

'Well, well,' said our Swiss friend with the calm of a mountaineer, 'all sorts of things are possible, it is a question of trying. I will write immediately to my cousin and you must make enquiries about the formalities.'

His cousin's reply was very positive, he consented to make an exception for the boys, to treat them as refugees and to deal with certain practical matters in the future – that meant when the war would be over. But that brought no solution to the problem of reaching Switzerland.

Now my father had to go back to Brussels and we would have to investigate the chances of such a utopian journey. But something was happening, there were hints of change on the horizon.

17

Visit to Grand'mère

Before my father's departure, we elaborated yet another project. The occupation authorities were apparently willing to grant permits to visit a sick relative in the occupied zone, according to the merit of the case. I had not seen my grandmother since 1939 and it was arranged that an uncle of mine would send me a telegram from Paris, backed by a medical certificate and I would try my luck.

Grand'mère was my very own, for the person I have referred to as my mother was in legal language my stepmother. My real mother had died soon after my birth and I was only two years old when my father married again and I found a new mother. My dear, sad grandmother, who looked after me in my early life, had accepted the situation, knowing that it was best for me. But I had always been in close contact with her, particularly when we moved to Brussels. I never failed to visit her during holidays.

Now I had not seen her since before the war and the only correspondence allowed between the two zones was on printed cards that could only contain the briefest message. What a joy therefore, when the telegram arrived, bearing the words: 'Grand'mère très malade' – since I knew it was not true – and I had the prospect of a trip to Paris and of seeing her again.

I was to take my telegram to Issoudun, a town near the border where a German commission would assess my case. The telegram had only been allowed backed by a medical certificate, so it was a valid document and I had with me all possible proofs of my identity.

It was late morning when I arrived in Issoudun where I confronted my first German in uniform. He took my papers, gave me a form to fill, never said a word, and on handing in my completed application to a civilian official, I was told to come back at five o'clock to see if it had been accepted.

All this time to kill in Issoudun! I had lunch in a restaurant which gave me a holiday feeling, then I visited the town which had some interesting churches and other ancient buildings, some quaint old streets, and I browsed in a bookshop. But it was an awfully long wait, wondering all the time whether 'they' would let me cross the line or send me back home. Before five, I was in the queue and when my name was called and I was handed out my permit, it was only with difficulty that I refrained from being thankful – for why should I be thankful to be allowed to visit my own grandmother in my own country?

I rushed to the station, where previously I had handed out my case at the left luggage office, bought a ticket and got into a carriage that actually said 'Paris' on it. I felt a mixture of emotions, joy, anxiety, and a profound sadness at the manner of my journey.

The train sooned reached Vierzon, the checkpoint on the demarcation line; it was already dark and there were no lights to be seen anywhere, the station was completely blacked out. Peering through the window, one could sense a lot of movement in the darkness, on the platforms and on the tracks, a lot of military movement.

Everywhere there seemed to be helmeted soldiers, some with rifles, some with machine guns. With their awe-inspiring helmets and their jackboots they looked like sinister robots roving in the night. Suddenly they invaded the corridors of our train, like a boarding party. One could hear teutonic voices giving orders. We seemed completely surrounded. Eventually our papers were checked, but the soldiers remained in our train for a long time, pacing up and down. There was the same pandemonium in trains on other platforms. I felt a little frightened and very hostile. A passenger discreetly explained to me that there were illegal crossings in both directions, which gave rise to these raids; they inspected the locomotive, the tender, the carriages, looking everywhere for people and documents. I was now witnessing the occupation in its stark reality.

'France, mère des arts, des armes et des lois' . . . wrote

the renaissance poet. Oh, my poor country, I thought, what a state you are in. Will you ever rise from the abyss? And the train rolled on towards Paris in the very dark night.

I had managed to sleep a little and I was fresh enough when I alighted in Paris, feeling in spite of everything, the unique joy of arriving in the town where I was born. Grand'mère of course, did not know when I would arrive, she knew what had been engineered for my visit, but the moment would be a surprise. I crossed to Gare du Nord in the old Metro, a familiar sight and sound of my early childhood and I caught the first suburban train to my destination. It was a long walk from the station to her house, about a mile, and my luggage was heavy, but when I turned into her lane and saw the fence of her little garden, my tiredness changed into warmth and I thought only of the surprise I was going to cause.

Yes, it was a moving moment for both of us, when she opened the door, and there were tears. We did not talk much after the first exchange of news about the family, it was just satisfying to be together, to be bathed in all that affection.

I gazed around me at the large family photographs in their gilded frames and the familiar ornaments, friends of my childhood. And when evening came, the oil lamps were lit. I am sure it was a unique experience to dine by the light of one oil lamp in this day and age. Not many people had them any more, certainly not in the Paris region. Grand-'mère was born in 1860 and she had seen many changes in her life, one of which was the advent of electric lighting. She had of course had electric light in her apartment in Paris, but when she bought her little house at some distance from the big town, she said she had known of too many fires caused by short circuits, she would feel safer with oil lighting.

For me, it had always provided the right ambiance for Grand'mère's stories of the past. She had a great gift as a raconteuse, she could recall her childhood, portray her parents, grandparents, people and events that were for me steeped into history. But just now, we had other things to talk about than the distant past: the war that had separated us, the hardships that she and other people like her were suffering, the dire shortage of everything in the Parisian region.

She had seen the war right on her doorstep. The battle that had raged around the capital had spilled as far as her own street, where there had been firing. Soldiers had been running back and forth, and when it was all over two dead soldiers lay on the ground, just by her house. One was French and one was German.

'They looked so young,' she said with a sad voice.

Her road was a cul de sac ending in a field and the next day, the two dead soldiers had been given a temporary grave on the edge of the field, just two rough mounds of earth with improvised crosses made from branches.

'They were so young,' she repeated. 'Every day, until they were removed, I took some flowers from the garden to their graves. They must have had a mother somewhere who would have liked me to do that.'

I obtained some ration cards, busied myself in the garden which Grand'mère kept very well although she was over eighty and we soon reverted to our old conversations. My father who could only have guessed the date of my visit, since we had no communications, turned up one afternoon, bringing with him butter, smoked ham, and other good things from Brussels.

He had risked the journey, having heard rumours that the German checks at the frontier and at the crossing points of the 'Zone Interdite' had completely collapsed through lack of personnel. Suddenly, the triumphal advance to Moscow had stopped and the German army needed all the men it could find. This was apparently the cause of the present disorganization at the Belgian frontier. We were a happy trio in the little house; I gave my bed to papa and I slept in the big brass bed with Grand'mère who wore a night cap trimmed with lace.

The infinite pity of my grandmother for the soldiers who had died at her front door had for a while deflected my thoughts from my wounded patriotism and I had seen through her eyes the senseless waste of war. She had lived through three armed conflicts with our German neighbours; she did not read many books or newspapers but she had formed the opinion that populations were pawns in the hands of the 'big ones', that is the heads of states who settled their quarrels by war without regard to the sufferings of ordinary people.

When the time came to leave, we told Grand'mère about the possibility of my return to Brussels and the hope of seeing her again in the not too distant future, which made the parting less sad. My father and I left on a Sunday morning, and after our long walk to the station, we found that we had just missed a train and there would not be another one for a long time. We left our luggage with the booking clerk and decided to go for a walk. The station neighbourhood had a general air of poverty and street names like 'rue du Camarade Lénine' left no doubt as to the political sentiment of the area.

We came across a very small church which was no more than a timber hut, where according to a notice on the door, mass was just beginning. More out of curiosity than piety, we walked in and were not at all surprised to find it nearly empty. There were just a few children kneeling in the front row, not a single adult.

When the ageing priest began his sermon, he spoke in a patronizing way; he seemed to be admonishing the children and was making the gratuitous statement that all sins shall meet their retribution. And to illustrate his point:

'Look at the Jews, look how they crucified our Lord, and look at them now, look how they are being punished.'

I glanced at my father, he appeared as shocked as I was. One cannot argue during a service in a church, but by common consent, we left and hoped that our dissent was observed.

We were now on our way to Paris where I would meet some old friends again, then we would pay a visit to my step-grandfather who also lived some distance from the capital; we would tell him about the 'telegram strategy' and hope he would find an accommodating doctor, so that my mother, in turn, could visit her family.

18

Exodus

Back home, my mother was hoping to follow in my steps and was preparing her journey so when her own telegram arrived, she was ready to leave. Her journey was to be more adventurous than mine because she went all the way to Brussels. To this end, my father had obtained for her an up to date identity card, since he now had the knack of playing the game in Belgium, behind the back of officialdom. Having delivered the card to her in Paris, their journey to Brussels was easy, for there was still no control at the checkpoints. They had at last had the joy of being back together in their own home, but only for a very short time.

Maman and I had seen and learnt much during our trips. We compared notes, exchanged observations, but the pressing question was still the boys' future. We were more than ever convinced, from our discussions with people in the occupied territories, that it was not prudent for my brothers to return to Brussels. Now that the Russian front was claiming more and more men, the Germans spared no effort to attract our work force to Germany in order to prop up their war industries which were getting short of men. How long would it be before this labour became compulsory?

The negotiations for the projected Swiss trip proved to be a nightmare, partly because it took so long to get a reply to any query, but mainly because the demands of both countries were so contradictory. The Vichy government would only allow a young male national to leave the country if he was so ill that he was practically incurable, and the Swiss authorities would only give a visa to a foreigner who could produce a clean bill of health. It would have been easier, had my father been here, for he knew many people, but there was no more talk of his return at present.

However, one late morning, to my utter astonishment, the garden gate opened and my father walked in, carrying a huge suitcase; he was followed by a woman and two children. My mother, who was nearby, uttered a cry of surprise and stared at the scene for a moment. Then she said:

'My goodness, I know who they are. It is Madame Plocker, the wife of a customer of ours; they are Jews.'

The little group walked towards the house, a blank expression on their faces. They were hungry and tired, including my father who had carried a suitcase the size of which I had never seen before.

The story that we heard was startling and alarming. The Germans had recently launched a raid on Jews of foreign origin in all the main Belgian towns. At such times, news travelled fast and families at risk started to look for hiding places. Plocker, a customer of our firm for many years, thought of my father who had his family living in safety in Southern France. He came to implore him to take away his wife and children from the present danger, whilst he himself could more easily live concealed in Belgium. My father did not think he could undertake such a venture, it was too risky, but Plocker continued his supplications and even went on his knees, painting a horrific picture of how the family would meet certain death if they were deported. In the end, compassion prevailed over prudence and my father agreed to work out a plan for the exodus.

Time was pressing and the children, Alex, four and Catherine ten years old, had to be trained to act responsibly beyond their years. Since my father was now in possession of my mother's new identity card, Madame Plocker could use it as her own and the family could travel as his wife and children. Unfortunately, Madame Plocker did not look a bit like my mother; she was short and plump with frizzy fair hair, whilst my mother was tall and slim and wore her straight dark hair in a chignon. But a dye, a treatment to straighten the hair and a false piece made into a chignon soon gave her some resemblance.

Catherine understood the situation easily enough, but it

was difficult for Alex to comprehend that he had now two 'Papas', his own and an adoptive one, and that he had to call him so.

Plocker had assured my father that there was still no control at the checkpoints, something he knew from a good source. So the expedition started for the station with as much luggage as could be carried. They found the station swarming with people, but they had not expected a line of German soldiers blocking the way of passengers trying to get to the trains. Papers had to be shown in order to board a train and fortunately my mother's identity card did the trick. Catherine, who was sharp of mind, slipped between two soldiers, pulling her brother behind her.

The journey to Paris went without mishap, without check as expected, and, the next day, they reached a small town on the demarcation line from where they would try to cross into the unoccupied zone. My father had preferred not to make use of the little churchyard he knew to cross the line because it could not easily be reached by public transport, and where they would have looked too obvious. The Jewish community was well informed about clandestine crossing points and after dark they went to an address where they were to meet the 'passeur'. They found other people there, waiting for the same expedition, which had to take place at night.

There were two passeurs, who first collected the money, then led the party to the ford of a nearby river. They took their shoes and stockings off to wade across and there was to be no noise at all. At a certain point, the dozen or so illegal travellers had to wait and observe the passing of the German patrol in the distance. They saw them very clearly in the moonlight and when they were far enough away, the party was able to climb up the bank on the other side, my father still lugging the enormous suitcase.

Now they only had to walk a few hundred yards to a village situated in the unoccupied zone. Alex had behaved in an exemplary manner, as though he was entirely conscious of the danger. And the passeurs knew everything about the German Patrols, their timing, their frequency – which made it all appear much easier than it really was. Now all the Plocker-Rey family had to do, was to find their way to our house by public transport.

We made our refugees comfortable, gave them the big bedroom, and my brothers pitched their tent once more. Little Alex suddenly decided to run amok, grasping any object he fancied and obeying nobody but himself – a reaction I thought from the stress of his nocturnal adventure.

My father had to remain with us for several days, in order to help the Plocker family settle down officially in the community, for they had no documents, no ration cards. To become residents, they would need false papers; the Vichy government was not in the business of helping Jews, even less now that Laval was in his second term of office.

Through his many acquaintances, my father was able to obtain the necessary papers and Catherine and Alex had yet another family name to cope with. People's readiness to help, often at their own peril, when others were in trouble, was a source of confidence and hope. It only made collaborators like Gérard Marchand, Alfred Helmond and others stand out in the population like a sore thumb.

It was during the same period that we were introduced to a doctor who could help us to apply for my brothers' visas to Switzerland; he was willing to underwrite the conflicting requirements of Vichy and Bern on the question of the boys' health. We could now carry on with the proceedings.

And the very last task my father performed before he returned to Brussels, was to introduce Madame Plocker to the proprietor of a small hotel where they could eventually reside in safety and no questions would be asked. The family appeared to be well provided financially and I learnt from Madame Plocker how Jews, through their turbulent history, had to be ready to leave at a moment's notice and how they chose occupations such as goldsmith or tailor which made it easy to carry with them the instruments of their trade.

Refugees, like other mortals, have their virtues and their failings, and it was unfortunate that ours were not of the adaptable kind. When they were staying in our house, the Plockers could not come to terms with our somewhat primitive style of living. Madame Plocker was one of those fastidious mothers, particular about her children's diet and hygiene and she deplored our lack of comfort. Whilst we frequently washed at the pump in the outhouse, she wanted buckets of hot water twice a day which we could not provide; the gas pressure was so low that it took ages to boil a kettle and we did not have much coal for our solid fuel cooker.

'And why could we not get more good meat? In Brussels if you had money, you could obtain anything!'

It certainly was not the case here where tradesmen might do you a favour, but where there was no organized black market as in Brussels. All the same, my father went to talk to a butcher of his acquaintance and came back with a luscious piece of rump steak – and we all enjoyed the treat. Madame Plocker would buy anything that was on sale to supplement the diet of her children, she seemed entirely dedicated to their material well-being. Given the danger from which they had escaped we found her preoccupation with such minor considerations difficult to understand for she would tell us of the horrific fate that awaited the family, had my father not saved them. I must admit that, in our ignorance, we only half-believed some of her stories, as the real truth about Hitler's treatment of the Jews had not yet been revealed. Soon after my father left, the Plocker family took up residence in the quiet little hotel that had been found for them and we returned to our affairs and our plans for the future.

We were not sorry to be on our own again for Alex had proved to be unruly and very spoilt. His behaviour after arriving in our house had really nothing to do with the tension of the clandestine adventure, he was simply always like that. His conduct at the moment of danger was all the more remarkable because he was so untamed at other times. As for Catherine, she was quite a nice girl, but I am sure that my brothers had felt a little pang of jealousy at the way she called my father 'Papa' with a show of possession, to prove that he was as much hers as ours. Now, Gilbert and Georges regained their proper beds and we resumed our peaceful life.

There was now a real possibility that my brothers' departures to Switzerland would materialize, and my mother, fearing the separation, suggested that we take a well-deserved week's holiday somewhere. Perhaps in some small spa, where hotels were still very much in business, for in peace as in war, the French take the waters to cure a multitude of ailments. It was decided that I should go ahead to a small town which had been recommended to us, to look for suitable accommodation. I was preparing to leave, when we found the Plocker family on our doorstep again, complete with luggage, saying they did not like the food in the hotel: please could they come back and stay with us?

It proved a difficult task for my mother to find a place acceptable to Madame Plocker. In the end, she opted for a better class hotel which, in our view, did not offer the same degree of safety. It is however a story with a happy ending; the false papers the Plockers had been provided with protected them till the end of the war, even when the whole of France was overrun by the Germans. When peace came and the family was reunited with their father, they never forgot those who had rescued them. Every year, on the anniversary of the exodus, they have visited my parents, presented them with a splendid bouquet, a bottle of brandy for my father, and some costly perfume for my mother.

In order to reach the chosen holiday destination, I had to change trains at Chateauroux. In wartime things do not work as they do in peacetime; my train arrived late and my connection had already left. There would not be another train until the next morning, so I started to walk round Chateauroux, a sizeable town, to find a hotel room.

For a reason that was not immediately obvious to me, all the hotels were full; there was not even a room to be found in private houses that normally offered accommodation. I would have to go back to the station and spend the night in the waiting room with all the other people who had missed the connection. At least, I could have a meal in a restaurant.

But that was not so easy. To my amazement, the restaurants were also full. I found one where they were willing to squeeze me onto a large table full of people. They were all men and they looked serious and tense.

Halfway through the meal, my table neighbour asked me: 'Are you looking for a place to hide?'

In a flash, the situation became clear to me. This town,

situated near the demarcation line, was full of Jews who had fled into the unoccupied zone for safety. It was the Plocker story many times repeated. I said, embarrassed,

'No thank you, I am not Jewish, I am just on my way somewhere.'

'Oh, we are not Jewish either,' they hastened to reply, their features belying their words, 'we just wondered if you needed help.'

We finished our meal in silence and I glanced around at the other tables. There were many families, some with very young children. On my way back to the station, I noticed how full the town was, full of people with luggage. I thought of the things Madame Plocker had told us and I realized the extent of the persecution. This was the second wave of refugees I had witnessed fleeing the invaders, only these people had to do it secretly.

19

Keeping Us Guessing

When the two incompatible medical certificates concerning my brothers' health reached us, they were immediately dispatched with the visa applications to the relevant authorities and we were aware that it would be a long business. Correspondence and questionnaires poured in from both sides; some did not receive a truthful answer.

To the gratitude we felt towards the doctor who had so willingly assumed personal responsibility for this affair, was added the fear that the manoeuvre might fail. But he, for his part, was not too concerned; he was absolutely sure that his word would not be questioned.

Never was a family so indebted to the medical profession! To think that our father had been returned to us because a doctor had consented to perform an unnecessary operation; to think that fictitious sickness certificates had permitted some of us to visit elderly relatives in Paris; and now this farcical situation had been made possible – by which my brothers would leave France consumptive, but a few yards down the road, on the other side of the frontier, they would have completely recovered. How different our life could have been, had these men not overlooked some conventional rules of ethics in favour of the solidarity and goodwill more essential in times of oppression.

The postman was soon to bring some very welcome news. The Swiss authorities consented to admit my very healthy brothers to their country, provided they were granted an exit visa from the French. The Swiss visa could only be delivered by the Consul in Toulouse on presentation of the French one but there was unfortunately a limit to its validity and so, no time to waste.

The long silence on the part of the French authorities became so worrying that in the end, my mother took herself to Vichy. Her brother Henri, now married, resided there and his home would be a base from which she could visit the officials on the spot, pester them if necessary and try to hasten the proceedings.

During my mother's absence, my brothers and I were invited to spend a few days with Marianne's family. Her father had now been transferred to a town upriver, a town of medieval grandeur which Marianne and I spent many hours exploring. Every street was a feast for the eyes and the sleepy squares with their houses of dissimilar shapes and sizes were a natural scenery for a period play. The surrounding countryside was no less attractive and it seemed that nothing had changed there for centuries.

The official house allocated to the Delambres was a modern construction in poor taste. It stood on raised ground above a country road but each of its windows looked out onto a restful landscape of forests, meadows and stone farmhouses.

It was ironic that the Delambres always lived in this kind of insubstantial, characterless house, for they owned some fine antique furniture, some Empire drawing-room chairs and a pedestal table that could not have looked more incongruous in their surroundings. Marianne succeeded in making something of her own room which had a certain cosiness for being under the eaves. I helped her to decorate and furnish it and while we worked, we resumed our conversations of the past years which I missed so much since she had gone to university.

With the boys, we made a good team and we went on merry cycle rides and picnics. Marianne's brother, Camille, had been to school with Gilbert and Georges and they had belonged to the same Scout troop, so for all of us, it was a reunion.

We could reach the river through woods and meadows and we had the use of a flat-bottomed boat which we launched from a shingle beach. The river, nearer its sources here, was narrower but very picturesque. The opposite bank was a sheer rock face along which we rowed the boat, and we were able to observe a variety of aquatic life; shell-fish anchored to the rock resembled large clams; and there were freshwater shrimps, all creatures that I thought lived only in the sea.

We dived from the boat into the water, so clear, you could see every pebble, every weed that grew on the river bed. Back on the shingle beach, a careful scrutiny would offer rewards, for there were fragments of stone-age tools and weapons scattered amongst pebbles. Those impressions of a leisurely holiday in a beautiful landscape would remain with us when we had moved to other climes.

My mother had returned from Vichy with little else than promises. The minutes were ticking away and the Swiss visa would soon expire. Our impatience grew and my mother wrote frantic letters to officials, spent ages at the post office trying to make telephone calls.

The project worked out by our friend Jacques Bailly could actually suceed, it was an undreamed of opportunity, and yet the whole thing would collapse if the French visa arrived only one day too late. Soon the time that remained could be counted in hours rather than days and the family, dispirited, prepared to make other plans.

When at last, the postman came, holding an official-looking envelope, we had nearly lost hope and we could hardly believe it. Yes, it was the visa!

But there was not a moment to lose. I was despatched to Toulouse with the precious document while my mother made preparations for the departure.

My journey was not so easy. If the railway system operated quite normally on the main lines, travelling across country and on branch-lines could be a nightmare. Connections were not assured and trains sometimes did not run at all. I found myself stranded in a town halfway to Toulouse and the only available train would reach my destination after midnight, not a suitable time to find a hotel room.

Luckily, I was able to locate someone my father knew, an old schoolfriend from his village; the family invited me to lunch and since they possessed a telephone, they tried to book a room for me in Toulouse, near the station. But the hotels were full and it was only by imploring the manager of one he knew well, that my father's friend obtained for me an attic room that was not really suitable for letting.

I knew that my host was an outspoken collaborator; he had belonged before the war to an extreme right wing party and the present situation vindicated his views. But I thought that with a little conversational skill during lunch, I could keep off the subject of the war and world affairs. It all went very well and we exchanged mainly family news until one of the daughters, a schoolgirl aged about fifteen, finished her meal in a hurry and rushed upstairs. Her mother explained that Céline had to change because she was going to a meeting and, to my utter dismay she reappeared in the black uniform of the *Milice*.

Céline's grandmother who was on a visit to the family and whom I knew well, gave me a knowing look for she was distressed at her son's opinions. I thanked my hosts for their help and took my leave hastily.

It was a very slow train ride to Toulouse and when I alighted just after midnight, the station approach was deserted and in complete darkness. As I groped my way across the square towards my hotel, I seemed, after a time, to be walking on some grass. I stopped carefully, straining my eyes to visualize what was around me, then my foot seemed to be walking over nothing. I stepped back and I perceived on the ground some very faint gleam, a diffused shimmer. I had just stopped short of an expanse of water which turned out to be the canal, without any kind of parapet or guard. I very nearly had a cold bath, and a disaster, for what would have happened to the precious papers I was carrying?

Somehow I reached a bridge and the hotel where my attic room was every bit as dismal as expected. The wallpaper was peeling off in places, there were damp patches on the ceiling and I saw some weird insects crawling on the wall. All the same, I had to consider myself lucky to have a roof over my head and to have reached my goal in time and I eventually fell asleep.

The hotel itself was very smart and breakfast in the stylish dining room was an unbelievable contrast to my accommodation. I did not linger however and at nine o'clock sharp, I was at the door of the Swiss consulate.

The interview with the Consul was most pleasant. He was a charming, relaxed man who was obviously happy to hand me the three visas – my mother had been allowed to accompany the boys to their destination. It was a strange feeling to talk to someone whose country was not involved in this global war, someone from a little oasis of peace. Perhaps that's why he seemed so relaxed.

After my slow return journey, I found the trio all packed and ready to leave. The boys were really quite excited: they knew that because of the location of their school, they would be able to ski in winter. But we parted sad at heart. The sense of belonging together as a family had helped us to endure the traumatic first years of the war and we hoped that the separation would not be too long. Things were looking up on all fronts, there was bound to be a landing in the months ahead! We promised to write a lot to each other, and we kept our word, giving the censors a vast amount of work; we had even worked out a code and so were able to exchange news of a more delicate nature.

20

Destination: the North

The house was very lonely when they had all gone, my only company being Moumousse, our tabby cat. Even my good friends across the road and their little boy Jean-Luc were away in the Occuped Zone, for they had obtained permission to visit their parents whom they had not seen since the summer of 1940. It was Jean-Luc that I missed most since I so often looked after him. He was such a sweet little fellow, with great big eyes, who loved everybody and was always eager to please. His latest joy, now that he could walk and say a few words, was to be a messenger between the two families, a sort of homing pigeon, who would carry a message pinned onto his little blouse. He would point eagerly to the piece of paper until it was unpinned and read, and somehow he knew that the message required an answer. We would watch him go across the lane with his reply, feeling very important.

My mother, in the turmoil of the rushed departure, had gone away with the ration cards, so I was very grateful if friends invited me to a meal. The Baillys took me out to lunch at the Hotel Bristol and we celebrated the happy outcome of the plan which at first, had seemed like an illusion.

I felt the absence of my brothers from the very first day, for we were very close, in spite of the several years' difference in our ages. And I wrote them long letters to ensure that we maintained contact from the start. I was also extremely busy, preparing our own departure. There was much packing to do and we had accumulated many things in those few years, which we could not take with us to Belgium, so I had to dispose of them; but above all, I had to find a home for Moumousse – yet another sad parting. I arranged to give him away to a young cousin of mine, back in the village, and she waited impatiently for the day I planned to arrive with Moumousse in a basket on the carrier of my bike but on that day, he was nowhere to be found. I called and searched for him with the help of neighbours but Moumousse never returned.

Not only was I very sad to lose him, but I later got the blame for his disappearance. A few months previously, I had had an argument with my parents who wanted to have him neutered. I thought it cruel and unnatural that he should not be allowed to live his life as a male and I had won the argument. Now, I was told, his fancy had taken him elsewhere. That was hard to believe, for he was extremely affectionate – even soppy! – to humans. When I had a sore throat, I used to put him round my neck, like a scarf, his paws hanging on each side of me, and he purred with delight. I was inclined to think that someone had stolen him.

The day my mother was due to return, a telegram arrived instead, stating that she was stranded at Annemasse, near the Swiss frontier, and that she would arrive the next day. But the next day, another telegram arrived, stating that she was stranded at Aix-les-Bains and that she would arrive as soon as possible. I became impatient, although I was familiar with the frustrations of train journeys.

The joy of hearing her relate her wonderful voyage in a land at peace had been well worth waiting for; also the details about my brothers' new school, the people she had met, made me feel that they would be happy there. My mother had been able to obtain a very limited amount of Swiss currency and she had fitted out the boys as well as possible, but it was a fact that they would be hard up compared to their well-off Swiss contemporaries.

There were fortunately other pupils of refugee status in the school, so they would not be singled out. Our good Swiss friend, Jacques Bailly, would if necessary arrange some small exchange transactions for us (which his Swiss nationality permitted) but above all, my father had promised that after the war, God willing, he would repay every penny owed, even if it meant selling his possessions.

Maman and I were now ready to leave, having obtained the necessary documents to join my father, and it was just a question of fixing the date. It was November 1942 and I was in my twentieth year. All this wasted youth, I thought. The only gain of those few years would be the completion of my education – a permanent acquisition, undoubtedly.

It is now that some wonderful, unbelievable news came through on the radio. There had been an allied landing in North Africa! A massive landing, and to lift our low spirits, the news that the North African Colonies had rallied to the allied cause, ignoring Vichy's command. France still had a substantial military presence there and those troops would now join in the struggle; we could once again look other nations in the face!

If our elation was great, the retribution was swift. To the pathetic strains of the Maréchal's feeble protests, the Nazis invaded the whole of France.

The fools who had agreed to sign a treaty with Hitler now found out what his word was worth. The people who had believed in the Vichy Government now discovered its futility; a regime that clad itself in legality, yet had never been endorsed by the nation. Its decrees were unquestionable and final; one of its great acts had been to condemn de Gaulle to death in his absence! Now those people would discover that Pétain's real master was Hitler himself, even if the Maréchal had some fanciful illusions of power.

The next good news we heard was that the fleet in Toulon, on which the Germans would dearly have liked to lay their hands, had scuttled itself. To many, it was only qualified good news, for if the Germans were denied the use of our still sizeable naval force, it lay at the bottom of the harbour instead of joining in the fight to liberate our country. What a waste.

'Why did they not escape?' was the question that came to mind.

Perhaps some antique rivalry with Britain, perhaps resentment at the destruction of the French fleet off Oran in 1940 by the British Navy, when 1200 French sailors perished. At least, they had done the honourable thing and Admiral Darlan did not have a chance to hand them over to his German friends.

With the new turn of events, my mother feared that our own departure plans might be affected. There was confusion for a few days although in the end, our journey was made easier, France was now reunited (albeit under the Swastika) and there were no more travel restrictions between north and south.

Just before we left, I invited Alice and Bobette Duteil to a goodbye lunch. It was the eve of the 11th November and the next day, the German troops were due to arrive in our town.

It was also the eve of the remembrance day for the one and a half million young Frenchmen fallen on the battlefields of the Great War. But an order came from Vichy, cancelling all ceremonies and forbidding all gatherings at the 'Monuments aux Morts'. We heard this news on the radio and Bobette Duteil was up in arms.

'They cannot stop people from honouring the dead,' she said, 'I think we should defy their order and go there tomorrow at eleven.'

Alice, who was of the cautious type, preferred not to risk it. I told Bobette I would go with her but my mother seemed to have some misgivings.

'We have got your brothers in safety, don't you go and do something foolish!'

We assured her that we just intended to pass by in silence.

The next day, Bobette fetched me just before eleven, and we picked a little winter flower from a bush in the garden, intending to drop it discreetly at the foot of the monument. But when we arrived in its vicinity, we found it completely surrounded by gendarmes and a special kind of armed and helmeted police I had never seen before. There was no way we could approach and we had to abandon our plan. We said goodbye, promising to meet again after the war, when our country would be free. I was never to see Bobette Duteil again.

Several years later, when peace was signed and some normality had returned, I discovered for myself the awful cost of the Nazi occupation. Bobette's life was part of that cost.

Late in 1943, she had found herself in the company of some young 'maquisards', when the Germans, who had been trailing them, sprung an ambush. They were all captured. Bobette, who was not herself involved in the Resistance – she was only talking to boys she knew – was sent to a concentration camp. When the camp was liberated, she still lived, a human wreck, and she was transported home, where she was soon to die.

The world has learnt with shock of the ordeal of women in those death-camps. How often, in late years, have I thought with grief of my jolly, foolhardy school friend, who was always raising her voice against injustice. She had a heart of gold and I remember well the day my brother waited for me outside the school to break the news of my father's return from captivity, how she had been as pleased as me, how she had jumped for joy.

My mother and I left by a night train, looking forward to being reunited with my father and to living in our own home again. As it turned out, we had got the boys away from France in the nick of time. In the blacked out stations where the train halted, the loudspeakers were blaring . . . Achtung . . . Achtung!

PART TWO

UNDER THE NEW ORDER

21

Home-Coming

After a short stop-over in Paris where my father had been able to meet us, thanks to the still unmanned frontier and border of the *Zone Interdite*, we were back on a night train for the last stretch of our journey. We had called on our relations, looked up some old friends, and I had bought some chemistry books, keen as I was to take the first steps towards my future occupation. We had even made plans for the new year, travel still permitting. We meant to spend New Year's day at Grand'mère's, a surprise we plotted with my uncle and aunt. For the moment, it had to remain a secret for we could not foresee the situation six weeks hence. There was also a scheme to spend New Year's eve with friends, two families whose sons and daughters were of my own generation.

The very full train stopped, as in pre-war years, at the two frontier towns. But suddenly something very strange happened. The corridors were invaded by a mass of people, a pushing and jostling multitude who soon filled the coach to capacity. In spite of the near obscurity, I could make out that they were no ordinary travellers. Instead of suit-cases, they carried parcels and sacks and there was a definite whiff of wheat flour about them. Some of the women, who wore aprons and woollen shawls, appeared rather fat and had some unnatural bulges under their clothes.

I was informed that they were an army of *smokkeleers* regularly boarding the train at one frontier post and alighting at the next. They were taking advantage of the lax surveillance and tomorrow, they would carry on their trade in the opposite direction with different produce.

On a grey November morning, I walked again through

the streets of Brussels. It was three years since we had left for a holiday from which we had not returned. The trams were just starting on their morning runs and made the streets immediately familiar again. They were the only traffic to be seen and now our only way to get about.

When I stood at last in the apartment where our family had lived for so many years, I felt like a visitor to a place I knew well but that was not really my own. It took a few days before I experienced the sense of home-coming I had expected, maybe because during such fateful years a chunk of my life had been spent elsewhere.

We were longing for our breakfast after our night's travel and we found everything organised in the kitchen by the new help my father had engaged. Then we went together downstairs to open the premises.

The people who worked in the firm greeted Maman and me like long lost relations. They were a little like relations, most of them having been with my father since he came to work in Brussels, and they had followed him to this firm when he had acquired it. My mother herself was part of the staff for she had always preferred to assist my father professionally and have plenty of help in the home rather than be a housewife.

Now we were gathered in the main office room decorated with dark wood panelling and mock tapestries that depicted falconers and hunters in a lush forest. This majestic décor, although not quite the right setting for an office, had always fascinated me as a child for it resembled a room in an old country mansion. There was so much to talk about and all took the opportunity to recall the fateful days of June 1940. Everybody except Madame Eveline, the secretary, had tried to get away when the Germans were nearing Brussels. Some had actually fled on foot when it had become impossible to board a train and they had soon been forced to return. Theo, the smelter, his family and other refugees had been bombed by the Stukas in northern France and his son had been wounded.

Their sad tales confirmed once more that my father had been wise to insist that we settle in his native province of France during the so-called phoney war. With him on active service and away from home, what ordeals had we been spared!

We went on to discuss day-to-day matters such as food and rationing, where we had much to learn and we got plenty of advice.

'Don't buy the ration bread, it tastes foul. Buy the ration flour, sieve it to get rid of the particles that are anything but wheat and mix it with an equal quantity of real flour from the black market and you will make a very acceptable loaf.'

So I tried my hand at this new craft and when I had made my first loaf I took it down to the office for approval. It looked crusty, appetizing, and smelt of wholesome bread. It was passed by everybody with full marks.

But a more sober purpose called me downstairs. It was about time that I undertook some serious activities. I had to become familiar with all aspects of the business and above all spend much time in the laboratory where I could watch the chemist at work and he would initiate me into the practical skills of making a gold assay.

22

The Sorrows of Others

There was a brief moment when I just surrendered to the joys of living in comfort again in our own home, furnished and decorated to our own taste, and to the bliss of having a hot bath when I wished. The apartment was warm for there seemed to be no shortage of coal and I found great pleasure in rediscovering my books, my possessions, and a variety of clothes I had forgotten about.

Yet I could not feel content: This was not the world as I wanted it to be. Nice as it was to have the undivided attention of my parents, I greatly missed my brothers and felt uneasy about our separation. There was no way we could see them until this dreadful war was over; in the meantime so many things could happen.

On returning to one's home town, one looks forward to meeting again former friends and acquaintances. The Bonar family, deeply grateful for the shelter they had found in our humble house at the time of the débâcle, gave us a warm welcome. The children had grown and altered and there was also a new baby, a reminder that life goes on, regardless.

Amongst the people we used to know, though, the war had often left its mark. Our elderly neighbours, the Denans, with whom we had been friendly for many years, lived in hope that their son-in-law had reached his secret destination: England. Like Captain Janson, who had stopped at our house the previous year, he was a career officer and his duty was clear-cut: he had to carry on the fight and liberate his country. Like Captain Janson, he had followed a trail to Marseilles where an underground network would organise his escape.

The Denans' only daughter, Armande, and their grand daughter, Nadine, now lived with them. Armande needed the companionship and also the financial help. The whole family was in no doubt that their loved one would return glorious with the liberating army. Never for a moment did they think that his escapade could have failed, although they had not received the secret message they hoped for. Little Nadine, when she heard the news from London on the radio, was quite sure the voices came from the country where her father now was.

She was a very serious child for her nine years. The great secret she had to keep, the pretence that father had just disappeared, kept her apart from other children; also the company of elderly people at home made her look a little too grave. But she was a sweet child, just a little deprived of the joys of her age, and I decided to make her my little friend. It meant that I sometimes indulged in the games and pastimes of a younger generation, but my little friend was also studious and one day, she asked me to teach her English. Having no experience in the matter, I had to think hard on how to turn the lessons into a game. We never devoted much time to it but she was indeed a good pupil who meant to greet the allies in their own language when they came.

Unlike the Denan family, our friend, Madame Timmermans, knew exactly what had happened to her husband. We had known them both for a very long time, and now, in their misfortune, there was not much we could do but to commiserate.

Madame Timmermans had been *la couturière* ever since I was a very small girl. She had come once a week to our home to make the children's clothes, rompers, dresses, pyjamas and all, some from new, some from old; she would patch and alter and she always enjoyed the day *en famille* for she had no children of her own.

Roger Timmermans was a gendarme who had once been an athlete of international repute and that had touched a chord with my father, himself a great lover of sport. Another entente between them came from the memories of the early years they had both spent in the trenches. The Timmermans were a Flemish couple who found our own language difficult and they simply loved to hear us speak French – the real French they said, not the French one hears in Belgium. On the 'couture' days, Roger would fetch his wife after work and enjoy a chat with my parents. He always wore his colourful, gold braided uniform which my brothers and I greatly admired, although it put the fear of God into us; we surely behaved in his presence!

For Roger Timmermans and some of his colleagues, the grim story began just a few days before the invasion of Belgium, a non-belligerent, neutral country, as it had been in 1914. The gendarmes had apprehended some very suspicious-looking monks who turned out to be none other than disguised fifth columnists who had just disposed of their parachutes. Enraged by this treachery, the police-constables put them through it before taking them into custody. Once in jail, all the infiltrators had to do was to wait for the Nazi invasion, which came like lightning. Then they were free again, free to turn on their captors.

The gendarmes were identified by the bogus monks. After a summary trial by a German military court, all but Roger Timmermans were executed by firing squad.

In his case, an extraordinary piece of luck occurred, an administrative error in the books, showing that he could not possibly have been at the given place on the given day. Although he had joined willingly in the rough handling of the Nazi spies, the military court could not build up a case against him. He had an alibi, the error in the book. This evidence saved his life but he was by no means acquitted, he was just thrown into jail and there he had languished ever since.

On the few occasions when his wife had been allowed to visit him, he had shown great courage but he had also tried to prepare her for the worst. For there had never been a word said about his fate. He feared that he might eventually be shot or at best deported to Germany and it was not just the detention he had to endure, but this cruel uncertainty.

One thing we could do for Madame Timmermans was to bring her back into our family circle. Although there were no more children's garment to make, there was plenty that could be done with the pre-war clothes we had discovered in our cupboards. It is amazing how a pair of man's trousers can be turned into a skirt, old shirts into blouses and other things altered to look like new. The shortage of clothing gave Madame Timmermans great scope to use her skill and she always looked forward to her weekly visits to us when we made a point of having an extended lunch-hour. I had always known back in the days of unoccupied France what misery and anguish the Nazi invasion had caused, yet witnessing its effects amongst my own friends had opened my eyes to its reality.

When my father tried to regroup the rugby club he had founded years ago, he noticed the absence of some players, who had been of the right age to serve in the army and were now prisoners of war. But it was no accident that those of Flemish origin had been freed whilst the Walloons had to sit it out for the duration - simply a Nazi scheme to win over the Flemish population in an already divided country.

The club mourned one of its members, a player who could be described as a 'tough guy' and who had been unable to come to terms with the German occupation. He kept a café in the 'Marolles', a plebeian, colourful district of Brussels with a clannish community that spoke its own vernacular, a mixture of ungrammatical Flemish and distorted French. He had declined to serve German soldiers in his establishment, and if they refused to leave, he would evict them by force for he was a fellow of enormous strength. Before long he was arrested. Maybe he put up a fight whilst in prison, the fact remains that he was beaten to death, as his family discovered when the body was handed back to them.

Such tales of barbarism were rife and for me in these early days in Brussels a tragic story could spoil a dinner I had come to enjoy with some friends. My hosts were relating in a way I found too casual, the plight of a Jewish woman who lived in their street. Her husband had already been taken away, and 'they' had come for her. But she was not allowed to take her baby with her and she was dragged from her home in complete despair, while the baby was left behind. Soon afterwards, the baby's cries could be heard but there was no way people could rescue it for the house was guarded.

I was a novice at living under occupation, and full of

indignation I asked why someone did not do something, get in through the back or plead with the soldiers. How naïve I was, they said, then recounted how the next morning the soldiers and the baby were no longer there.

I began to ask myself how human beings could commit such deeds. Who had shaped those men's moral value? Was there no baseness to which they would not stoop? I nearly felt guilty at my own well-being.

What could I write to my brothers about our life back in Brussels? I did of course reassure them about our everyday existence but I tried to convey the sadness behind the seemingly acceptable life and I told them how wicked Aunt Philomène (the Germans in our code) was with children and how it made us broken-hearted.

No doubt the boys would have liked me to describe the noises of war that were now with us, the occasional rattle of a machine-gun in the night, the distant roar of allied bombers high in the sky and the pounding of the German flak. But I could only hint at them because our letters were opened and censured.

23

Friends and Foes

My work in the firm was enjoyable but they were not days of great commercial activity and I had plenty of spare time. I wanted to take up the thread of my former social life and perhaps rejoin the club where I used to play tennis, also look up people from my old school.

Brussels itself had a more inviting atmosphere than cheerless Paris or the sleepy little town where I had spent the last three years and the trams tended to give a look of normality to the almost trafficless streets. I had soon caught the mood of how to behave in a tram if a German sat next to me. You stood up the moment the soldier sat down and you felt gratified by the wave of approval passing through the crowd.

All the rumours about the Belgians not being too affected by shortages appeared true.

'With money you can get anything in Brussels' Madame Plocker had said.

You could certainly eat some delicious cakes in the patisseries, just like pre-war, only they were less in view. A number of restaurants served normal meals. To my surprise, buying a pair of shoes was also a near normal affair; I had the choice of several models in the size I required, but they were so expensive, I sold the pair I had just bought in France with my coupons in order to afford them, for they were dull and did not quite fit.

Reunion with former school acquaintances happened in a quite impromptu manner one day when four boys turned up at the office and asked for me. They had heard through the grapevine that I was back and they whisked me off to an ice-cream parlour they favoured. In our small gathering was a former class-mate of mine who was still doggedly trying to get his second Baccalauréat after several failures. The other three had been in the form below and two of them were also working at their second attempt, not astonishing when the closure of our Lycée in June 1940 had made learning so difficult for them. Then there was Marc Ruben for whom studying seemed effortless. Marc and I had been friends since our early years at school and I was really glad to see him again. Because of the small number in our lycée, classes had sometimes very few pupils and friendships formed across the divide of forms.

Nibbling our succulent ice-creams, we recalled the good old days, reviewing school events, analysing teachers and laughing at pranks for which their form had been famous; particularly the kidnapping of Nestor, the skeleton, from the biology lab. Nestor had been taken for a picnic to the Bois de Lacambre, a fashionable pleasure ground on the outskirts of Brussels, creating the expected sensation. It had not been easy to get hold of him on a Saturday morning when the school was closed. One of the gang had gone to see the caretaker about some possession forgotten in her class-room and she had helped the others to find their way into the building. Nestor had to be dismembered to fit into satchels, yet the following Monday, he was back in his place of honour a few minutes before the start of the lessons. Oh, those carefree days, without a war.

A war that could not for long be left out of the conversation.

'Did you know, there is a chap from the old philo class who has gone to France to join the *Milice*, our glorious French equivalent of the SS?'

It was also rumoured that someone in my year had made for England and succeeded. And did I know little Alain Mathieu?

'Yes, he used to be in the Scouts with my brothers.'

'Well, he transferred to a Belgian school when our lycée was closed and there another boy denounced him for possessing some leaflets dropped by the RAF and passed round the school – jealousy over some girl. The Germans came to arrest Alain Mathieu and effectively found some leaflets in his pocket. He was only sixteen at the time and they beat him repeatedly to obtain the name of the person who had brought the leaflets to school. All he ever said was that he had found them in the playground and after three weeks they released him, when his poor widowed mother was despairing of ever seeing him again.'

The closing of our school was a problem for those who insisted on obtaining French state exams, for now they had to study on their own or have recourse to private tuition. My friends had joined a small group that took lessons with a lecturer from Brussels University, another insitution which had been closed by decree. Unlike Louvain, the Catholic university some distance away from Brussels which had remained open, Brussels, a lay establishment, had incurred the wrath of the Nazis. Its academics had in their time expressed liberal and radical views and condemned Hitler's regime. Now some of them could only exist by offering private tuition but courses and examinations went on in secret, albeit on a reduced scale.

The arrangements seemed happily casual for my friends suggested that I come to one of the lessons.

'The prof won't mind, I am sure.'

One of his colleagues was actually a friend of my family and he received me very courteously. How I would have enjoyed my year of 'philo' in this manner – a stimulating teacher in surroundings that conveyed erudition. The study was cosy, richly carpeted, the walls lined with bookshelves right up to the ceiling, the highest books could only be reached with the help of elegant library steps.

Marc had also come with us. He was already a 'bachelier' but was looking for a direction in further studies after attempting a subject at a French university which he had found uninteresting. He had changed so much in those last three years. He was now very tall and attractive, still more prone to joking than serious conversation, but with a more mature sense of humour. Perhaps we might go out on our own one day without the others.

At the next gathering at the ice-cream parlour, Marc announced that he had to leave the country. Not entirely unexpected, for if Marc had the good fortune to have a Swiss nationality automatically passed on to him from a Swiss ancestor, he also had the misfortune to be of Jewish descent. The family was suddenly given short notice to pack their bags and go to Switzerland. They had been established here for three generations and it meant leaving their livelihood behind and starting all over again.

I felt resentful that so much in my life was dictated by the invaders. Yet Marc himself must have been grateful for that Swiss nationality; where would he have been sent otherwise?

Before he left, he promised to telephone my brothers for whom I gave him a lengthy message which I knew his memory could cope with. We corresponded for a while, his were entertaining letters but it was not the same thing.

The sports club we had belonged to before the war had had to quit the grounds it rented from the state. It was a great pity for it was vast and had many trees, and fresh air being a commodity sadly missing from the continental urban life, week-ends at the club were one of our most pleasurable memories. The membership had now fused with another club a good tram ride away and I decided to take up hockey there. Working in the laboratory and breathing acid was not too healthy and going down to work just a few flights of stairs was hardly exercise so I took my new sport seriously. I was not very good at it, though, and I attended the training sessions on Thursday afternoons as well as the games on Saturdays. I also met again young people I had known at my former club.

It was during a Thursday afternoon tram ride to the club that my audacity was put to the test. The coach was completely empty and I was sitting in one of two facing seats by the window. At a tram halt, a German in uniform got into the tram. Although he had the place to himself, he decided to sit opposite me, a very cosy little arrangement indeed. I had seen him from the window, a short, fat NCO with a cheeky face. And there I was, lumbered with his offensive presence.

Well of course, when a German sits near you, you just get up and sit somewhere else! But it was not as simple as that. The revelation suddenly hit me that heroes are only heroes because they have an audience. There was no support in that empty tram and I felt incapacitated. Yet I was thinking 'I must move, I must not let that Boche get away with it, I know he is looking at me, I must move.'

The tram halted at the next stop and to my horror, one of the men we called the 'blacks' got in, a Belgian traitor in an SS like uniform. Gosh, that was not the audience I wanted, he might arrest me if I insult the Boche!

The 'black' was reading his paper so I thought: now! With the desperation of someone about to jump to her death I gathered my hold-all and my hockey stick, I rose from my seat like a Jack in the box and moved to a seat where I was turning my back to the soldier.

I heard the door to the platform open. Then, from my window, I saw that the German had jumped out of the moving tram and was stumbling, trying to regain his balance.

24

Into Another Year

The approach of the festive season made my parents more acutely aware of the parting from their boys. On the 6th of December, the day Saint Nicholas comes down the Belgian chimneys where little shoes wait to be filled with toys and goodies, my mother decided to hold a children's party. The Bonar children, our little neighbour Nadine and others made our home alive once more with pitter-patter and young voices and when Christmas came, we would have felt quite sad, had not the Bonars invited us to their *réveillon*, the Christmas Eve party. There were quite a few guests there and the meal was good and copious, washed down with excellent wine, for Carlos Bonar, Spanish by birth, was a wine importer. Suddenly his nationality had become an advantage to him, a factor of safety in an occupied Europe, in spite of the fact that Carlos himself had shown open opposition of the Fascist regime during the Spanish war. His wife Fernande was Belgian, like most of their friends, for Carlos' family had settled in Brussels when he was a child.

We were grateful for the Bonar's invitation and their excellent fare but I missed the intimacy of a Christmas *en famille*. In some Belgian circles, this *réveillon* meant revelry, rollicking fun with lots of doubtful jokes, getting tipsy and dancing through the night. This was not our way and I longed for a Christmas tree, the smell of burning candles and I found myself wondering how my brothers were spending Christmas Eve.

We could only return home early on Christmas day, when the trams started again at around six in the morning and then we exchanged presents. It had been possible to do some Christmas shopping as long as we did not seek useful or practical gifts: instead the traditional crafts of Belgium adorned some shop windows and my mother was delighted with the large circular mat of real Bruges lace that we gave her, a present which before the war would have been very pricey. Now there was no outlet for such luxuries and they were real bargains. We regretted not having been able to send a present to the boys, although I had despatched a small gift to them, an article that at the moment was all the rage.

A poem called 'Si' had recently appeared in display windows, written in ornate writing on parchment-like paper and prettily framed. It was on sale at stationers, in gift-shops and at other traders. No author was mentioned but the word had soon gone round that it was a translation of a famous poem by Rudyard Kipling and, in our present mood, it reflected the admiration we felt for the nation still unconquered by Hitler which would soon come and liberate us. It sold like hot cakes and I posted a copy to my brothers, without the frame, quite sure that the censors would have no idea that it was a translated English poem.

At the year's end, our projected trip materialized. New Year in Paris could sound romantic, but the city of light was in darkness and when the snow fell it was clad in silence.

We spent New Year's eve with our friends as planned and dined in a restaurant *sans tickets*, for if the rations were pitiful in peoples' baskets, smart restaurants remained open and thrived. To set one's conscience at rest, the black market was always upheld as something patriotic as the products so obtained were mainly diverted from the Germans who were commandeering foodstuffs and other commodities. Anyway, the passing of a year of occupation when one was still alive and in good shape was worth celebrating; the war situation was more auspicious and with every toast was expressed the hope that the next one would be a liberated New Year.

Our table companions were the Vaillants and their daughters and the Chevaliers and their sons. The Vaillants were friends of my father since the time he had settled in Paris, just after the first world war, but the Chevaliers were of more recent acquaintance. We had met them as refugees in the south where they also had some family connections and I knew Jacques Chevalier who had attended my brothers' school, but I had never met his elder brother Yves who was a few years older than me. It was good to make the acquaintance of a young man rather than a boy as most of my present friends were. Yves was nice; perhaps his face was too round, a feature accentuated by the thick rimmed spectacles, but he was cosy and solid and we got on well together.

Alas our enjoyable meal had to end early because of the last metro and the curfew. The young generation at one end of the long table took a poor view of that. We wanted to see the New Year in, so we schemed to persuade M. and Madame Vaillant to let us spend the rest of the year and the beginning of the new one in their home. We wrote a humorous petition signed by all concerned on the back of a menu and it was accepted somewhat reluctantly because it meant putting up with the company until at least 5.30 am the start of the first metro. We went on foot to the Vaillants' who lived quite close to the restaurant and Yves and I walked arm in arm in the snow. On our way, we crossed other groups of happy people chatting and hurrying home before the curfew. As the party progressed at the Vaillants they soon admitted that it was a good idea after all. We danced to the screech of an old gramophone and to Andrée Vaillant's piano playing and the parents did not take much persuading to join in till the small hours of the morning. When somnolence became noticeable amongst the guests, M. Vaillant produced a game called 'billard Nicolas' which caused much merriment. The miniature balls of this game are not pushed by a cue, they are set in motion with the aid of rubber bulbs which all the players were soon squeezing frantically to send the balls into the opposite camp. The energy people found in spite of the sleepless night was astonishing.

After a few hours' rest, we caught a suburban train on our way to surprise Grand'mère, a plot we had organised with my uncle and aunt. They had arrived first with the victuals and Grand'mère had immediately declared that there was far too much for the three of them.

'But we have invited some friends to join us for New

Year's lunch,' replied her son, 'don't worry, they are very nice and we shall do all the work.'

Grand'mère was a little taken aback by this intrusion into her tranquillity but when we knocked at the door and she realized who the friends were, she could not contain her emotion.

'Oh you great big teases,' she said, when she recovered her capacity to speak, 'what a surprise this is for me.'

All through the day she expressed her joy at the unexpected visit. Her small dining-room was filled with people she loved and she was very happy, forgetting no doubt the age we lived in, the third great war in her life time.

In the evening, we had to rush back to Paris, for we had booked seats at the theatre – altogether an exhausting twenty-four hours, but the most enjoyable for years. There was however another aspect to my journey. My father wanted to introduce me to M. Laurent who owned an assay and analysis laboratory and who had agreed to employ me as a trainee in his establishment for a few weeks. There I hoped to acquire the practical experience necessary for my future examination.

My stay in Paris was fixed for the end of February, when I would reside in the small hotel where we had always stopped on our visits to the capital, and which was situated conveniently near to my place of work. There was no problem about my board as a number of friends insisted that I should be their daily guest and I would visit them in turn. I did look forward to those coming weeks, when I would have a taste of independence and a new way of life.

We spent our last evening in Paris as guests of the Chevaliers. Jacques entertained us with his imitations of the popular singers in vogue, but Yves, of a more placid temperament, preferred conversation. We discussed our tastes and interests, and he promised to take me to see a play when I returned to Paris.

I never did go out with Yves. At the time I started my work at Laurent's, the S.T.O. – *Service du Travail Obligatoire* – had just been decreed by the Germans and Yves had to go into hiding where he remained until the liberation. Because they had so little response in attracting the French workforce to the war-factories in their homeland, in spite of all their inducement, the Germans had now decided to conscript the young people they needed. But few were willing to submit to this mode of forced labour. I was to learn one basic rule: not to form an attachment to any member of the opposite sex or the Germans would somehow contrive to keep us apart.

Back in Brussels, I applied myself to my work in the laboratory, eager to give a good impression when I started at Laurent's. As I appeared keen to prepare for my examination, our chemist seemed less disposed to impart his skill to me and I sensed his misgiving. He clearly thought that he might lose his job if there was another assayer in the firm. Only after my father reassured him that such was not his intention, that he simply wanted his children trained in some of the skills necessary to a bullion firm, did I get more attention from M. Gallois. He even let me complete an assay on my own.

By this January of 1943, I had become accustomed to life in the occupied world. It was impossible to go far without meeting the green uniforms so hated by the population; all the good hotels were requisitioned by the Germans and the large cinemas (now renamed 'Soldaten Kinos') reserved for their troups and the Gestapo reigned supreme over all other authorities. Ostensibly wearing civilian clothes, they were sometimes so obvious with their black trench-coats and black wide brimmed trilby hats, that no-one could mistake them for peaceful citizens.

But morale was high. There was no Maréchal Pétain here to sow the seeds of hesitation. The BBC was our source of news whilst people ignored the write-ups in the press, now run by traitors. But it was necessary to buy a daily paper if only to find out about decrees and official announcements that affected our everyday existence. We also received secretly *La Libre Belgique*, the clandestine newspaper, and we passed it round to other readers for its publication was perforce limited due to the great danger involved in printing it. Its columns reported the real version of events, the truth about people disappearing, and it reflected our mood and our hopes.

Listening to the BBC at news time could require a great effort of concentration. All wavelengths in our language were jammed, but by playing with the knobs, it was sometimes possible to discover a station the Germans were themselves listening to, and where the reception was good. Fortunately, the transmissions in English were not so distorted by jamming and this is where my understanding of English was a great advantage.

If one could stand listening to the official radio, it was revealing. According to their figures, the Royal Navy and the Royal Air Force had by now been destroyed twice over; it was a wonder they were still in the war! But the news of an important local event, whether distressing or heartening, always travelled like wild fire amongst the population.

This is precisely what happened on the 20th of January, at the end of the working day, when a customer came in with a beaming face and related the fantastic story he had heard from people in the street: a Spitfire of the Royal Air Force had dived to roof-top height in the Avenue Emile De Mot, a short, wide thoroughfare that met the Avenue Louise just at the point facing the dreaded Gestapo building, and, firing its cannons at close range, it aimed at the Gestapo quarters, turning the place into a shambles! No better heroic deed could have given the beleaguered population more satisfaction. The pounding of this most dreaded, most infamous Nazi institution was not only an act of courage, it was an act of tremendous skill.

The BBC was soon to confirm the attack by a Belgian Flying Officer, the Baron Jean-Michel de Lelys Longchamp. How we loved this pilot for performing a solitary action in breach of discipline, but in the cause of liberty! Would he be reprimanded?

It was rumoured that many of the occupants of the building had rushed to the windows on hearing the sudden thunderous noise and that quite a number of the torturers of the Avenue Louise had been killed. We would never know the extent of the damage, for nothing was mentioned in the press. We were informed by a friend who visited us the next day, that the SS had cordoned off the area. Just after the event, the avenue was teaming with people who had come to gloat over the discomfiture of the oppressors and those who jeered had been seized and taken to the still intact cellars of the Gestapo, where they were beaten up. So it would be wise to wait a few days before our curiosity could be satisfied, but what a wonderful start to the year!

25

Correspondence

The attack on the Gestapo building would have been a wonderful story to write to my brothers and to my friends, if it were not for the censor, who stamped little red and black swastikas on all our correspondence. Just the sort of sensational news I used to enjoy sharing with Marianne Delambre and Bobette Duteil in our school days; they listened to the BBC, so maybe they knew about it. Marianne had written to me, but her letter had taken so long and had to be so cautiously written, it was hardly news when it arrived. As for Bobette, she had preferred to send me a card via Gilbert and it had been just as quick.

The mail from Switzerland, usually more regular, allowed my brothers and I to carry on an assiduous correspondence. We wrote about events in our life, people we met, what we read, and so we felt near in spite of the distance that separated us.

We gathered from their letters that the Christmas vacation had been fun, with their school turning into a boarding house for young people on skiing holidays. There were parties and dances, but the boys felt the shortage of pocket money at that particular time. They rarely went into the town which was so full of temptations, unless someone invited them to partake in a cake-guzzling session in the celebrated patisserie.

School matters were always prominent in our epistolary exchange, so I took on the role of mentor to my brothers' studies. My letters were full of encouragement and advice and theirs of information about their class-work and their textbooks. Had they still been living at home, they would surely not have put up with all this patronising from their sister, who had not always been a model of studiousness herself. I found myself disserting on the Latin authors Gilbert was translating, maybe with some regret that I had not paid enough attention to them when I had the chance. The boys certainly progressed well despite the lack of parental supervision, especially Georges for whom the small classes were a blessing. He, who had always been inattentive and dissipated during lessons, now discovered an interest in several subjects and he blossomed. His letters, at first full of spelling mistakes, now contained very few, and I hastened to congratulate him and to theorise on the importance of good spelling. I would also advance the theory that our country would soon need educated men to restore it to its former place in the world and I hoped that those patrotic words would spur their learning enthusiasm.

Gilbert, who was going to attempt his first baccalauréat the following July, was beginning to think about a career. A film he had seen, he wrote home, a newsreel of the battle of Stalingrad had effectively stamped out his boyhood fascination for a career in any of the armed services. These images of war had shocked him, the human suffering he witnessed horrified him. No, he would do his duty if called to, but he would not enter the military profession. His future, he decided, was in the small family firm where he would take the place reserved for him; and he would write to Papa to discuss the best course to follow in his studies. Georges followed suit and suggested we would make a nice trio. Perhaps it was because they missed their family that they felt that way, perhaps it was because I wrote about my work and about the efficient way Papa ran the firm. If in our letters, we complained about our parting, we never failed to stress that we were lucky to be all safe and in good health.

Then came the letter from the headmaster's wife. Gilbert had had a skiing accident: a bad fracture and a damaged tendon and he would be in hospital for a few days. Then he would be immobilised for several weeks. Of course, when the letter arrived, the accident was days old, and my parents worried until the next mail, when they learnt that the patient was progressing normally. It was very unfortunate news, but the boy was well looked after, and in such times as we lived, we had to admit it was no tragedy. Gilbert himself took it as well as he could and it gave me an excuse to write more philosophical letters on how to endure his plight and occupy his enforced rest.

Now, Georges wrote longer letters and one could detect that he was upset and missing the company of his brother, now confined to his room.

'Sunday morning, I went to mass at the little chapel in the valley,' he wrote, 'and I prayed for Gilbert and for all of you.'

Never before, had I known in him this religious fervour. He went on: 'When the collection came, I fumbled in my pocket and discovered I did not have a *sou* to put in the bowl. I had forgotten I had spent all my pocket money.

26

The Old Gentleman

It had been all too easy to cross the frontier into France during those few months and to assume that we could go to Paris at will. If trains were sometimes slow and overcrowded, rail fares at least were still cheap in comparison to other things.

Unfortunately, several weeks before I was due to go to Paris, the news got around that the situation had changed. The Germans had reasserted their grip and it was now impossible to cross the frontier and the borderline of the *Zone Interdite* with an *'Ausweis'*, that is an official pass delivered by the military authority. They were impossible to obtain except on very compassionate grounds, such as the serious illness of a close relative and that had to be well documented by doctors' certificates. Or of course if you were a businessman whose business was of benefit to the occupation authorities.

My chances of being granted such a document in time were obviously nil. I thought of all the arrangements that had been made on my behalf and I was incensed. On reflection, the situation was as it was meant to be, and as it had always been, except for that short period following the collapse of the Russian front when, through sheer lack of personnel, the check-points had remained unmanned.

But far from yielding to the will of the invaders, people always tried to find ways to defeat their intentions and pass round the obstacles. In this instance, our problem was solved by being introduced to a person who had access to the right German quarters and who claimed she could obtain documents in return for a consideration. She was a lady with a Rumanian name and a German education who cared for her sick husband, and she made a living out of this little traffic.

With time, the German military administration, which was leading a soft life in Brussels, had become corrupt and some of its members were willing to sell an *Ausweis* for cash or coffee or cloth or some other commodity in short supply, but easily obtainable in the flourishing black market of Brussels; plus, of course, the commission for the Rumanian lady.

Through this contact, we were able to resume our travelling to France and also help some of our friends. We once obtained a permit for someone who had to leave Belgium in a hurry when the place became too hot due to his activities in the underground. After the liberation, the lady in question was arrested for collaboration with the enemy; but testimonies and evidence from those who were indebted to her helped to secure her acquittal.

And so it was that I could after all attend my training in Paris with an *Ausweis* valid in both directions for many weeks. My father came with me to the station to help me with my luggage for the trams were pretty full at this time of the morning. We had long forgotten what cars and taxis looked like and my luggage was heavy because it contained books and a number of things for relations and friends that were unobtainable in Paris. I had found some real flannel pyjamas for little Jean-Luc. His mother would never believe her eyes. I felt happy because I have always enjoyed travelling by train and my father had treated me to a second class ticket – in those days there were three classes – to make my long journey more comfortable.

In my compartment were a young couple and an old gentleman, at least he seemed old to me for he had white hair and a neatly trimmed little white beard. The four of us soon began to exchange a few cordial words and I had the feeling that we would be good travelling companions. The old gentleman, very smartly dressed in a navy blue suit had a hearty laugh. He soon informed us that he was going to Paris on business. The young couple, recently married, had not been able to go on honeymoon, so this trip was in lieu of. I explained the aim of my journey and very soon we were all friends; it was a time when people found a great need to communicate.

It all started as the train went by a level crossing where some motorised troops were waiting. One of us young ones passed a casual remark about 'them'. We often felt the need to mention 'them', to get them out of our system. Some joke, some sarcasm, and we had established our togetherness in this matter.

However, as the conversation went on in this tone, it became obvious that the old gentleman was not joining in. He was listening with a slightly vexed expression on his face, until finally he butted in as if he meant to give us all a telling off.

'You don't really believe all that propaganda from London do you?'

Stunned and upset, we then had to listen to the usual arguments of sympathisers and collaborators: the German hegemony was a fait accompli, we had better accept it whatever our misgivings, the allies would never land in Europe because the German machine was too formidable and its people too efficient; anybody with any sense might as well make the best of the situation.

'Anyway, I find them very nice people to deal with in business.'

So, he did business with them! He certainly looked prosperous. He was obviously not a creepy collaborator, nor an informer, these were just his opinions and he would let us argue. So our eloquence knew no bounds, we fought for our cause with determination and from every angle: the humane, the patriotic, the political. It all took place in a civilised manner because he was a nice fellow; yet such matters seemed to have the importance of life and death. We talked of arrests, of hostages, of all the things we knew by hearsay and by London, but of course we could not offer him any proof. He was sometimes taken aback by the logic of our arguments and was obviously impressed by the sincerity of our convictions, by our faith in the final victory.

He became quiet. Perhaps he was wondering what the future held in store for him if we were right.

The train stopped at the frontier and 'they' came in to check our papers. A tall officer in his impeccable green uniform and jackboots had a look in the compartment, up and down, left and right, and he picked up the book that I had intended to read and which lay on the seat next to me. He fingered a few pages, then put it down again. I breathed an inaudible sigh of relief and hoped that anxiety had not shown on my face. The book was in a leather book-holder, and between it and the book cover, I had hidden letters. They were from French friends in Brussels to their families in France – but it was absolutely forbidden to transport uncensored mail.

As the train rolled on, we remained silent for a while and I began to feel hungry. The restaurant-car attendant peeped in the compartment to announce that lunch was being served but I reached for a bag where my mother had packed me a picnic. The young couple were about to make a move.

Before I had time to open my bag, the old gentleman said:

'Well, I think we ought to seal this discussion with a nice meal. I invite you all to lunch, I think you are such interesting young people. Although I don't share all your views, I have really enjoyed this discussion, please be my guests.'

I looked at the other two, wondering what to do. The old gentleman was pleasantly insistent and we tacitly agreed and followed him to the restaurant-car.

The meal was certainly a pleasant way to occupy a long journey. We now kept off politics and amazingly, there were many other subjects of conversation. The wine was excellent, we became more jolly and he insisted that we finished the meal with a bottle of champagne. In the happy torpor that followed, sipping the partly 'ersatz' coffee, I felt vaguely guilty, but only vaguely, because we had fought gallantly for our cause.

Had we convinced him at all? Perhaps we deserved this reward, and anyway some of his ill-gotten money was now being spent on the right sort of people!

27

The Star of David

My hotel room was none too luxurious and in need of some redecoration. It was not very warm either for coal was not so readily available here, but I liked it all the same because I relished the prospect of a few weeks on my own in Paris. I felt tired after hauling my heavy luggage in the long corridors and up and down the steps of the metro, then in the street to the hotel, so I tucked myself up cosily in the double bed and fell asleep. It was not long before I was awoken by a deafening, piercing noise, so loud that I sat up in a panic, wondering where I was.

When I came to my senses, I realized that the uproar came from an air-raid siren, a siren that sounded as if it were in my very room. I opened the window and came to the conclusion that it was located on the tower of the little church, just a stone's throw from my hotel. The street was dark and deserted, and when the wailing had ceased, I could hear the droning of bombers high in the sky, on their way to Germany, I hoped. Then the repeated thumping of the anti-aircraft guns, and I prayed that they would miss their targets. I closed the shutters, something I had neglected to do, and I found that it helped to muffle the strident noise in subsequent alerts.

Having planned a short-cut to the 'Laboratoire Laurent' through a maze of small streets, I set out in good spirits on a sunny morning that seemed to herald the spring. My route took me into one of those ancient and picturesque districts of Paris, with tall, shabby buildings, faded grey shutters, and an array of small shops. A poor district, where, at that early hour, the housewives were already in quest of scarce provisions and queues were beginning to form at the bakers' shops.

A woman was walking towards me, and I noticed on her coat a bright yellow star in the centre of which was the word 'Juif' in black letters – a very large badge that could not pass unnoticed. It was my first encounter with the practice of labelling Jews and I was staggered.

Another woman, similarly branded, passed me by, then a young mother, holding a little girl by the hand. The girl, poor little mite, also had the yellow star stitched on her coat. The sight of a baby in arms with the badge on its woolly clothing made my heart ache.

This was obviously a Jewish quarter of the city. I was surprised, as well as shocked, to come upon these people, for in Brussels, the Jews had been deported or lived under assumed identities.

I noted that there were no men wearing the yellow star; perhaps the men had already been 'fetched'! All the men I passed were non-Jews.

This was a walk I had meant to enjoy, but every morning the spectacle of the yellow stars turned it into a heart-ache. Until one day, I saw them no more. They had been 'fetched'.

An eye-witness described the raid to me. It was not the Boches that had fetched the mothers and children out of their homes and loaded them into the waiting coaches, the mothers in one, the children in another; no, it was the French police. The Boches evidently preferred to delegate their dirty work, and the passers-by witnessed these harrowing scenes, totally helpless. I thought it was monstrous that the French Police were made to perform such a task, it made me feel ashamed.

The people who lived in these streets were the poor Jews, the ones who could not afford to go into hiding, the ones who had no well-off gentile friends capable of sheltering them. If there had been some warning of the raid, perhaps the little children could have been saved – it was the helplessness of it all that sometimes made one lose hope.

28

My Spell in Paris

I gained sound experience from the weeks I spent at Laurent's, as I had never had an occupation outside the family circle. On the first day, M. Laurent introduced me to members of his staff before leaving me in the charge of those who would initiate me into their methods of work. There was an air of efficiency about the place, where the different stages of an assay were carried out by separate people, well trained yet unqualified, M. Laurent being the only qualified person entitled to sign the certificate. These repetitive tasks must have been monotonous, but it was just the practice I needed and everybody seemed very happy and chummy; everybody except a young man called Julien, who never said a word. At the back of the premises was the laboratory proper where more expert and detailed analyses were performed by qualified chemists.

It is said that you cannot start work in a Parisian firm without being thoroughly teased; I had not been there an hour before someone sent me to find the gold magnet. I did not fall for it and it earned me some respect.

'Do you know,' they said, 'there is a new girl in the lab, she is a qualified chemist, and yet she went all over the place to find it.'

My first week had been spent with that strange fellow Julien, and it was as much as I could do to extract a yes or a no out of him; so I just watched his nimble gestures and soon became less clumsy in my handling of the precision-balance and in manipulating tiny quantities of metal chips. Fortunately, my other sponsors were more pleasant and much more cooperative.

My favourite was Roland. He looked after the cupelling

furnace and preformed the cupellation and other smelting jobs that might be required. His was a hot and dirty job and he wore blue overalls. Roland, who was about forty, had the fair hair and healthy complexion of people from the north and his frank blue eyes were a nice change after Julien's shifty look. He loved to talk about his twelve-year-old daughter who had just been admitted to a 'Lycée' and of whom he was very proud. He had ambitions for her, she was not going to be uneducated like himself, no, she would have an interesting career. Much to his pleasure, I was a willing audience because of the interest I was taking in my own brothers' schooling.

In spite of the taciturn Julien, the people who worked at Laurent's were a friendly crowd, from the odd job man to the laboratory manager, and difference of status was no barrier to an occasional get together after work at the little bar across the road. It was a quaint old place, with its sign so faded, you had to guess it was a bar; a few steps led down to a room below street level which still had an old zinc counter, and there was saw-dust on the floor. But its real attraction was that it served absinthe and other alcoholic aperitifs unobtainable elsewhere. Not that I cared much for absinthe, but I joined the group once or twice, purely for the atmosphere.

When the chief chemist was about to go on an early holiday, I was convened to a drinking party with a difference. He had brought to work a large bottle of red vermouth, something not easy to come by, for he wanted to give us all a good-bye drink.

It was a Saturday, when the firm closed at noon, and we were all gathered in the lab, including M. Laurent, when our host said he could provide the drink, but not the glasses, and we would have to find ourselves a suitable vessel and give it a good wash.

'And don't think that by choosing a large one you will get more, because I shall measure out the rations.'

To find a dozen drinking vessels in a small laboratory is not so easy and I could see that people were not competing for the size, but for the oddity of the shape. We clinked glasses – after a fashion – and when we began to drink, any pretence that this was a serious occasion vanished in laughter, which was catching. Some sipped through a tube, others made contortions to bring the liquid to their mouths and all showed great imbibing talent, not made easy by the giggles. We were still in that state of hilarity when we left the premises, leaving the puzzled passers-by to wonder what there was to laugh so much about.

My last few days in that otherwise happy workforce were marred by the arrival on the scene of the *Service du Travail Obligatoire* to which the firm of Laurent, like all other enterprises, had to contribute a quota. The Germans wanted their pound of flesh and one of the people they took was Roland. Heads of firms were quite powerless and sometimes tried in vain to prove that their employees were indispensable and the only choice for a reluctant victim was to go into hiding or to make for the Maquis.

But it is not so easy when you are a breadwinner, so Roland submitted. After the first shock, he decided that in one way he was lucky; he was not being sent to the Ruhr or some other part of Germany that suffered repeated Allied bombings, but to a gunpowder factory 150 miles south of Paris. It was nice to be allowed to remain in France and not too far from his family which he hoped to see occasionally. He resented working for the German war machine, but so was his fate in common with many others.

The disaster happened after I had returned home to Brussels and I only learnt about it during my subsequent visit to Paris. There had been a mighty explosion at the gunpowder factory, one of the largest in France, and Roland, with numerous other French workers perished in the accident. It was kept quiet, of course, but news of the tragedy rapidly spread. I thought of the little girl I had heard so much about, and of Roland's wife, and the happy family picture he had painted.

I also learnt that another person was missing from the roll at Laurent's, the taciturn Julien. He was in jail. Not a hero's jail, just plain jail. It was an astonishing thing to hear about nowadays; being arrested meant to most people being apprehended by the military police or the Gestapo.

There had been a burglary at the firm, one day when a sizeable consignment of gold ingots was being delivered for assaying. A gang had sprung on the deliverers at the right moment and disappeared in a well organised escape. From the start, the police had suspected an inside job, and what led them to Julien, was his sudden lavish spending, his generosity to his colleagues at the little bar across the road where he had unexpectedly become sociable.

The tragedy for M. Laurent was that he had trained Julien into his job because the boy, the son of a friend of his, was a misfit and had proved unemployable. For Julien, it was a way as good as any of avoiding the STO and when he came out of jail, it would no doubt be in a liberated country.

29

Hospitality

If training at Laurent's had been an interesting experience, being entertained by friends every day had been like a holiday. The long lunch hour afforded plenty of time to reach their homes in the crowded Metro, but in the evenings, I always had to watch the time in order to get to my hotel before the curfew. If there was an alert, the trains stopped because the power was cut, and they stopped more often in the tunnel than in the stations; that usually meant an acrobatic descent onto the line and a walk to the next station, which was quite safe, as there was always plenty of warning before the line became live again. Alternatively, it meant a very long wait in a stationary train.

    I enjoyed having lunch at the Vaillants, who tended to spoil me. As my father's oldest friends, they had known me from birth, they had known my real mother, and they had been a comfort to my father when she died. They still called me 'l'enfant', and with them, I had the feeling of going back to my roots. There was something so Parisian about the style of their formal, yet elegant flat, about the sound of their voices, here I could rediscover the impressions of my early childhood. My father always used to say that Madame Vaillant was the best cook he had ever known, but these were sad times for her to exercise her talents. M. Vaillant grew wonderful vegetables in the garden of their weekend house, and for them, quality was the word; if they served radishes, they had to be of the right size and tenderness, and so it was with all produce, with which Madame Vaillant made simple, yet excellent meals. She did not find it as easy as the Bruxelloises to obtain the provisions she needed and like many other Parisian housewives, she made long train journeys to the country where she might know a farmer. She would come back with her luggage and baskets full of the foodstuffs that had evaded requisition.

The Vaillants had a daily help to whom they seemed to show much solicitude and generosity. The reason became apparent when I saw the lady put on her coat; it bore the yellow star of the Jews. One morning, she did not turn up. The Vaillants thought that perhaps she was unwell, but she never returned and there never was a message.

The Vaillant daughters both had jobs in Paris, and they brought home the latest political jokes circulating in the Capital, jokes at the expense of the Germans, but more often at the expense of the Maréchal. Subtle or crude, they showed irreverence for the man who had changed our cherished national motto 'Liberté, Egalité, Fraternité' into 'Travail, Famille, Patrie'. The issues were not confused here like in Vichy. This verbal disrespect, the stories of tricks played on the Germans, the listening to the BBC and the circulation of clandestine newspapers were all the expression of a growing passive resistance.

When I spent a Sunday at the Vaillants' weekend house, I was full of admiration for the way M. Vaillant tended his garden, nearly alone, in spite of having lost his left arm in the First World War. In the afternoon, I went for a walk with Andrée and Suzanne in the forest of Sénart where we followed a stream that wound about in the woodland. Suddenly, in a clearing, we came across a group of boys who seemed to be engaged in a very absorbing game under the supervision of a couple of adults; they all wore similar neckerchiefs.

'Clandestine boy scouts,' said Andrée, 'they meet here every Sunday and when they go home, they tuck their scarves in their pocket.'

It was heartening to see such an activity taking place in the depth of the forest, for it had been banned by the Germans in the occupied territories.

It was a measure of the hospitality that my parents had shown to their friends in the good old days before the war that so many doors were now opened to me. At such a time, it would have been very difficult to fend for myself in Paris. Occasionally, I would lunch on my own in one of the little eating-houses that had once offered such good fare at a modest price to office clerks and shop assistants, and found that they now offered a meagre diet. The regulars who gave some ration tickets may have been slightly better off, but my lunch consisted of some very skimmed curd cheese, a bit of spinach, one small piece of bread and an apple, a very frugal meal indeed.

I lunched for a whole week at the Chevaliers and I enjoyed the company of Jacques who had now better things to do than to imitate the singers in vogue. He was attempting his 'Bac de Philo' in June and was in a serious mood. The family had news of Yves through an intermediary, but I had no idea where he was hiding.

Those relations and friends who lived further afield, I visited in the evenings and of course there were plays and concerts to go to. The theatre flourished – in spite of the heavy censorship – and there was a wide choice of concerts, also 'censored', because composers of Jewish origin, like Mendelssohn, were banned from programmes.

When Paul, the son of a business friend of my father, whom I had known for many years, invited me to see a ballet at the Opera, I was delighted and I wore my best dress. Paul was a second year student at the Sorbonne and was therefore safe from the STO – for the time being. Paul was very serious and I had never really felt relaxed in his presence. He was also thrifty, although he was extremely well off, the sort of person who will not spend a penny where a halfpenny will do. So he booked some seats on the highest balcony where he claimed the acoustics were better and one had a panoramic view of the stage. Before the start of the performance, I looked at the stalls down below and I gasped. I had a panoramic view of plush red seats completely covered in green – green uniforms. Paul said it was always like that, the stalls must either be requisitioned by them, or they must reserve the lot. So here they came to enjoy their culture! I could not reconcile this scene of well-mannered civility with the predicament of the people in the little streets on my way to work.

Of all the people I called on during those Paris weeks, two young friends, Odile and Lucile Mosalsky were the most eager to invite me to their home. Before the war, their parents had had a house in the same street as Grand'mère's where they spent weekends and holidays, and whenever my brothers and I had stayed with Grand'mère, the girls had been our holiday companions. They were a family that kept very much to themselves; I don't think Odile and Lucile had any close friends, so I was received with open arms. Now in their teens, they were aiming for a musical career and they were pupils of the Paris Conservatoire. The small house with a front garden where they lived was situated on the edge of the Bois de Boulogne, but bordering on the industrial district of Billancourt. Whenever I paid the family a visit, my young friends insisted that I stay the night, which meant sharing a double divan with Odile; Lucile was furious because at sixteen, she thought she had as much right to my friendship as her sister, who was nearer my age, and we usually finished three to a bed, chatting most of the night.

I appreciated having musical friends. I had never learnt an instrument myself, but I enjoyed listening to music and it was therefore a treat when they smuggled me into the Conservatoire with a group of music students to hear the resident orchestra rehearse on the eve of a concert.

The Mosalskys, as their name implies, were Russian emigrés. In 1918, the father had been serving with a contingent of Russian soldiers in the French lines and remained in this country when the revolution flared up, whilst the mother had come to France as a child and was very much a Parisienne. The girls were completely French and did not even know Russian, which their parents used as their private language. The whole family had cycles, a very sensible means of transport in those trafficless days, and one sunny, warm Sunday, Odile, Lucile and I went for a ride after lunch. The girls wanted to visit a teacher who had been ill and who lived near the Etoile, so I set out with Odile on her parents' tandem, Lucile following on her own bike. The ride through the Bois was exhilarating, the trees were coming out in buds and droves of people were taking their first stroll in the sunshine; some dressed as if summer had already arrived.

When we reached our destination, there was an air-raid warning, a distant rumbling noise, then the sound of anti-aircraft guns. At least the alert did not stop us cycling, as it stopped the people travelling in the metro and the ride back was just as pleasant.

As we were approaching the Mosalsky's home, we were suddenly overtaken by ambulances and on coming closer, we became conscious of a tumult, of some sort of a commotion. Odile asked me to pedal harder on the tandem. As we turned into their road, which was full of people, there was a smell of broken masonry and an unpleasant dust in the air. Then we saw their house, sliced in half. It looked like an open doll's house, with the furniture still in place, but the fridge was hanging down, with its door twisted; a pile of smoking rubble lay in the front garden.

The scene of devastation and the impact on my young friends left me breathless. We dropped our cycles and Odile charged frantically through the crowd of onlookers and policemen towards the house, while Lucile, holding my hand, started to cry aloud. We followed Odile and a voice was heard saying, 'Don't worry, your parents are all right!' In the next moment, we saw M. Mosalsky standing amongst the rubble, a great bear of a man with his arm around his little wife, who was in tears. It would be difficult to describe the emotional scene that followed, for the girls had feared that their parents had been killed. Father Mosalsky tried to restore calm in everybody's mind; there was only material damage, he said, they should rejoice that all the family was alive.

The target of the American bombers had been the Renault works, some distance away, but the bombs that fell astray had killed people and damaged property. The Mosalskys had rushed to the cellar on hearing the first explosion, and just in time too for the next bomb had been for them. They were quite sure that had we all been at home it would have been a different story.

I stayed as long as I felt useful, then the family was driven away to a friend's house where they would stay while things were sorted out. The façade of the house had been removed in one fell swoop, and it seemed that they would be able to recover some of their possessions.

I had never taken shelter during an alert, in Brussels or Paris, nor had anybody else I knew. We always assumed that the bombers were on their way to Germany.

30

Vive le Roi Albert!

Letters brought across the frontier by friends kept me in contact with my parents and I knew that my father intended to join me in Paris for the last few days and that we would return together. He wanted first of all to thank M. Laurent for giving me the chance of such valuable training but it was also time to enquire about the syllabus, the timing, and the possibility of my taking the assayer's examination set by the Paris Mint. This French qualification, like others in the professional field, was valid in Belgium, but not the other way round.

The news my father brought from Belgium was disturbing. The STO was now in force, playing havoc with peoples' lives and crippling firms. German officials had recently descended on our firm and claimed the smelter, the accountant, the secretary and the chemist. They were all the key people and it was only by arguing frantically that my father had succeeded in having Madame Eveline struck off their list; she was a person of very nervous temperament and she had nearly passed out on hearing the news. In the end, by evasion or by ruse, none of the others found themselves making ammunitions for Hitler's war.

People chosen for the STO had to be in good shape physically and were required to attend a medical examination. M. Gallois, the chemist, decided to skip this and to disappear forthwith. He had the chance to hide in his native provincial town, where he would be helped to obtain another identity and even a job. As for Theo, the smelter, who sometimes had digestive problems, he ate all the wrong things several days before the appointment and made himself convincingly unwell; he was not accepted. M.

Devos, our accountant, had no wish to go to Germany either. So he confided in the doctor where his wife worked as a housekeeper, and he was advised to take a certain dose of caffeine at an appropriate time, which he did without hesitation. Not only did the medical panel turn him down, but one German doctor, horrified by the state of his heart, advised him to take an early retirement.

It was a happy ending for our small staff. Nevertheless, I was surprised and worried to find women on the STO list. So far, it had not been the case in France. My father decided that I must not be on the list of official employees, although my presence was needed now that M. Gallois had gone into hiding. I could not sign assay certificates, but I would be useful for tests wanted within the firm.

An appointment was made by telephone with the Director of the Mint Laboratory, who was the person responsible for setting examinations. He received us courteously but regretted to inform us that I had unfortunately missed the exam session for this year. He thought my level of practical preparation very inadequate; I would have to do much practical work in a laboratory for there are certain things that cannot be learnt in books. Candidates for the Assayer's Diploma were usually qualified chemists and he did not hold out much hope for me.

Disconcerted, I explained how difficult it was for me to sit an exam in Paris because I lived in Belgium and correspondence between the two countries was extremely difficult. That seemed to touch a chord.

He was a frail-looking man, bald, with a dark moustache and matter of fact brown eyes behind gold-rimmed spectacles, everybody's idea of a serious and diligent civil servant. On hearing that I came from Belgium, his expression became friendly and his eyes more animated.

'I am very fond of that little country,' he said, 'King Albert of the Belgians is one of my heroes.'

We made a point of stating that we were French, just residents in Belgium. But he went on singing the praise of 'the Roi Soldat' of 1914, paying tribute to his unflinching courage at the head of the small army which resisted the great barbaric power.

'He was a truly great man!'

Inevitably, this lyrical evocation of a period not dissimilar to our own led to talk about our present situation, where we were much in agreement.

'I would like to help you, Mademoiselle Rey,' he said at the end of our little discussion. 'I'll consider you an exceptional case, in memory of the Roi Albert!'

I was taken aback and felt a bit of a fraud, although I had told him I was not Belgian.

'I'll make a special exam session for you in October and if you would like to come and work here for two or three months with our chemists, I'll teach you personally all the practical work regarding the exam.'

We did not know how to thank him for this incredible offer, and all in memory of the Roi Albert!

'Has your daughter somewhere to stay in Paris? . . . then we could start in mid-August.'

'I am an imposter,' I said later to my father, looking forward to yet another and much longer period in Paris.

That evening, we visited my friends, the Mosalskys who had now been rehoused in an apartment in central Paris. The accommodation was spacious and pleasant, and enough of their belongings had been saved to furnish the flat comfortably. The whole family seemed happy that the unfortunate event had ended so well.

When Odile and Lucile found out that I would return to Paris for a long period, they begged their parents to take me as a boarder. They agreed willingly and we made arrangements; I promised to find my own lunch for I knew well the difficulties of providing food for a family.

Walking back to the hotel, my father and I were chatting happily about the day's events when the sound of sirens suddenly broke the serenity of a spring evening. The experience of the Mosalskys had not changed my attitude to taking shelter – the Allies had no reason to bomb the city of Paris. It was different, alas, for those who lived near a marshalling yard or a factory of military importance for the Germans. People there were suffering severe air-raids and were often the casualties of their own friends!

The familiar droning of the aircraft in the sky, the thumping of the Flak suddenly became more uncomfortable when bits of shrapnel began to fall around us on the pavement. I was sure those little projectiles were lethal, but my father was ignoring them and went on with the conversation as if they did not exist. Then a red hot piece of metal fell at our feet.

'That one just missed us,' he said.

Maybe he had been toughened to this kind of thing during his youth in the trenches, but I did not find it at all funny and I ran towards the porch of the hotel.

31

The Easter Break

I would have over four months to wait before my next visit to Paris to which I was earnestly looking forward. The Brussels I had returned to was losing the mood of optimism that had reigned after the North African landings and things were getting tougher. In spite of advances on all fronts, the Germans did not seem on the verge of collapse and the hope I had cherished of spending next Christmas with my brothers in a liberated country now looked like a utopian dream. It mattered to have things to look forward to since we had to be armed with more patience before our great hope could be realized.

Having the laboratory to myself gave me a chance to show off what I had learnt. I felt useful, although my usefulness was limited since I could not sign any assay certificates. Customers who required an official 'bulletin' had to be sent to another firm – not a good practice according to my father – but hopefully I would be in charge at the end of October.

Working alone in the spacious white laboratory on the first floor was very satisfying; when the weather was nice, I could open the two French windows that gave onto wrought iron balconies and watch the comings and goings in the street while I waited for the action of the boiling acids in the glass vessels to be terminated. The small smelting furnace was in the back room where the temperature could be uncomfortable in the summer and I found the equipment inferior to what I had been used to at Laurent's. The tongs to put the cupels in the furnace were too short and I tended to burn my fingers owing mainly to my slowness and inexperience. But I felt rewarded when I wrote down the results at the end of an operation.

There was not enough work to keep me constantly occupied in the laboratory and I spent the odd moment downstairs with the rest of the people. It was all relaxed and happy again after the STO scare until Theo announced one day that his son Gustave had to undergo a medical examination by order of the Germans.

Gustave used to pass our house every morning on his way to work, only two streets away. He was the boy who had been wounded on the roads of France when the Stukas bombed the columns of refugees. He had in fact completely recovered, in spite of a small piece of shrapnel still lodged in his thigh. This foreign body gave him no trouble, but Gustave pretended otherwise in order to appear unfit for labour in Germany. He had learnt to limp very convincingly and to walk with two sticks for he was by nature a comedian. I must add that he was a member of my father's rugby team and every Sunday, he would jettison his walking sticks in the dressing room and give an excellent performance on the pitch.

Gustave took his X-ray pictures with him that morning, to show the German doctors the cause of his limping. He had a beaming face when he came to tell his father the result.

The Germans had not been entirely convinced by the X-ray and insisted on taking away his walking sticks. Gustave, seemingly helpless, fell flat onto the stand loaded with smart Germany Army greatcoats, and they cushioned his landing onto the floor. The angered Germans gave him back his sticks and sent him home with a certificate of dispensation.

Gustave's description of the scene had kept us in fits. Theo hugged his son and remained in high spirits all day, which he showed by non-stop joking and teasing people – particularly Madame Eveline who was easy game. She had during the lunch hour gone to buy a leg of mutton from a 'smokkeleer' for her weekend meal and she had shown it to the others, very pleased with herself. Theo looked at the piece of meat and said:

'I would not trust these black-market butchers if I were you, it looks to me like the leg of a big dog!'

She rebuked him, offended, but every time Theo passed by her shopping bag, he would bark and that nearly put her off her Sunday lunch. That was Theo's way of giving vent to his joy.

There were now so many dodgers from the STO that the Germans, who were losing more and more men in Russia and needed this forced labour at all cost, started to round up people in the streets, theatres and cinemas. It was of the utmost importance to carry an official discharge paper or some other proof that you were not required for the STO.

I had not received an invitation yet – it was bound to come – but I had been able to exchange my identity card for one stating that I worked for 'The Industries', that is industries vital to the German war effort. A clerk we knew in the local council office had willingly done that for me, as he had procured for my father a completely bogus identity card if he ever were in danger. He had accepted a reward, but he did not make a trade of it. The civil servants were the same people in the same positions as in prewar days and many helped people within their capabilities. The Germans certainly could not rely on their loyalty.

Our everyday existence now took place against a background of roundups, early curfews and occasionally an announcement in the press that hostages had been shot. It was not infrequent for a tram to be halted by helmeted soldiers and all the passengers to be turned out. The men would have to stand with their arms raised, facing the wall, while the soldiers searched them and the women had to stand in a row with their handbags opened for scrutiny. Passengers were only allowed back in the tram when the soldiers were satisfied they had found no weapons.

However undignified and humiliating this harassment, it was a sure sign that the underground Resistance was becoming effective and giving our oppressors something to think about. Unfortunately, after a successful sabotage, the whole population would be punished by an early curfew. It disrupted social life and was not to be taken lightly; you could be shot on sight if found in the street after hours. The most sinister revenge against the success of the Resistance, however, was the execution of hostages. The list of victims would appear in the press and would send a shiver down one's spine, particularly the day my father recognized the name of someone he knew, a personality in the world of sport. To be twenty at such a miserable time when one wants to live and have fun was wretched. You may be safe for the moment but all around you there is suffering. A sad Madame Timmermans now came for her weekly couture day. Her husband, like the other prisoners in his jail, had been sent to Germany and she had no address to write to and received no news. But she was an optimist and was quite sure that he would come back; she polished with unflinching energy the innumerable silver cups he had won in his sporting life and that were cluttering their flat in the Gendarmerie buildings.

Life was not devoid of entertainment and it was sometimes full of surprises. When I went to the pictures with one of my old school friends, I was astonished to find that all lights were turned on during the newsreel.

'They are forced to do that,' said my companion, 'because people were throwing things at the screen. But be careful, we are being watched!'

Sure enough, I saw some vigilante walking up and down the aisles. All because when people had been forced to have the lights on to prevent them throwing missiles at the German news on the screen, they had brought their books to read or their knitting. Now if anyone indulged in such activities, he or she would be marched out of the cinema. What happened to them outside, I know not. I must say, I was so sickened by the newsreel – to call it blatant propaganda would be a gross understatement – that I chatted discreetly with my friend, my eyes away from the screen and I swore I would not go to the pictures again.

As for early curfews, they did not necessarily deter from social life. There were ways in which they could be turned into a friendly occasion; guests would arrive immediately after work and stay the night, bringing sleeping bags if needed.

During such an occasion, as I was spending the night on a sitting-room floor with others, I was invited to join in a camping expedition in the Ardennes at Easter time. Camping is something of a misnomer since living under canvas was forbidden. Our sleeping quarters were to be a gardener's hut in the woodland of an estate and we would lead an open air life like in the days of real camping.

We left some days before Easter and some of our parents were to come and stay in the village in a small mill-cum-baker shop-cum guest house during the Easter days. It was a hilly yet lush farming area where there was little sign of the war. No Germans. The nearest ones were some miles away in the town. The rural population seemed to feed itself pretty well and by chatting people up, we soon obtained the produce we needed.

The local owner of some caves had given us permission to enter them and to explore them, but because they could not at the present time be opened to the public, the main entrance was padlocked. Our only access was through a small hole in the ground, but being all young and supple, we had no difficulty in penetrating inside. Our torches were the only lights and it was occasionally a little dangerous, but extremely interesting. Some of my companions were young, perhaps in their last year at school, although Norbert was at an engineering college – so everybody was OK concerning official papers. This young crowd expressed its feeling about the war noisily and enjoyed doing forbidden things. We made a campfire in the wood every night – God knows what punishment we could have incurred for that – and made jokes about British parachutists that would see it and descend in our midst. Around that campfire, we sang all the national anthems of the allied sides – another serious offence – but since we did not know the Russian one, we sang the Internationale. Norbert, whose sympathies tended this way, taught us the words we did not know.

We were quite 'liberated' when we went to meet our parents at the little station and we greeted them with 'It's a long way to Tipperary' which we sang in complete abandon. The look of horror on their faces when they heard us.

'You are crazy, what about the Germans?'

'There are no Germans here.'

But we agreed to stop to pacify them. After showing them to their quarters, we returned to ours.

We cooked our meals at the entrance of the grotto where a rocky porch would shelter us from wind and rain, and a great shock was awaiting us. On the road, just facing our cooking area, a car was parked – a German army car, a resplendent open Mercedes and by it, stood a resplendent German officer. The driver was still in the car.

My heart missed a beat; we could not run away, so we proceeded towards our open air kitchen, ignoring the visitors. The officer, who must have been very high-ranking to judge by his elaborate uniform, joined us and tried to explain that he wanted to go into the cave. Was he a geologist or someone interested in caves? He could not be looking for 'Maquisards' dressed as he was and without protection. We explained that the caves were not opened and my girlfriend gave him a demonstration on how to get inside through the little hole; she reappeared on the other side of the iron bars of the main gate, a monkeyish smile in her eyes. We invited him to do the same, but he had no sense of humour. He got hold of our axe and tried to chop open the chain of the padlock, damaging our useful implement in doing so. Then he got his driver to help him shake the gate, in the hope of breaking it, I suppose. We decided to get on with cooking our potatoes. Eventually, the intruders left, to our profound relief.

It was not quite the end of the story, for after relating the experience to our parents and other people, the whole village was soon to know about it. In the evening, when we were all settled for the night in our sleeping bags, some steps were heard approaching our hut, followed by banging on the door with what sounded like a rifle butt; then the words 'Feld Polizei!' A shiver ran through our little group. Who was going to be brave enough to open the door? Someone did and was greeted by a horse laugh!

The Boches were none other than the young man who owned the property and was playing a 'good' trick on us. We did not appreciate the joke and some of us sprang at him in anger and in the process I tore his jacket, which I mended the next day in sign of reconciliation.

In the slow train that took us back home, there was renewed singing of 'It's a long way . . . ' and other banned marching songs, including:

> *A l'appel du grand Lénine,*
> *S'elevèrent les Partisans*

Norbert who taught us the song had a definite penchant for the Russian revolution. But there were no Boches in the train and no harm came to us.

The open air holiday had made me healthy, I even found it difficult to sleep in a comfortable bed, rather than on a floor. I met my camping companions some weeks later when one of them had a birthday party. It took place in the afternoon, so there were no curfew problems.

Norbert was the last to arrive. A fellow not usually demonstrative, he came in smiling and impatient to tell us what he had witnessed.

The tram he had been travelling in had suddenly been stopped and commandeered by German troops and all the passengers who were in the trailer were moved to the front coach. In the trailer climbed Germans soldiers, and 'Would you believe it, a British airman in RAF uniform!' He must have just been picked up after coming down in his parachute according to Norbert and the people in the tram realized at once what was happening; they crowded onto the back platform to have a look at a real Englishman! They waved to him, cheered, gesticulated and generally made him feel that everybody was on his side, quite unconcerned by the presence of the German soldiers.

32

The 'Zone Libre' Revisited

Sadly we sometimes saw bombers being shot down by the flak and the crew descend in their parachutes, but being actually close to an airman, like Norbert had been in the tram, was unheard of. It was an open secret that an underground organization rescued some of the fallen airmen and helped them to return to England. I was not told who approached my father about sheltering fugitives in an emergency, but the idea appealed to me very much. It would only be for a very short stay, a stop over on their way to a safe place. I lived in hope that one would turn up, certain that I could be of much assistance with my knowledge of English, but we were not rated a secure house because we were right in the centre of Brussels, nor were we altogether immune from a visit by the Germans; they had come before, to inspect our stocks, and were likely to come again. In vain did I wait to welcome my flyer, but the opportunity never presented itself.

There was a growing desire to do something for the Allied cause, but how did one set about it? It was not the sort of thing where you could go to an office and join! Contacts were the only way.

My father had many friends in the French Colony – the French are an insular lot when they live abroad and tend to move only in their own circles – and he was recruited by one of them into a group of FFI (*Forces Françaises de l'Interieur*) which was eventually attached to the Belgian Resistance Organization. Behind the scenes much preparation was taking place to help the Allies liberate the country when the time came; there would also be a need for a provisional administration until normality returned. The duty of the FFI group would be general policing and taking care of French affairs and interests in Belgium. The members met occasionally, but at present there was very little activity, except perhaps recruiting more people whom one could trust.

The *Werbestelle* had now caught up with me. The *Werbestelle* was the German recruiting office who sent me a questionnaire in order to assess my suitability as a recruit and it had to be answered within a week. The next thing of course would be the medical exam, so I tore up the questionnaire and threw it into the fire. I just pretended I had not received it.

This may seem foolhardy, but it was in fact common practice. People had become wise in their dealings with the Authorities and it was reckoned that the *Arbeitsdienst*[1] was so overworked that it would take months before they sent another questionnaire. The war might be over by then! The time to worry was when you were sent a registered letter. You could not pretend you had not received it and it was preferable to decamp.

In a letter to my brothers, I explained how Aunt Philomène was taking a sudden interest in girls of my age, but that I ignored her. 'The old so and so will not be missed when she dies and we shall enjoy the inheritance, but I very much fear that the death duties will be heavy' were some of my comments. The censor must have thought I was a wicked niece.

What with my father's illegal activities and myself not being in order with the *Werbestelle*, it was wise to make contingency plans in order to disappear at a moment's notice if need be. This is where the lady with a Rumanian name who could obtain passport documents from the Germans with a bribe was so invaluable. Such an *Ausweis* was perfectly official, even if it had been bought with coffee beans; it gave us a right to temporary ration cards when in France, a welcome contribution if you stayed with friends.

Being so well documented, there was nothing to prevent me from returning to former unoccupied France for my summer holiday. With no more demarcation line, I was free to travel anywhere in the country – except in the *Zones*

---

[1] The organization in charge of labour in occupied countries.

Interdites – and it would give me an opportunity to go and see my old friends.

Anyhow I was expected in Vichy at the end of July for the christening of my new baby cousin. My uncle Henri and his wife Madeleine had asked me to be the Godmother. That meant a holiday with much travelling, neither easy nor comfortable nowadays, but I would call on friends and relations, stopping perhaps a few days at the little Spa where I had once spent a week with my mother and brothers.

Many months had passed since I had last seen my friend Marianne and during the few days I spent with her, we had much to talk about; I was keen to know how things were now in the former *Zone Libre*. She commented on the changes that had taken place since November 1942, on the press that was now openly pro- 'New Order' instead of being just pro-Pétain. Officially the Vichy Government was still in charge, in contrast to the 'Occupied Zone' which was directly under German military rule, but the Nazi Army and the Gestapo were now established in every town. Pétain's illusion that he was still governing had become ludicrous. Marianne told me how an increasing number of young men avoided the STO by joining the Maquis and how the Vichy Government was sending the French *Milice* after them. Laval was again Prime Minister and there would be no quarter for dissenters.

But we did not just talk about the war, I described my life in Brussels and Paris and I was interested to hear about Marianne's studies, how she had dreaded giving her first injection and how she was rather proud of not having fainted when she attended her first operation. Her present assignment was the inspection of prostitutes, who by law had to carry a card in order to prove that they were not infected by venereal disease. But Marianne was happy in the confirmed knowledge that medicine was her calling.

I was sorry to miss the Duteil girls who were on holiday in the country as I had been looking forward to a good laugh with Bobette. Nor could I hug little Jean-Luc who was staying with his grandparents; at least the abolition of the demarcation line was giving a chance to families to get together again. But Jean-Luc's parents gave me a warm welcome and we had some fun together.

The lack of transport in those days could be a real nuisance. On returning from a party with my good friends, the prospect of a long walk back was rather daunting. Jean-Luc's father had come to the party straight from work with his bicycle and rather than pushing it all the way home, he thought he would try to give us both a lift. I was sitting on the handle bars whilst his wife, side-saddled on the cross bar, complained bitterly that she was being squashed between us, but we made some progress – the driver with a tremendous effort, the passengers in great discomfort. When we were nearly home, the bike got out of control and we all finished in the ditch, luckily with nothing worse than bruises.

Bicycles are also the focus of an event which will remain in my memory from that holiday, which was not without encounters and incidents. It took place when I was returning with two others from a group excursion which had been very enjoyable. We were cycling three abreast on a country road which wound its way through fields and woodland, chatting as we went along. In spite of the tranquil rural scene, our minds could never be far away from the war, for my two companions, a young teacher from far away Normandy and Walter, a student from Strasbourg who had fled his native Alsace, now incorporated in the Reich, had papers that were not strictly in order – particularly Walter who was a Jew. He did not wear a yellow star but his identity card had the word 'Juif' printed across it in thick black characters. He seemed to move from place to place when he felt his safety threatened and I had the impression that he was engaged in some underground activity.

Contrary to what we thought, we did not have the road to ourselves, for on the brow of a hill, two cyclists suddenly appeared. They were gendarmes. Typical village gendarmes, peaceful looking and casual in their less than trim uniforms. As they came closer, they waved us to stop.

In a flash I remembered a recent article in the Vichy Press, castigating the Gendarmerie for not pulling its weight in the hunt for STO dodgers and other *réfractaires*.

'If the gendarmes don't do their duty,' the article went on, 'they will have to bear the consequences.'

We were asked to show our papers and after close examination those of the young men were declared not in order. They would have to come immediately to the Gendarmerie!

My companions did an about turn as they prepared to follow the constables and they glanced at me with unease. My first reaction of anguish and shock had turned to one of anger, an anger that I could no more contain. All at once, inside me, emerged another person that I could not control, and I gave the gendarmes a piece of my mind. The words came easily like the day I had tried to stop Captain Lapie from joining the LVF.

'You are going to hand them over to the Germans, aren't you? Your own compatriots! How can people who wear a French Military uniform[1] do such a thing?'

One of the gendarmes was middle-aged and, changing the tone of my voice, I said:

'You are old enough to be their father, have you not got a son whom you love?'

'And you,' I said to the younger one, 'are one of them. You both make me ashamed of being French!'

The older man muttered something about duty.

'Fine duty!' I went on, 'nobody is watching you, you can pretend you have not seen us!'

My oratory fire had come to an end and I waited for the consequences. Without a word, the gendarmes mounted their bicycles and went on their way, leaving behind three people stunned with amazement.

'This is how a field commander must feel after a great victory,' I thought after my outburst. I never saw the two young men again after we parted that day; I hope they were not caught by zealot-gendarmes or anybody else.

After that holiday, I looked forward more than ever to my forthcoming spell in Paris because of a chance encounter that had worked upon my sensibility. I felt flattered to have been noticed and to be courted by someone I had found attractive. And because he lived in Paris, it would not be

---

[1] The Gendarmerie is legally part of the French Army.

long before we met again. Perhaps it was the fact that
Frédéric had been one of the fishing-rod students[2] that first
aroused my interest. His health seemed to have been
affected by the few weeks in jail for he suffered from
asthma, but he also considered it a blessing in disguise
because at the present time, he was not considered fit for
the STO. He was working for a diploma which still gave him
a student status, so his papers were in order and he did not
fear going out. Soon after meeting him, I thought I was
experiencing the early symptoms of love.

Vichy was the last lap on my journey, where I met my
parents who had also come to the christening. It was a
modest affair due to wartime hardship, not the great
celebration French families used to indulge in, but it was
better that way, with the baby the focus of attention, rather
than the feast.

My godson, Alain, was an endearing little boy. How I
would have loved to watch his progress and mother him as I
had Jean-Luc. Unfortunately I lived too far away, it might
be a very long time before I saw him again.

I could not leave Vichy without satisfying my curiosity
and taking a glimpse of the Maréchal. Although he worked
for the national Press Agency, my uncle Henri was no wiser
about the real world news, but rumours of items received
and then suppressed circulated amongst the clerical staff.
Anyway, he knew where and when to find the Maréchal and
he took us to see a little ceremony that occurred daily
outside the *Hotel du Parc* where the *Chef de l'Etat* resided
and worked.

He came out and stood for a while in his field-marshal's
uniform, as a few soldiers of his personal guard presented
arms. Yes, he was the man who figured on our postage
stamps, the victor of Verdun who had abolished the
Republic, the misguided old fool who had confused many
Frenchmen into thinking that he was the saviour of France.
He was nearly ninety. The only sentiment I had was of
looking at a picture in a history book; my real resentment

---

[2]University students who demonstrated in the Champs Elysées on
Armistice Day, holding fishing-rods (Gaule in French) and shouting 'Vive
De . . . ', then raising their gaule into the air.

was for the politicians and the military in his entourage who so hated democracy, they did not mind serving Hitler. My father was most upset; he was hurt to see the man and the uniform he had respected in such pathetic decadence.

33

Wagon-lit

Even after a short absence, it was possible to detect changes brought about by the intensification of war. On my return to Brussels, I found that there were more frequent alerts, lasting sometimes as much as two hours, when all the trams would stop and the life of the town come to a standstill. In some cases they were more than just alerts, for the aerodrome of Evere, in a northern suburb of Brussels was subjected to repeated air-raids. We could often hear the explosions.

One day the explosions were much louder, for the bombs were falling over the town itself. The target was a group of very important barracks now occupied by the German army, and possibly other military objectives; but in spite of its accuracy, the RAF could not help killing many civilians in bombing such an urban district.

As details of the raid emerged, we realized that the Gendarmerie flats, adjacent to the Barracks, had been hit and we immediately thought of Madame Timmermans. Before our enquiries were complete, she turned up at our house in a state of disarray, with bloated eyes and covered in bruises. She was not a person to cry easily, but she had a good weep before she could tell us her story.

Madame Timmermans luckily had not been in the building when the bombs fell, or she would have been killed like the other residents of the block. She was just returning from the shops and before she had reached her front door, she was projected into the air, to land a good distance away, stunned but in one piece.

Madame Timmermans became agitated when she related, not what she had suffered, but what she had seen.

During the raid the overhead trolley wire had collapsed onto a tramcar, and the vehicle had literally exploded in flames, burning alive the passengers and the people who had stood near. On coming round after her flight into the air and her severe fall, she had found herself in an avenue strewn with carbonized bodies.

'The corpses were that small,' she said, outlining with her hands the size of a baby. 'These were real people, that small! . . . and completely black!' She looked haggard as she recalled the vision of horror.

We offered to put her up for the time being, but Madame Timmermans was an independent person. She preferred to stay at the centre where she had been housed while waiting for new accommodation – and new furniture, and new clothes, for she had lost absolutely everything. She accepted to come to lunch every day however, and we did our best to help her return to a normal state of mind. The official radio and the press did not spare us the propaganda against the 'British murderers', but it did not win them any converts.

Some days later, when she was feeling more relaxed, Madame Timmermans wondered:

'What will Roger say when he returns to find that all his cups have vanished?' And with a voice that expressed relief and a smile not without irony,

'Thank goodness I shall not have to clean the blooming things any more.'

By the time I left for Paris, I knew that she was becoming herself again.

Travelling was increasingly tiresome and journeys seemed to last longer; the trains between Brussels and Paris were full of exhausted German soldiers – maybe some had been on the Russian front – lying everywhere in the corridors, and it was nearly impossible to reach the toilet without treading over them. To make my journey to Paris less tiring, my father suggested that I travel by a night train when it was sometimes possible to book a berth in a sleeping car. There were very few available, and it was advisable to grease the palm of the clerk in the 'Mitropa' agency. He used to work there when it was a French Travel Bureau which the Germans had now taken over.

Having obtained my berth, I felt excited at the idea of my first trip in a *wagon-lit* and I made sure to arrive early in my compartment which I would have to share with another woman. When the attendant appeared at the door a few minutes later, to my surprise and incredulity, it was not with another woman, but with a German officer. There had been a booking error, said the attendant, he was very sorry. I pointed out that I had arrived first and that I was therefore entitled to my berth. A discussion followed, when I tried to stand my ground, but the arrogant officer was not prepared to argue with a mere girl like me. He got hold of my case, landed it in the corridor, and ordered the attendant to take me off the train.

I burst into tears. The guard and another member of staff were standing nearby and the *wagon-lit* attendant who felt sorry for me had a quick word with them; there was apparently another sleeping car at the front of the train where they would try to accommodate me. But the train was about to leave. The two Railway Officials got hold of my arms, picked up my luggage, and propelled by them, I raced to the front end of the train. During our run, we found time to curse 'them' and the railwaymen reassured me with a 'don't worry Mademoiselle, on les aura, les Boches!' – the daily slogan that came after the news on the Belgian programme of the BBC.

After what seemed a never ending run we reached the other sleeping car where it was confirmed that I could have a berth. I thanked the two men with all my heart.

The other woman in my compartment was sitting on the lower bunk, and to my dismay, she too was wearing a uniform of the 'Wehrmacht'. The attendant brought in my luggage, showed me my bunk which was the lower one, then closed the door on us. I realized I would have to stay here with her, the whole night long, and I felt like a prisoner.

At first we sat in silence. I did not know where to look, what to say. She was about thirty, slim and blonde, a good looking woman. It was too early to settle for the night so we would have to sit like this for a while. She ventured to speak a few words of French to me and I replied politely. Her French was not bad at all and for a while we exchanged banalities; then I collected my book from my case because I thought the conversation might become uneasy. She glanced at my book and I thought I would risk a feat of great diplomacy. Feeling really magnanimous I said: 'I am reading a book by a German author!'

'Oh yes, who?'

'Stefan Zweig.'

Silence.

Then: 'He is a Jew, he is in prison,' she informed me in a cursory way.[1]

I was punished for my ignorance, why had I not known he was a Jew? I tried to keep my countenance.

'Well, he has a good grasp of his subject, makes interesting reading,' I said. No reply. We went on talking about this and that, the difficulty of learning foreign languages, specially hers and mine. She told me she had just been home on leave and was going back on duty in Paris. What was her job, I wondered? Maybe she worked in the Commission for Jewish Affairs or some other dreadful branch of the occupation machine.

She seemed human enough and harmless enough just chatting like that but I feared that this dialogue might take an awkward turn. Trying to sound polite and affable during our casual chat, I was at the same time performing mental gymnastics, working out a verbal escape route, should the conversation take an unacceptable slant. I would then try to give meaningless replies without betraying my integrity.

She decided to go up to her bunk and I breathed more freely. I lay down on mine and went on reading my Stefan Zweig. She knew I had the book anyway. It was a biography of Erasmus, the fifteenth century Dutch scholar, advocate of free thinking and tolerance. Books can be burnt and men silenced, but the ideas of men live on, for generations, for centuries. This reassuring thought lifted my spirit.

---

[1] She was oddly ill-informed. Stefan Zweig, I learnt later, was safe in South America. When after the war the whole horror of the holocaust unfolded itself, he could not come to terms with it, sank into deep depression and committed suicide.

34

The City of Beauty and Sadness

The Mosalsky household was a happy, if noisy one, where I settled down comfortably. It possessed no less than three pianos and I must say I was thankful for the French law about 'tapage nocturne' – disturbance of the peace at night – which ensured a quiet evening, at least after nine pm.

Frédéric was away, staying in an Alpine village until the start of his course, where the air was most beneficial to his asthmatic temperament. It was just as well really, for his presence in my neighbourhood at this stage would have distracted me from the real purpose of my visit to Paris.

At the Mint, the director of the laboratory who admired *Le Roi Albert* wasted no time in commencing my instruction and acted as my tutor. The entirely male staff of chemists and helpers were intrigued by the new arrival, but I was set to work in a small room well provided with the implements, chemicals and samples I would require. My days were spent watching over reactions, producing precipitates of amazing hues, and taking lots of notes. The separations and analyses I had to perform became increasingly complex and I could see why my tutor had said it could not be learnt in a book. He was a very kind man and a keen teacher, who would occasionally digress into his favourite subject, rare minerals, on which he had done research and written papers.

I was invited to the Director's flat, on the upper floor of the Mint, to meet his family. Their married daughter now lived with them, waiting for the return of a husband she had hardly known, when he was taken prisoner in 1940. In spite of our government's total allegiance to the invaders, the bulk of our army remained in captivity. Even *la relève*, the scheme[1] contrived to atttract our industrial workers into their factories, had proved a fiasco for the Germans.

The Mint is a majestic eighteenth century building situated on the Quai Conti, and the top floor flats, allocated to high-ranking officials, were spacious and stylish. Above all, they commanded a magnificent view over the Seine in this historic quarter of the city.

My fascination for this view gave me the taste to explore the district in my spare time. Strolling along the Seine in late summer was a pleasurable experience, when I would browse at the stalls of the 'bouquinistes' that line its banks, and stray into adjacent streets where some unexpected edifice would excite my attention. Hitherto, I had only seen the well-known Paris, the sights in the tourists' guidebooks; now I discovered the medieval *Hotel de Sens*, the harmonious *Place des Vosges*, and palatial buildings in the Marais district that had once been the town houses of Louis XIV's courtiers – all in various stages of decay; but the shabbiness did not detract from their appeal. Venturing into a courtyard, I would not have been surprised to find Molière's *Bourgeois* and *Gentilshommes* pacing up and down the graceful stone staircase.

If there can be nostalgia for the unhappy era we lived in mine is the memory of those wanderings and the architectural gems revealed to me, in a metropolis without noise and without fumes. While the weather lasted I made the best of the long lunch hour and ate my picnic sitting on a bench in the little island of the Vert Galant, below the Pont Neuf. A friend sometimes joined me, Jacques Chevalier or one of the Vaillant girls, and we would go for a walk together.

Travelling to and from work was less idyllic. A few buses were still running – their silhouettes deformed by the huge gas-bag they carried on the roof – but the Metro was by far the most effective way to get from A to B. I shall never cease to wonder at the human capacity for self-compression. 'Packed like sardines' may have been a peace-time description of a crowded train, but no metaphor could accurately portray the crush of the wartime rush-hour. When a train

---

[1] One POW would be freed from captivity for every three workers accepting to go to Germany.

stopped at an interchange station, one gasped at the never-ending multitude pouring out of it.

To avoid the worst of the discomfort, I would cover part of my route on foot or leave long before the rush-hour. It was in the early morning trains that I encountered the lean faces and sad expressions of the Parisian population; industrial workers on scanty wages, people who did not get enough to eat. Yet most of them had declined to work in Germany for a better pay.

At certain times, the underground passages of the Metro were teeming with humanity; what better place could there be for public announcements? I had not been in Paris long when I discovered for what sinister purpose the wall space could be used.

Just inside the entrance of a station I saw a small group staring at a poster, more exactly at the enlarged version of a traditional French announcement of death, a white letter with a black edging. It did not start in the conventional way: 'We regret to announce the death of . . . ' The letter read something like this: 'In view of offences committed against the Forces of Occupation, this morning at dawn the following persons were executed by firing squad as hostages.'

There followed a list of names, one under the other. The paper was still damp with the paste that stuck it to the wall. The hostages had just been shot – for crimes they had not committed. The people who had read the poster did not speak, their eyes met in silent anger.

These haunting letters generated more anti-German feelings and bitterness against those who collaborated. When I had been invited to the Director's flat, I had been shown from a back-room the goings-on in a flat that was overlooked by the Mint building. A party was in progress, windows wide open, music blaring. The men – at least those I could see – were in German uniforms. There was no attempt at concealment, on the contrary, it seemed a blatant piece of ostentation.

'It is the home of X, the actress,' I was informed by my hosts. 'It happens quite often, the inhabitants of the district are shocked.' Such resolute fraternization by well-known people was offensive to the oppressed nation.

My tutor was not a healthy man, one could tell by his complexion and his tired features. He saw the need to consult his doctor and was told that he had a stomach complaint that required an immediate operation. The patient went into hospital, quite confident that he would come out feeling better.

He never woke up from the anaesthetic: something must have gone wrong. I attended his funeral with the rest of the staff and it took us ages to reach the cemetery by Metro, by bus, and much walking. By the graveside, the widow and the daughter, in their deep-mourning clothes were disconsolate and I shed some tears for the man who had been so kind to me and had died so suddenly.

I had looked forward to my second spell in Paris, yet now I found the town so sad, I sometimes wished I were back home. Fortunately things did happen that relieved the gloom.

Going to dinner after work at my uncle and aunt's flat, I found myself as usual walking with the multitude in the underground passages of the Metro – and some are interminably long. At some distance, an accordion was playing. The corridors of the Metro have always been a favourite shelter for beggars and street musicians.

The accordion was playing one of those repetitive but nostalgic refrains, typically Parisian. The music stopped, then started again, louder. Something about this next tune went right through me, it was immediately familiar. I must be dreaming, I thought. The atmosphere around me became electrified when we all realized we were hearing the Marseillaise! The anthem was forbidden under German military rule, yet it resounded loud and clear, enflaming our hearts and bringing broad smiles to people's faces.

I hurried to the spot where the accordion was playing; the daring musician was a blind beggar, sitting on the ground. While he was squeezing away with gusto, the coins and the notes were pouring into his hat and I added my contribution. For the time being we were liberated – what could the Germans do to him, a blind beggar? All the way to my uncle's, I hummed to myself 'Allons enfants de la patrie-i-e . . .'

35

Life With My Friends

The noisy world of the Mosalsky household meant that I could only revise my notes and study my texts late in the evening. On the other hand I had free 'concerts' and an insight into the pressure on musical students, the effort required to reach a high standard of piano playing. In a highly competitive ambience, both the girls were aiming for a Conservatoire prize award at the end of their training and Odile's technique was already advanced.

M. Mosalsky was himself a musician whose classical training in his own country had been interrupted by the First World War. As an exile in France, he had been able to earn his living in the world of light music and, before the war, he had his own band that played on transatlantic liners. Now he had formed a small orchestra that played in a night-club. Night-clubs were frequented mostly by Germans and their henchmen and there was no curfew for them – entertainment had to be provided – so Stéphane Mosalsky had a pass that allowed him to return home in the small hours of the morning.

I slept on a sofa-bed in the living room, where the baby-grand stood, and there was another piano in the dining room and one in the girls' bedroom. At weekends Father Mosalsky would go round the household, playing a velvety tune here, a jazz rhythm there, with his delightful touch, in order to call us to breakfast, a sound infinitely more congenial than the buzz of an alarm clock.

The girls' musical careers were the main preoccupation of their parents. Their mother's trained ear was always watchful of their practice, whatever she was doing about the house; whenever the Chopin Etude changed tempo and turned into a boogie-woogie rhythm for my entertainment, she would erupt from the kitchen thundering 'Odi-i-i-le'! – once brandishing the saucepan she had been about to use, only to be told by her daughter: 'My little mother, please get back to your pots and leave me to my music' and to be physically removed by her like a baby under her arm, for Odile was much bigger than her. It was all done in fun for Odile was one of those people who would turn everything into a joke, irritatingly so, sometimes.

When Frédéric returned to Paris, my heart leapt and we arranged to meet at a smart café terrace halfway between our two homes. The reunion was sweet and we planned to meet again, go out together on Sundays and perhaps spend our lunch hour on my little island of the Vert Galant. The prospect of the next encounter now gave a new perspective to my life.

To arrange a meeting, we had to telephone each other, or we would simply phone for the pleasure of a chat, and this is when I learnt to curse French telephones that always have a spare receiver. For my two young friends, who felt like sisters towards me, also felt they had a right to know my affairs. When Frédéric was on the phone, one of them would pick up the second receiver and listen to every word we said; she would then pass it to her sister, after which they both had a good giggle. It sometimes finished with the girls having a conversation with Frédéric instead of me! Odile was about eighteen and Lucile sixteen and I found their girlish behaviour very irritating. So did Frédéric. However it was something I had to take in my stride, together with the hours of piano practice. Perhaps I got even on the day Odile and Lucile took me to the maiden concert of a 'First Prize' of the Conservatoire, a young lady of their acquaintance. After the performance, I was dragged behind the scenes where the soloist was being fêted and toasted. The musical pundits were discussing the fine points of Schumann's piano concerto in A flat which had just been performed. Odile and Lucile were longing to say their piece, but the pundits preferred to talk to an adult young woman like me than to my bobby-soxer friends. Although a little embarrassed and striving to hide my ignorance, I was laughing inwardly at their growing impatience.

On the way home, I suggested they should grow up a little if they wanted serious people to talk to them, though Odile as usual saw the funny side of it. But we were really good friends and I was quite interested in their musical studies; by the time I returned home, I was more or less able to turn the pages of their score for them. Odile was very conscious of missing out on general education, for there was no formal teaching at the Conservatoire except in music, and they had been very young when they left school; so she asked me to help her choose textbooks that could redress the situation. Whether or not this was the right way of pursuing one's education, the effort was commendable. She was also gifted for languages and she had returned from a short holiday in England in 1939 with a good fluency in the language, although she had been only fourteen. So we practised much English together, as well as our own mixture – qu'est-ce que tu mean? – and we listened to the BBC news in English which was much easier to pick up than the French language equivalent. Madame Mosalsky's young brother had escaped to England and was a fighter pilot in the Free French Air Force, so hearing voices from England brought the family nearer to him; after the war, they learned that he had been killed on active service.

M. Mosalsky and his emigré friends had surnames that seemed to aggravate the Authorities of occupation. A Slav name awoke suspicion; the bearer might be a Jew!

Although he provided entertainment at the night-club for high-ranking Germans and prominent French traitors, Stéphane Mosalsky was not shielded from the humiliating stratagems of the Commission for Jewish Affairs. Those suspected of being Jewish were summoned to go and show the ultimate proof of their irreproachability, that is to say, that they had not been circumcised! We were informed that M. Mosalsky was safe on this point, and Odile managed to turn the episode into a joke. Not only was this demand degrading, but it was a mockery, for many non-Jew little boys had been circumcised in the twenties when it seemed to have been a medical fashion.

The Mosalskys became scared. What if some zealot decided you were a Jew or a Gipsy or just pro-Russian, for being an emigré did not mean that you wanted your former country to fall into the hands of the Nazis. Once in their grips, however hard you tried to prove your innocence, the Germans rarely released you.

Once when I came home late from an evening at the theatre with Frédéric, Odile appeared at the door the moment I rang the bell, put her hand on my mouth to stop me talking, and hinting that I should walk on tiptoes, hid me in the kitchen and asked me to be absolutely quiet. Later I discovered the reason for my confinement. Her father had invited to coffee one of the sinister characters who visited his night-club and who claimed to be fond of music. The idea was that he might then be somebody to appeal to if the worst came to the worst. So he was shown this model happy and musical family who minded its own business, and the girls had performed their best pieces and been made to discuss music with him. I had not been told because they thought the man would have left before my return, and anyway I was not considered safe or diplomatic enough to be face to face with such a villain.

36

Mein Onkel

My friends and relations did not see me so often since my leisure time was otherwise occupied, but I made sure of visiting Grand'mère often enough. I tended to replace the Sunday by an evening in the week, then getting up very early the next morning to catch my train to town.

The railway line passed through some of the industrial suburbs of Paris and the conversation of the early morning travellers who lived and worked in those areas left one in no doubt where the real hardship lay. This used to be a nation where life was good; now the systematic plundering of the economy by the Nazi invaders had reduced many to the breadline; worse really because the bread ration was not sufficient for working men or growing children. If we had been a nation at war instead of an occupied territory, the resources could have been shared – now the little that was left after the pillaging was out of reach of humble purses. I did not bring flowers to my grandmother, but some provisions that supplemented her meagre rations and that my better off friends in Paris knew how to obtain. Grand'mère thought everything was rationed and she could never quite understand how I came across those things.

The situation was hardly better at my step-grandfather's. He lived in an outer suburb with his second wife and Pierre, their young son of twelve who was growing fast and needed more food than the rations provided. So the garden had been turned into some kind of smallholding where they kept a few hens – very few because animal feed was not available – and a goat. These animals would apparently feed on such things as leaves and twigs and I remember eating some delicious fresh goat-cheese for my supper.

Once I took an afternoon off to spend it with Grand'père who had promised to show me his painting den, a wooden hut at the bottom of the garden. The old man had the reputation of being a loner, not much of a family man. But I remember that he had been very sweet to me when I was a small child; he had made me a tiny gold ring with a pearl, because he had been a jeweller of talent, an excellent craftsman who was more interested in his work than in making money. That's why – Maman had told me – they had always been hard up but also because he was a painter. Painting was his 'own thing' in which he had always indulged in the afternoons – purely for his pleasure; he would not contemplate selling his works. So it is easy to see why the family always lived on a small income.

I had never seen a painting or a drawing anywhere in his home, although Maman had told me he liked to paint in the Impressionist fashion. It did not prove difficult to persuade him to allow me into his hut, he was even flattered by my keenness to see his work. Maybe his family in the past had not shown sufficient interest in his pastime.

The hut was a revelation. For there worked a fine draughtsman and a delicate painter. The sadness was that all was on a very small scale for he could neither obtain nor afford the materials he needed. Canvasses were cut to make several small ones and painted over again and again. But that was the life he enjoyed. To my surprise he gave me several little canvasses, like miniatures, and some drawings done on a brownish-yellow paper, for that was all he could get.

After my grandfather's death, his widow was to allow me to search the loft. That's how I eventually rescued some oils he had done in his youth and that nobody knew about.

During one of my visits, I said I was going to Brussels soon for a long weekend and my mother had expressed the wish that I take young Pierre with me if his parents were agreeable. She wanted to fatten him up a little and fit him out with clothes that had belonged to my brothers. He could stay for a while and Maman would take him back herself.

They all agreed, particularly Pierre who had never travelled and for whom it was an adventure. We got him well documented and thought that if we were stopped at the frontier, we would just return by the next train. As he was my step-mother's step-brother, Pierre's kinship with me was always cause for a joke and I would greet him with a respectful 'bonjour mon oncle'.

The great day came, and when we arrived at the station we found that our scheduled train to Brussels was more of a troop train with only the first two coaches at the disposal of civilians. Now, I had heard a rumour that, owing to constant attacks on railway engines by the allied air forces, civilians would have to travel in the first coach behind the engine, that is to say as hostages. This must have been the reason for the odd train formation. Ours was an old uncomfortable third class coach where the seat was covered with a thin upholstered pad. It soon filled up and when the train left many were standing in the corridor.

When we arrived at the Franco-Belgian frontier where passengers now had to leave the train to be checked, we were quite pleased to stretch our legs. We had to file past some Germans in uniform, show our passes and they would pick some passengers at random to be thoroughly searched. What were they looking for – arms, seditious literature, money? (for we were only allowed to carry a limited sum).

As Pierre and I were about to enter the customs house, one of them stopped me and asked in German:

'Who is the child'?

I was secretly surprised and pleased to have understood those few words, for German had not been my strong point at school. To show off my linguistic talents I declared:

'Mein Onkel!'

The German stared at us for a second, then burst into loud and prolonged laughter. People watched in wonderment, smiled with astonishment – one did not expect a German official to laugh – then he waved us on with a friendly push on the shoulder.

Eventually we were all back in the train and it chugged along past the vast flat countryside where the ploughed fields seemed to meet the horizon. Suddenly an aeroplane appeared from nowhere, flying quite low alongside the train. It disappeared, only to reappear again some minutes later.

Someone said: *'c'est un avion anglais!'*, which prompted the passengers to make an instinctive move towards the window. Before we had time to wave at our ally, the whole place was engulfed in an infernal fracas and the train stopped in a succession of jerks. In a few seconds it was all over. We were more bewildered than frightened as we had hardly had time to realize what was happening.

'We have been machine-gunned' said a man in our compartment and Pierre asked: *'j'me fous sous la banquette?'*[1] – a very pertinent suggestion since there might be a repeat performance and maybe we just had a narrow escape.

The aircraft just above us, the train attempting to stop, and the machine-gun sounding as if it was in the compartment itself had combined to make a terrific noise and the boy was justifiably shaken. I did not know whether to stay put or leave the train with my charge.

Quite a few people had alighted from the train and were looking at the engine, many soldiers were at the side of the track, others were wandering away into the countryside. There was much coming and going, animated conversation, but the aircraft did not reappear so we stayed put like most people in our compartment. We soon heard that the footplate crew had not been hurt and there was no sign of anybody being wounded. Unquestionably the rumour about the travelling hostages was true and I could now substantiate it.

Half an hour passed and we heard the engine make a tentative noise. The civilians and many German soldiers boarded the train again and after a while, amazingly, the damaged engine started to puff away and the train accelerated steadily through the countryside. There were sighs of relief and satisfaction amongst the travellers but in the corridors some kind of hushed gossip seemed to be in progress, coupled with muted laughter. We were soon to learn that a number of Germans who had wandered rather far away, perhaps thinking that the engine was really *'kaput'*, were running like mad to catch the train – but it left them behind!

It was nice to be home with my parents for a short time.

---

[1] A rather crude way of saying: 'shall I fling myself under the bench?'

That weekend I met the leader of the FFI group my father had recently joined. Afterwards I thought that I might be of some use there as well, if only as an interpreter when the time came, and my father promised to find out for me.

'Mein Onkel' stayed behind with my parents and my journey back was uneventful – except for having to come off the train at the frontier where we queued to have our papers checked. I was carrying a compromising paper to take to an address in Paris, an address which I had learnt by heart, and it was hidden in a large box of face powder, for which I had made a false bottom. Although I felt it to be a safe hiding-place, I did not want to be caught by the woman in German uniform who searched female travellers at random and compelled them to undress. So I waited until she had picked on somebody and taken her into a little room before I attempted to pass through the barrier.

37

Farewells

The joys of travel were certainly a thing of the past – and of the future it was to be hoped. Now I would remain in Paris until my examination and it was time I did some revising – not always so easy when Odile was strumming the part of the orchestra on the dining room piano for the concerto which her sister was practising on the baby-grand in the sitting room.

The weather was turning colder and I could not picnic on my little island anymore. Therefore the suggestion from my acquaintance, Denise Dumont, that I should lunch at the pension in the Latin Quarter where she was residing, was welcome.

It was a quaint place, a venerable house with a forecourt shaded by a tree. Through the open oak portal a grand staircase with its wrought iron railings could be seen, a reminder of the fine residence it must have been when it was built two centuries earlier.

Denise Dumont's parents lived in Brussels and I would carry a letter to their daughter whenever I crossed the frontier. She was about ten years older than me and was involved with the art world, striving to be a stage designer. At the pension lived and ate a kind of intellectual Bohemia, struggling actors, students, and the proprietress was forever to be seen running after bills that had not been paid. There was a long *table d'hôte* in the dining-room, always full at lunchtime, and small, more private tables in the corners. The meals – very cheap – were strictly on the rations and not very exciting. The place evoked for me perhaps a page of Balzac, certainly something I had read about the Paris of another age.

Sometimes I lunched at the *table d'hôte*, and there I got

into conversation with a lady engaged in medical research, who turned out to be – it's a small world – the aunt of our 'Soldier for Christmas' of 1941. At other times I sat at Denise Dumont's table amongst her own friends; the aspiring actress with the distinctive voice who spoke with a flourish and borrowed clothes from a famous designer, other people connected with the stage, and the young girl with striking black eyes and long curling lashes. She was just sixteen, with a peach complexion and generous curves which she accentuated by wearing a tight-fitting black velvet dress. She could not pass unnoticed and she seemed to be everybody's pet for she was living here alone since her family had been arrested by the Germans.

When Denise Dumont phoned me one evening to ask me over to a party, I could not forsee the terrible worry it would cause the Mosalsky family. It was not Denise's fault, it's just the way things turned out to be.

My invitation seemed to have been an afterthought, coming so late; however fascinating the milieu at the pension, I was something of an outsider in it.

The smart apartment where the party took place was newly decorated, the modern furniture and *objets d'art* were of faultless taste. I recognised some of the people from the pension, and I learnt that the owners were away, but that their nephew was using the flat to give his own party. Denise seemed to be his particular friend. Two couples were dancing, but soon the music had to stop because of the law on noise in the evening. It was clear that the guests had come in pairs and that I had been invited as a partner to a young man who had come alone. It was also clear that it was 'that kind' of a party; the young girl with a curvy shape was sitting on a man's lap with her blouse unfastened and everybody became flirtatious, including my partner. Why on earth had Denise invited me to such a party? I had not told her I had a boy-friend, but she could easily have found out that this was not my scene.

On the whole a conformist, how could I avoid conforming this once? I had seen 'my' young man at the *table d'hôte* in the pension. He was a student in architecture, a touch 'zazou'[1],

---

[1] A nickname for trendy people who in 1942 had adopted an eccentric style of dress and hair.

but quite nice, only I did not want his amorous kisses.

Now I thought the clock would help me to escape because I did not want to miss the last metro, but I was told it had already gone from the local station. I would have to spend the whole night here, so I made for the telephone. Alas, I was told, the telephone was being installed in the block but was not yet connected! I could not even phone from the neighbouring flats and there was no way I could warn the Mosalskys that I would not be home that night. I just hoped they would guess I was not on the phone, and I had another drink to forget my worry. I don't think my concern about contacting my home was appreciated by this totally emancipated company.

Then people settled in pairs for the night in different rooms and I was left with my architect in the living room, my next concern being to convey to him that I had not come to this party with the same ulterior motives as everybody else. Trying not to appear naive, I talked about this and that with much mentioning of my boy-friend. In the end he took his bad luck in good part and we made ourselves comfortable on the couch and in armchairs and fell asleep.

Leaving all together by the early metro the next morning, we must have looked like a band of revellers. Denise came close to me and tried to say how sorry she was about the whole thing – I am not quite sure what exactly she was sorry about, my worry for the Mosalskys or perhaps the impression I formed of the party?

I had good grounds to be worried. The moment I rang the bell the whole family rushed to the front door, Lucile embracing me and saying 'Oh my dear, you are safe!'

Their relief at my return was manifest. None of them had slept a wink for they feared that something dreadful had happened to me, like being arrested for being out after curfew. I realized the terrible anxiety I had caused and when I explained the circumstances I got thoroughly told off, for there was nothing they could have done to find me. They did not know the address where I had been, and as far as the police were concerned, they would not be prepared to look for missing persons who might have been arrested by the Germans. It took some days for the flutter to die down, but my guilt remained.

I did not mention the party to Frédéric. We did not meet as often as we used to, for it was a sad thing that getting to know each other had not brought us any closer. When the enchantment of our early infatuation had died down, we found we had little in common. That should not have mattered, had there been acceptance on both sides, but Frédéric tended to be disparaging of my tastes and of the interests I had in common with my own friends. The image of him I now had – when the world would be at peace again – was of someone arriving at a fashionable resort in a dashing car with a wife wearing the latest trendy clothes. I like fun and I like frivolity, all in moderation; I decided that Frédéric was superficial and he no doubt found me a bore. We ceased to find pleasure in each other's company; we still had the same attitude towards the war, but that was all.

The parting was unpleasant because he would arrive later and later at our meeting place, until one day, I realized he would not turn up at all, and I went home. It left me disenchanted and I meant to be wiser in the future, my own inflammable nature permitting. At least my mind was free of emotional commitments when the time came to apply myself to my revising.

After the Director's death, the atmosphere in the Mint laboratory had altered. The three other chemists, men about forty, proceeded with my instruction, but there was more fun and rather less teaching. They visibly enjoyed my company, for the laboratory was a dull, cheerless place, and their work a little solitary. They now entrusted me with some of their own jobs such as the analysis of aluminium-magnesium alloys from which our present weightless and worthless coins were made. They also let me operate the Brinell machine to test the hardness of those alloys – that was fun for I thought I was sitting at the controls of a modern aeroplane, watching instruments and taking readings.

One of the three chemists was promoted to the position of Director of the Laboratory. As they were about the same age and equally qualified, there was the usual resentment from the other two who thought they should have been given the job. One would gossip to me, the other make derogatory hints. But they all went on preparing me for my exam.

There were also two helpers in the lab, general dogsbodies who cleaned and tidied after the chemists. It always puzzled me how the five men would get together at slack times to start a political discussion and argue about the newspapers they favoured, the columnists who wrote in them, until I realized they were the papers of yesteryear, the prewar journalists they were talking about – as if the war had not taken place. The men in blue overalls and the chemists in their white coats indulged in an amiable class-warfare with much teasing, in a bout of nostalgia for the days when France was the country of endless political discussions. A taste of things to come?

I sensed that the most junior of the chemists drew satisfaction out of embarrassing me and putting me on the spot. I had no clue about his motives, but he would wait until all were assembled to say:

'Are you still meeting your "girl" friend in the lunch hour?'

I had once asked to leave early to meet Andrée Vaillant because her office was a long way away and she did not have much time. But he must have spied on me and seen me with Frédéric and other male friends like Paul or Jacques Chevalier with whom I sometimes lunched and he proceeded to describe my so-called 'girl' friends! Taken by surprise, I blushed with embarrassment, just the spectacle he had wished to create.

Another time it was my ignorance about the duration of an electrolysis that gave him a chance. I started much too late, yet he saw it and said nothing. When the time came to go home, he laughed and asked me when I expected to finish? It was not something that could be interrupted and I had to stay until 8 o'clock, under his supervision. At least I was allowed to phone home and say I would be late.

I thought his tricks were mean and I began to ignore him, until one Saturday morning when he brought his toddler to work – a funny little boy with whom I made friends immediately, and I spent more time mothering him than doing my work. His father's attitude towards me changed completely and he treated me with more respect. Perhaps he thought that a woman's role was to look after children rather than fiddle with test-tubes and Bunsen burners. The rapprochement was timely as I was about to sit my exam and take my leave of my entourage.

Never had I felt so confident about an examination. I was sure that the men who had taken so much trouble to instruct me would not deliberately fail me. The Director of the Laboratory was setting the written paper and I had a good idea of the subjects he favoured; also, some of the practical tests had to be described in writing rather than performed because there was no gold or platinum available at the Mint, not even the minute quantities required for a test – no doubt the Germans had taken it all. I would have been quite happy to do a gold assay, but I had no experience of the more difficult testing of platinum by the wet method, and I was relieved that it would be in writing. Everything can turn out perfectly on paper but not always so in practice.

On the day of the special exam session that had been created for me thanks to the Roi Albert, everyone tried to appear solemn; the helpers walked quietly and refrained from chatting, and whatever I was doing, I had the feeling of being watched, watched protectively. Nobody wanted me to go wrong, yet nobody dared to interfere.

Only the next day I learnt that I had been successful and that I was now a fully fledged assayer. There would be some administrative work to do, like choosing my own mark and being officially registered, but hopefully, it could be done by correspondence.

The goodbyes were effusive and I had to promise to call at the Mint whenever I came to Paris. I also paid a visit to the ex-Director's widow who had not yet vacated the beautiful flat on the top floor and I told her how thankful I was for what her husband had done for me.

Now I wanted to return home, hoping to come back to Paris in better times. The cold weather seemed to be coming early and the coal ration was insufficient. I wondered what it would be like for the Parisians if we had a severe winter. The city was sad and chilly, I had taken my fill of its beauty, although there were things I would miss, like the excellence of its theatres where I had been privileged to see great actors; in Brussels, I could never be reconciled with hearing the classics in a repressed Belgian accent.

In this autumn of 1943, there was undeniable progress on the war front. The allies had a foot in Italy, the Italians had changed sides, Hitler's armies made no headway in Russia, which proved to be a graveyard for them, but the general feeling was that the Germans were nowhere near collapse. Hope there was, but for those at risk, the urgency was to survive, to hold on until the final victory. And the number of those at risk was increasing. Notwithstanding the hundreds of thousands deported to German factories and living under constant allied bombing, those avoiding the STO swelled the ranks of the Resistance as was clear even from the totally servile Parisian Press, who presented them as bands of criminals roaming the countryside. There were articles about the glorious *Milice* and the German Army fighting those bandits. The ill-equipped and badly fed Maquis formations that sprang up in different parts of France had great logistics problems, and it is true that they raided banks and post offices – where the Postmaster sometimes turned a blind eye – for they needed money and food to survive. They raided Pétain's *'chantiers de jeunesse'*[1] to obtain clothes and equipment and they requisitioned food, which did not always bring them friends. This was what provoked the vilification in the press. It was only when the war was over that we learnt how some of these boys had been savagely massacred in skirmishes with the Germans and the *Milice*.

Maybe those who hid in Paris found it easier to make themselves invisible, there is more anonymity in a large town, but there was always the question of ration cards and false papers. And if they were in the Resistance, they lived under fear of death and torture.

I took my leave of my country with sadness, not of leaving Paris, but sadness that things were as they were. I had no reason to come back until the world stood on its feet again, but how much suffering would there be until then?

---

[1] Camps in which the young were conscripted to perform a variety of hard manual tasks in lieu of the prewar military service.

38

Working For Father

There were large amounts of work waiting for me on my return, work that I was now qualified to do. Yet due to delays in the post between the two countries, it was not until the end of December that I was officially registered in the Paris Mint with my own assay-mark. Then, I had to obtain legal ratification of my document in the Belgian Mint. I had however a letter from the Director of the Laboratory stating that I had passed my examination, so I went on with my work and signed my assay certificates.

The choice of a personal mark had posed a problem, for there were many already deposited with the Mint Administration. I had to choose an original personal symbol or a completely different version of an existing one. Having no clue how to symbolize myself, I was glad when a family friend came to the rescue with a little amulet he had found decades ago in the ruins of Mycenae.

Our friend was an art historian, one the academics sacked by the Germans when they closed Brussels University. He was also a painter and sculptor of some talent, but like his other dismissed colleagues, he tried to exist by giving private tuition. We had met him and his wife at the Helmonds' manor house in 1940 and we had remained friends ever since, our friendship reinforced by our common chagrin over Alfred Helmond's volte-face. The dismissed Professor was not idle in the struggle against the invaders, his contribution being a cache of arms in the cosy cottage style house where he lived with his wife. They were also willing to shelter people in danger if the occasion arose.

I was very satisfied with their offer to let me copy the winged griffin carved on a small gem and unearthed in

Greece, for had life given me complete choice in the matter, I might possibly have found myself on an archaeological site rather than in an assay lab. So the mythological creature surrounded by my name was engraved on a die that I could now use to stamp metals which I had assayed.

In a small concern like ours the scope for laboratory work was very limited. We tested always the same range of alloys, and ingots of similar compositions. Little of what I had learnt in Paris would ever come into use and my syllabus had been mastered only to be forgotten. At least I was now fully occupied in a productive way.

In fact, the laboratory was becoming the busiest place in the firm, because the client who wanted an assay was not required to have his identity checked, as was the case at the counter downstairs. He could call himself Mr Bloggs if he wanted to and nobody would investigate his affairs or query the origin of his goods. The trafficking in the jewellery trade was causing the demand for so much testing; there were shady operators in the market place, selling items of a showy and shoddy character to satisfy the demand of the racketeers. When these objects, usually stamped '18 carats' were sold for scrap and smelted, the metal was never of the right fineness. Somewhere on the line, someone had been done.

Unfortunately, the racketeers were part of the economic scene, in France as in Belgium – people who made a fortune selling goods and services to the German army, or took advantage of the general shortages to launch into vast black-market enterprises. Although every trading concern operated in a parallel market in order to survive and everybody had recourse to the black-market for something, the racketeers were another breed altogether, people who thrived in the chaos. Nor must they be confused with industrial firms who were forced to produce for the Germans, their management and work-force helping the enemy against their will.

The income from the laboratory was welcome because it was official income, and a firm had to prove viable and capable of paying its personnel, otherwise, the authorities would find better ways of employing them! It was gratifying for me to know that my contribution was so important after years of an uncertain role. One thing I had to adjust to was working under pressure when a customer wanted his results quickly, and that sometimes caused friction with my father. I had been trained to work with precision and at a leisurely pace, whilst his point of view was purely commercial.

Otherwise I picked up the threads of my life in Brussels after the novel experience of my months in Paris. My query about joining the FFI group to which my father belonged had been answered:

'No, we don't want girls in the section.'

But the leader had come to see me and said that on reflexion, since I was so keen to join, he would accept me as a messenger, calling upon my services whenever possible. The prospect of being even a tiny cog in a big wheel, was very satisfying, and, deciding that I ought to become more mobile, I went on a quest for a second-hand bicycle.

While I was away, my little neighbour Nadine had been waiting impatiently for the resumption of our English lessons; that was 'her' small contribution to the cause, she would greet her father in English when he returned with the Allied Armies! I was more than ever convinced that had he and his brother reached England in 1940, a message would have been received by now through some secret agency; it was the case in other house-holds in the same situation and their blind faith in a happy ending was disturbing.

Correspondence from my brothers had piled up during my absence. I had myself been very lax in this matter while in Paris and I now redressed the situation by pouring out epistles to the boys. The long separation was beginning to weigh upon them, especially upon Georges–Gilbert was due to take his first baccalauréat in June, and, being devoted to his studies, he had plenty to occupy his mind. But Georges displayed a melancholy that neither his beautiful surrounding nor my affectionate letters could dispel. It was upsetting for my mother, who tried to obtain a visa to visit her sons. It took her weeks to collect the documents required by Vichy, where she had to go in person, only to see her request turned down; it was obvious that the Germans would not allow anybody out of the country.

Gilbert's letters were a detailed report of his studies. He was already worrying about having to take an oral in the main subjects as well as a written paper, an oral that I had been lucky to skip in 1940 when France was overrun. When he stated that he felt all right about geography, history, maths, literature, but that he feared physics, chemistry, Latin and German, I remembered what a weight off my mind this 'no oral this year' had been. But Gilbert was a more studious person than I had been.

He was taking German as a modern language, where I had switched to English which was so much easier. I was impressed by the titles of his essays – *'Die Idee der Freiheit'*, *'Sturm und Drang in Werthers Leiden'* – in a language I had found so difficult, yet I was myself revising it with the aid of my old school text-books.

Paradoxically, the German language on which we commented in our letters was the expression of a culture, a subject in which we were interested; it did not relate to the people I called 'the Boches' in my everyday life and 'Tante Philomène' in our code. Somehow at a deeper level of our consciousness, Hitlerism had not succeeded in warping for ever our perception of all things German.

39

Freedom of the Press

Listening to the BBC news was a ritual that could not be missed, even when friends visited friends. Trained ears were sometimes necessary to sift the words through the ouaouaouaoua of the German jamming, but programmes like *'Les Français parlent aux Français'* and the Belgian voice repeating daily *'Courage! On les aura, les Boches!'* reassured us that we were not forgotten in our captive isolation. Then there were the personal messages after each news bulletin, meaningless phrases like 'the little dog has jumped three times' which we knew to be important communications to the underground movement.

During the summer months, when people's windows had been wide open, we had noticed that we were not alone; from the back of houses that overlooked a patchwork of courtyards, the first bars of the fifth symphony had resounded loud and clear in all directions, followed by the jammed voices of our overseas speakers. Nobody had bothered to turn the volume down, every open window seemed an encouragement to disobedience.

The clandestine press offered a different kind of satisfaction, more like live theatre as opposed to films, where the players had to perform a daring act to print each edition. The audience was smaller, but the very fact that their production involved danger made them exciting. Several were published in France right through the war, reflecting different tendencies, but united in the great struggle.

The one I had access to was the Belgian *'La Libre Belgique'*, a news-sheet of small format that appeared every two weeks and had been famous for the same reasons during the First World War. It was amongst other things a source of information about internal events that were not divulged by the authorities, such as arrests and executions. We learnt for example in the issue of 15th November that 750 hostages had been shot to this date. It also documented the passage of Himmler in Brussels, after which there was an increase in the number of executions. Traitors were denounced, especially those responsible for the death of their compatriots at the hands of the enemy. And the newspaper showed no indulgence for the companies of Gendarmerie that had just been armed to fight the *'STO Refractaires'* who lived in bands in the Ardennes. Cheerful news appeared also, and with some interesting figures. The STO was now claiming 600 people daily according to an article, but only about a tenth of those conscripted would board the train taking them to Germany – in one case, on 14th October, 20 out of 400.

The editor of this newspaper gave his name as Peter Pan and his address as a park somewhere in Brussels, the address of the offices was the *'Oberfeldkommandantur'*, that is the German high command. The puzzling thing was, how did they come by some of the material they published? A photograph of American bombers in action over enemy territory, of a new type of aeroplane being exhibited in London in front of St Paul's cathedral, a section drawing of a Lancaster bomber showing innumerable details!

Those exciting pages provided a diversion from the official daily press which we read out of necessity, to find out about rations, curfews, ordinances and such like, and where the traitor journalists poured their pro-German platitudes. Our own daily had been *Le Soir*, a major Belgian quality paper and we continued to buy it, even in its vilest hour.

On November 9th, my mother went as usual to the nearest news-vendor to buy our five o'clock edition and returned commenting:

'They must be getting short of news, because the paper is rather thin tonight.'

Something about it looked different, although the usual adverts appeared on each side of the title. But the pictures! Flying Fortresses dropping their bombs with the caption *'En pleine action'*, and below, a photograph of Hitler looking angry and yelling – like the Kaiser before him – *'das habe ich nicht gewollt'*, apparently aimed at the bombers! That was bizarre enough. Reading just a few lines of the articles and communiqués, it dawned on us that the paper was a hoax, a superb hoax. Everybody gathered round my father who was now reading aloud about an imaginary peace conference in Berlin where a number of prominent Belgians were present, notably Léon Degrelle, the head of the Rexist Party[1] and called here the '*Obersturmbahngefreitersonderhauptmannführer*'. Then someone else volunteered to read the comic comments from a couple from the *'Marolles'* in its dialect of coarse Flemish mixed with ungrammatical French. We were laughing away, yet realized that the practical joke was enough to get the writers and the readers shot. My mother hurried to the news-vendor to get some more copies. Alas it was too late. The papers on sale now were the genuine article.

The old lady at the kiosk had been completely foxed. The delivery van of *Le Soir* had arrived a few minutes early, the driver had apologised for the small bundle of papers, saying that more would be delivered soon, but nothing had seemed out of the ordinary. Only when people had come for more papers, and the regular van had appeared, had she become aware of the deception.

For this successful and most humorous coup, a *Le Soir* van had been 'borrowed', a delivery planned to the minute, and small bundles of papers deposited at all the main kiosks in the centre of Brussels. They provided much pleasure to the readers and much anger to the collaborators.

For once I read *Le Soir* from beginning to end, ads and all. If some articles were written with humour, others had a serious tone. The editorial was a moving appeal to people, whether they were catholics or communists, artisans or industrialists, workers or civil servants, to support the struggle for freedom and work towards the victory that would restore the high spiritual values swept away by the Nazis. Also an appeal to avenge the victims of the Gestapo, who were suffering odious torture and death in the camp of Breendonck near Antwerp – the only camp we knew about

---

[1] The Belgian Nazi Party.

in those days, before the discovery of even more sinister ones scattered all over Germany. Articles that normally appeared in the regular version of the paper were parodied in this number under the very names of their usual authors. Altogether a clever publication, witty down to the last ad – a certain tailor Mr O. Portune, was offering his services to turn coats! And the films and theatre titles were entertainment in themselves. This daring hoax was the talk of the town for many days.

40

The Rugby Match

In order to depict this memorable rugby match, a little history of the game in Belgium is called for. When my father was sent to Belgium to represent a French firm in the early twenties, one of the things he missed from his native France was the game of rugby. Born in the South-West where this sport was prevalent, he had begun to play early and eventually had his place in one of the well-known Parisian teams. But in the early days in Brussels he had to content himself with watching Association football, when he would take me with him to a match, while Maman stayed at home with the baby and the toddler. My father, always eager to further my education, explained why the men in bright coloured jerseys were so intent on kicking that ball and what they were trying to do with it; a game easy enough for a little girl to grasp.

Well-documented in my father's archives are the years that follow his discovery that the British colony in Brussels had its own rugby team, and his bid to join it. Although the British club was a closed circle run specifically for the recreation of British residents in Brussels, my father and two other Frenchmen were exceptionally admitted, and to his great joy he could once more handle the oval ball.

The team only ever met its counterpart in Antwerp. It was not the serious rugby my father had played in Paris, and the three Frenchmen sometimes were left out of the team if there were enough British players to make a fifteen. They did not integrate too well, mainly owing to language difficulties, and because in those days the British abroad seemed even more isolationists than the French.

Before long my father conceived the idea of a 'Rugby

Club Français'. He launched an appeal in French circles and sport organisations for players, or would-be players, and was happily surprised by the response – not quite fifteen, but with the odd Spaniard, like our friend Carlos Bonar, the club was founded.

A pitch was found at Waterloo, on rather sloping ground, which meant the players had to run uphill one half and downhill the next. The *'Morne Plaine'* became once more a battle ground, this time between the Rugby Club Français and the Brussels British Sports Club. It would have been presumptuous of the French to expect victory on such a fateful location, but the defeat was honorable, only 3-nil. Several years passed before the French beat their British opponents, and not at Waterloo. As I ran along the side-line with my little brothers, I could never understand why my father had chosen this new game, so messy and unclear, in preference to the other one.

The club expanded and soon the Belgian players outnumbered the French; the word Français was dropped and it became the 'Gallia Rugby club'. Other clubs were born and, suddenly in 1931, my father saw the need to form a 'Fédération Belge de Rugby' to maintain the amateur status of his 'noble' sport and keep it out of the claws of some rapacious entrepreneurs who saw in it a form of mass entertainment on the line of 'catch-as-catch-can!'

The British stayed aloof from the new Fédération but continued to play friendly matches against the Gallia. Eventually I understood the game and my brothers and I – and my mother – became great supporters of the team that my father captained. The words 'Papa a marqué un drop!' would send us jumping for joy. The Gallia now rented its field from a sports club that had extensive grounds surrounded by woods and where we played tennis in the summer; they were enjoyable week-ends in the open for the urban dwellers that we were.

Until the onset of war, the game of rugby saw a growing activity with international matches against Holland, France-Nord, and even the reserve of the French National team and of the German National team. The Belgian team, without the support of its more experienced French and British team-mates could only give a mediocre performance and was thoroughly beaten by France and even by the German second fifteen, who won by 34 to 6. The international encounter took place in October 1937 in Düsseldorf. It would appear from the programme of that match that the game was no better understood in Germany than in Belgium, for it explained in detail how all the points are obtained. But the German team was good, selected it seems from a fair number of rugby clubs in the country.

It was precisely the existence of that game in Germany that would cause my father a headache some years later during the occupation. Someone in the German Army, who was interested in rugby, decided to approach the Belgian Fédération with a view to organising matches. The Belgian officials were seized with panic.

'It is unthinkable,' said my father. 'We must find a solution immediately! Knowing what normally takes place in the scrum during a heated club match, can you imagine what it would be like if the chaps played German soldiers? Anyway, they would refuse to play and we would all be in trouble.'

Under the circumstances, the solution was to dissolve forthwith what remained of the pre-war clubs and replace them by an organisation called 'L'Ecole Belge de Rugby'. It had no official team as such, its objectives were physical fitness, practice and blackboard instruction.

It worked, and there were no more scares about a 'friendly' match with the enemy. Yet there were more than enough 'pupils' in the school to form two teams, who were eager to continue with the game. So 'demonstration matches' were given in colleges or wherever they could avail themselves of a ground.

Early in 1944, the Red Cross offered its own sports ground for such a demonstration match, when the proceeds would go to that organisation (if proceeds there were, for the sport was not popular, nor understood, and spectators were always few).

That day we brought our own 'claque' of friends, arriving early, as my father, who was refereeing the game, wanted to inspect the ground. The big surprise was that we were not the first; more than a dozen spectators stood already on the side-line. Pretty satisfactory for a charity match, and on such a cold day too.

Later when the match was in full swing and I was explaining the finer points of the game to some of our friends, my mother suddenly tapped me on the shoulder, and pointing to the privet hedge that enclosed the ground,

'Look,' she said, 'here they come!'

Along the medium height hedge I saw military lorries slowly moving, then coming to a halt to allow the soldiers to jump out. We were surrounded.

Without hesitating, my mother ran onto the field amongst the players calling:

'André, André . . . stop the match, they are here!'

With repeated blows on his whistle, my father ended the game abruptly. At the same instant I saw one of the players rush to the side-line and make for his overcoat.

A lady in our group exclaimed in a panic that she had too much money in her hand-bag – for we were restricted as to the sum we could carry, unless officially documented. Maman and I took a few notes off her and stuffed them inside our jumpers. By this time the soldiers had entered the grounds and were completely in control. They formed a line to separate the players from the spectators and the teams were marched to their dressing-room under armed escort.

When the spectators were at last allowed to filter out of the ground, the player who had rushed to put on his overcoat left with them. The Germans never noticed that he was wearing red and blue striped socks instead of trousers.

Our little group did not reach the exit. We were suddenly approached by a giraffelike *Feldwebel* with a face as hard as stone who, pointing at us 'ein, zwei, drei, vier, funf, sechs . . .' ordered his men to take us into a tennis court and keep us under guard.

To what did we owe this special treatment, of being kept in a cage like beasts at the zoo, while everybody else was allowed to go? I began to piece together the elements of this situation when I saw the so-called early spectators in the company of the *Feldwebel*; I also understood scraps of conversation in German accusing us of passing papers to each other. The men who had come here before the match, looking quite innocuous – one had his little boy with him – were none other than Gestapo informers. They had obviously seen us share out our friend's banknotes which they thought were documents. As quietly as I could, I told the others what I had gathered; at least we had an explanation. We were quite sure we would be taken away in one of the lorries and I ought to have been afraid; but I so hated the hard-faced *Feldwebel*, the soldiers pointing their guns at me and the nauseating Belgian informers that the stronger emotion triumphed.

The soldiers' uniforms were of a grey I had not noticed before, and we had no idea who they were – for you could be arrested either by the *Feldgendarmerie*, the *Abwehr*, the *Sicherheits Polizei*, or the *Gestapo*! Finally we were searched on the spot, pockets and handbags; and since the soldiers did not find any *'Papiere'* they had a little conversation with the *Feldwebel*, who decided to release us. It was not really us they were after.

The dressing room was still being guarded and we waited anxiously for my father, who came out last with some of the Germans. He too was allowed to go home.

After the tension, the irony! The bird they were after had flown – in his overcoat and his rugby socks.

No member of the team had of course seen him that day! The Germans had not been very astute, for there must have been one more set of clothing than the number of players in the dressing room. What a farcical operation – and my father, who had rejoiced at the sight of keen spectators, at last! Mind, they had paid their entry fees, which all went to the Red-Cross.

41

The Challenge of the Curfew

Early curfews were punishments that interfered with everyone's life; business and trade in particular, and social life in the evenings. Such days must have been responsible for improved literacy, for there was not much else one could do but read. The regular curfew however was not without problems. Concerts, plays and other public entertainments were well timed to give people a chance to get home by tram. But when visiting friends, it was up to you, for being caught on the streets after curfew meant certain arrest, or being shot at if you tried to run away.

My parents and I were always very prudent in this respect. Thus when we were returning from a pleasant evening at the Baillys one winter night in 1944, we had given ourselves plenty of time.

It was an exceptionally cold winter and we were happy to reach our front door. But try as we may, we could not open it. The key would not turn in the lock because the lock was frozen. Repeated efforts remained unsuccessful, even after breathing warm air through the keyhole, so we had a quick count of our money and decided that between the three of us we had enough to spend the night in a hotel. There were several on the near-by boulevard and we still had plenty of time. At the Hotel Central, a well-known comfortable establishment, not in the luxury class, the man at the desk looked at us as if we were peculiar, asking for a room.

'Did we not know that the hotel was reserved for officers of the Wehrmacht?'

He informed us that the same applied to other known hotels in the district. At least he let us use the phone to call the Bonars, who lived within a reachable distance. We could still get there by walking at a brisk pace.

Carlos Bonar was not very cooperative. They had people staying and could not offer us a bed; he did not think we would be comfortable spending the night in their armchairs.

'Why did we not try a certain street in the vicinity, there was a small hotel there, where we would surely find rooms.'

After a further walk in the cold, we found the hotel and went in in search of warmth and a roof. One glance around was sufficient to realize where we had landed.

Pearched at a high desk, a blonde past her prime, and outrageously made up, agreed to let us have two rooms, while two women of a similar genre, sitting idly in a corner, eyed us with distaste on discovering that we were not customers. The awful decor of red plush and garish wallpaper added to the atmosphere.

We ordered hot drinks that we consumed concealed in one of the secluded recesses behind high-backed seats. My father saw the funny side, Maman was only half amused, and I scanned the place with a mixture of curiosity and uneasiness. An odd world which one knew existed but never came in contact with.

The place was extremely quiet, there were no visitors because of the curfew. Our rooms were decorated in the same red-velvety style as the downstairs saloon, with the addition of mirrors over the beds and in other strategic positions. I had never viewed myself from so many angles. Admittedly it was better to sleep in a brothel than in a German jail. In the morning the problem of our lock was resolved, but Carlos was never allowed to live down his recommendation of a 'small hotel'.

My other curfew incident was rather less picturesque, but rather more frightening. I was alone at home because my parents had rushed to Paris after receiving news that my step-grandfather had become fatally ill. The news had upset me, but what upset me even more was to find myself alone at night in our rambling building of four floors, attics, basement and cellars; with the possibility that the alarm system might go off if a mouse accidentally brushed against a wire. And there were other hazards.

One of our jeweller customers had been robbed at night

by rogues who posed as the Gestapo – there is no limit to human villainy. If the bell rang at night, it could be the real Gestapo or the bogus Gestapo! I slept with my hockey stick by me, a weapon unlikely to be effective, yet it gave me some measure of confidence. In reality I hardly slept at all and was not very bright in the morning when I was supposed to be in charge of the firm.

It was therefore a tremendous relief when the mother of a friend of mine asked me on the phone if I would meet her daughter at the station and bring her back to stay the night with me. She had discovered that her daughter's train would arrive late from Paris, with the risk that she might not reach her home before curfew. They lived miles from the centre, while I was within walking distance of the Gare du Nord. I had recently renewed acquaintance with Martine who had been at school with me in the early years, and she would be a most opportune guest.

The train would be very late, I was informed at the station; but the longer days of the approaching spring made the waiting more bearable. All the same, after nightfall, when the station became deserted, I began to worry about the curfew.

There were hardly any trams left, but I could not simply race home in the time that remained and leave my friend in the lurch. Fortunately I knew for a fact that special provisions existed for people whose train came in after curfew; they were given special passes to allow them to get home within a time limit. This was confirmed when another train arrived and I saw the ticket collector hand out passes to the passengers.

After a wait that seemed endless, Martine's train arrived, and I stood close to the barrier as the first passengers were handed out their passes. It was long past the curfew and it was fortunate that my parents were away for they would have been beside themselves with worry.

I caught sight of Martine, looking worried, and when I waved to her, she understood immediately the reason for my presence. As she was handed out her pass, I asked for one for myself, explaining why I was meeting my friend.

– Oh no, you were not on the train, replied the employee.

- But I had to meet my friend.
- We are only allowed to give passes to people who were on the train.
- Surely, you have not counted them, and I must get home somehow.
- That's your affair.
- But you know the danger of being out after curfew, you can't abandon me like that!
- *Le règlement, c'est le règlement!*
- How do I get home with my friend then?
- That's your affair, walk along the walls and hide in doorways.

He would not budge and there was nothing more I could do. One of the passengers suggested that I go to the German 'Kommandant' on the station, but what if I were arrested for being out after curfew? We decided to hug the walls and hide in doorways. At first we went along with the other travellers, but they soon dispersed, and we found ourselves on our own on the boulevard.

It was now a question of remaining inconspicuous, of looking, listening, walking as far as we dared, hiding for a while in a doorway, then surveying the situation anew. It was not easy in the total black-out, and at first I was frightened.

We learnt to navigate successfully along the walls, taking cover at intervals in the darkness and the silence, communicating only in whispers, when suddenly we heard steps coming from a side street. Then we heard a voice and we hid in the first available doorway. The voice started to sing. As it came closer we realized that it was the voice of a drunk, blissfully unaware of patrols, curfews and the war.

'He can't do us any harm, but he could attract the attention of a patrol,' I whispered.

We distanced ourselves from him as fast as we could and we reached the end of the boulevard where only a few streets separated us from my house. Crossing them on tiptoe, we soon came to my own front door. Even now I had to take care and close the door cautiously.

How safe it felt indoors, how wonderful to breathe freely, to have no more anxiety. It had not been so difficult after all to beat the curfew, we had not met with a single patrol, and it looked so simple now. We thought we deserved a drink, but first Martine had to telephone her parents to say that all was well.

42

Heavy Seas

The start of 1944 did not look promising, with the intense cold, scarcer food, and the Germans intensifying their pursuit of the defaulters, as well as becoming more skilful at tracking down members of the Resistance. Impatience was growing in the population, who began to wonder whether the liberating offensive, so often promised by the *'Radio Anglaise'*, would ever take place. People were tired of oppression and tired of privations.

Now a smart new police was being trained to catch *'smokkeleers'*, thus restricting an expedient flow of food on the fringe of official rations. Marie, the nice girl who was our home-help, could tell a thing or two about the new police. Her marriage had just broken up, and the last straw had been when her husband had become a member of this new force. They were real thugs, who kept a substantial portion of the booty for their private consumption, and to indulge in their own illegal trading.

However some relief came on the food scene with the arrival of the herrings. They were the miraculous draught of fish that even the Germans did not try to hinder. Shoal after shoal unfurled close to our shores, and the fishermen, normally restricted by the coastal defences of our 'protectors', only had to cast their nets. The herrings flowed in, more than they could catch, it was said.

They were transported to Brussels by the trainload, giving the town a particular odour. Fish-shops that rarely had a thing on display were now selling herrings by the bucketful; customers had to bring their own containers. We ate them fried, grilled, baked, and since they were dirt-cheap, there was no excuse to be under-nourished – that is if you liked herrings. In order to preserve the miraculous food, we learnt to fillet, to pickle, to souse, for refrigerators were still unheard of in the average household.

It was not only our kitchens that effused the penetrating aroma, our hands after a filleting session sent out a whiff that remained impervious to soap and water. Just to make things worse, my mother bumped into Monsieur le Comte de Mandeval who was paying my father a visit. Anticipating his gesture and unable to retreat, she held out a firm hand in order to shake his, but noblesse oblige, a blue-blooded Frenchman kisses a lady's hand – that day, with unromantic consequences.

How far-reaching the odour must have been, we discovered one evening while eating our meal – of herrings – when we clearly heard steps going down the stairs. With some alarm my father opened the dining-room door, very gently, then we caught sight of the offender: a large rat on his way down from the kitchen, holding in his mouth a sizeable herring. Before my father could get hold of a blunt instrument to chase the animal, it had reached the ground-floor and disappeared. We never knew where the intruder came from nor where it went, we guessed it was through a small crack of the back door into the courtyard. We had it repaired, but ours was not the only story of this kind. The rodents, also on a wartime diet, had no doubt emerged from their subterranean refuges to share in the unexpected bonanza.

I received my second invitation from the *Werbestelle*, which followed the way of the first, being duly and ceremoniously thrown into the fire. This was the last communication I could treat thus with impunity for I knew that the next one would come by registered post and would have to be answered. Not for many weeks though, and for the moment the matter could rest.

Despite my 'safe' identity card, stating that I worked for the War Industries, the more frequent raids staged by the Germans were a source of worry; my papers would not have stood much official scrutiny. When a defined area was surrounded, every individual within its orbit had to produce identity documents; some did not comply and the rest of us watched helpless as they were taken to a waiting lorry. I acquired a form of intuition about an approaching raid that allowed me to run off into a side street before they had time to block all the escapes.

But the Germans' desperate effort to net more workers did not always take the form of an army raid. More sinister were those civilians wearing black trenchcoats and black felt hats. They walked in pairs and were easily recognizable by their shifty looks as well as by their apparel; better step out of their path if you spotted them in time! Unfortunately, they could be concealed in doorways and suddenly spring in front of their prey.

Two of these characters were once making a bee-line towards me when they suddenly noticed a young man. They set their sights on him instead – a better catch than a female – which gave me time to turn left and make myself scarce. Yet there was no joy in dodging them when you knew it was at the expense of someone else.

The most unfortunate victim of this kind of chase was an old class-mate of mine who had managed to live concealed and undetected in his parents' house for months on end. He never set foot in the street until news came to him that his fiancee was seriously ill. The young man took the risk of walking the 200 yards that separated him from his sweetheart's home and was immediately stopped by two Gestapo men, who arrested him on the spot as his papers were not in order.

The punishments for defaulting were severe and came under military law: deportation to a labour camp, even death. Women who were enrolled in the STO were more likely to be found a job in Belgium than in Germany, all the same I had pledged to myself that they would never get a scrap of work out of me. When the time came I would go into hiding.

How were we to reconcile with the realities of our life the preposterous rumour that the Belgians were very lucky to have as their Military Commandant General von Falkenhausen, whose family connections with Belgium insured us a 'milder regime' than that of other countries? If this was the case, God help the others! For news of arrests were commonplace, made intolerable for the families and friends of those arrested by the complete silence about their fate.

The existence of a camp of torture and death like Brendonck near Antwerp was well known and we suspected there were many more. Someone found innocent by a German court, or released after serving a sentence was a rare bird indeed.

The arrest of Father Fraisset came as a shock to my father. He had much respect for this priest, whose dedication to the welfare of underprivileged children was well known. When Father Fraisset used to pay him one of his discreet visits, it was not just because we subscribed to his organization; he sometimes assisted young men who tried to reach England and my father could provide him with safe addresses in France and before November 1942, with locations and instructions for crossing the demarcation line.

Father Fraisset's secretary was also arrested, but the charity work went on without them. In 1945, I had the privilege to meet this churchman, whose spiritual strength and vitality allowed him to survive beatings, solitary confinement and a period in a concentration camp. His lady secretary did not survive the horror of the camps. My father, who had met her on several occasions, described her as 'a person entirely dedicated to serving others, with a total sense of duty, always greeting graciously the many visitors that came her way. A legendary figure who compelled respect and admiration.'

Was the German defeat any nearer? There was no sign of it in our streets. Yet the air was filled with the hum of aircraft, night and day. There could not be anything left of Germany by now, why didn't they give in?

To think that my father had emerged from the Great War a pacifist, when its senselessness and cruelty had become manifest to him. That was the way he had brought me up. He had befriended Germans, who unfortunately had in time espoused the cause of Hitler. Now we cheered the bombers. Compassion for Germans had been wrenched from our hearts by the brute force of the Nazi oppression.

Passive resistance in the streets and in the trams was kept alive by the cheeky humour of the Bruxellois. When Germans were running to catch a tram, the drivers' strategy of pretending to wait, then of accelerating away when the soldiers thought they had made it, always drew a laugh if not cheers from the passengers.

In memory, I can still see the spectacle of the tram conductress whose vehicle had been halted by a march past of Rexists – the Belgian Nazi Party of Léon Degrelle. With total insouciance, the comic little woman was haranguing the passengers who were convulsed with laughter.

'Look at our brave Rexists having a parade! But don't be dazzled by their numbers,' she clamoured, 'it's the same lot going round and round the block to create an impression. I see the great Léon is not at the head of his troups, maybe he is having a conference with the Führer! . . . Here they come again!'

And she blew her small brass trumpet[1] with a martial bearing. Every word she uttered could have got her arrested, but she drew courage from the response of her audience, and she was for us the fillip we needed to go on enduring.

Sometimes, a Bruxellois would express his feelings with a mixture of humour and hatred. The man in a cloth cap posted himself squarely in front of the Belgian soldier in German uniform – a member of the 'Légion des Voluntaires Belges' – who was finding it difficult to step down from the tram on his crutches. With arm and forehead bandaged and one leg in plaster, he had obviously copped it on the Russian Front. The man in a cloth cap, eyes blazing, thundered at the traitor in his disctinctive accent: *'C'est dommage que c'est pas ta gueule qui est cassée!'*.[2]

---

[1] Part of a tram conductor's gear in those days.
[2] Very loosely translated 'what a pity they did not bump you off properly!'

43

Confidential matters

Amidst the stress and difficulties of everyday life, cultural activities offered an escape. There was no lack of painters, talented or not, to exhibit their work, and no lack of visitors flocking to the galleries. Owing to the scarcity of consumer goods, people who had some spare money and saw its value steadily decline, spent it willingly on works of art and antiques.

Small private libraries sprang up, that offered amongst their books works by British and American authors, some actually in English, which gave me the opportunity to practise that language. I also welcomed the chance to improve my knowledge of those authors I had discovered in my school days with the books I used to borrow from Marianne Delambre. Libraries, art galleries, and conference halls were places where one could usually forget the Germans.

Lectures and talks on learned subjects were the vogue, a pleasant form of recreation to which Jacques Bailly's wife Esther contributed. She chose to talk on a lesser known period of ancient Egypt, a subject on which she had lectured and researched in her days as a university teacher. Now she evoked for her delighted audience the Pharaohs of a certain dynasty and their queens. The court intrigues, religious dissent, the problems of governing an empire, were recaptured and made present by this talented speaker.

My parents were forever grateful to the Baillys for their part in arranging my brothers' Swiss exile, but we also enjoyed their company. Esther's mother was American and spoke French with a pronounced accent, so did Esther's friend from New Zealand. These ladies' voices sounded like a melody from a forbidden world and a challenge to our present condition. Having been married to Belgians, they had espoused their nationality and were therefore protected from being interned as enemy aliens. We met interesting people in the Bailly's entourage and above all we were of one mind about the present predicament of the world.

Jacques had much to be thankful for, being a citizen of a neutral country, hardly affected by the war. But from an early age he had lived in France, then made his home in Belgium when he had married Esther. These two countries were also homelands to him and he could not accept the sufferings and humiliation imposed on them. When he had returned to Belgium in 1942, soon after us, he had stopped a while in Paris and had witnessed the crack German troops marching past the Arc de Triompe. He could not take this violation, he told my father, it had actually caused him physical pain.

Early in 1944 we became conscious of a slight change in the Baillys manner, something that could not easily be defined. Maybe they had become less talkative, less relaxed, and in time less accessible if not a little distant. We found it puzzling because we thought we knew them so well. The answer came during a visit Jacques paid to my father early one evening, after the staff had left for home. They remained in conversation for a considerable time, a conversation that seemed very confidential and hush hush. And my father was very quiet when he came up to dinner.

In time I learnt the reason for it all. Esther's was a family of serious academics and people who involved themselves in human affairs. One of her forbears was a historical figure, a founder of the Belgian state, while Jacques' activities were in the more mundane world of life insurance. Together they had a wide circle of acquaintances, which in pre-war years had been international and no doubt contributed to their present adventure: they had come into contact with and were involved in the world of wireless transmissions to London; it explained their slightly enigmatic conduct and a certain change in their lifestyle. In this new risky exercise, they acted as messengers, watchers, and general protectors to the wireless operator.

Vital to the functioning of the 'line' were safe premises

for the actual transmissions and this is why Jacques had come to see my father. He had no doubts about his commitment to the German defeat and he also knew him to be a man of courageous character, willing to take risks. What he sought was permission to transmit from our house, as well as help in finding other locations; it was essential to keep moving to avoid detection.

This was not the sort of activity you gossiped about light-heartedly. Jacques had approached my father because he had great hopes of an affirmative answer, yet it needed a little pondering, even if it met with our aspirations. My mother and I would have to be consulted about such a grave decision.

We were at once unanimous about this prospect of direct involvement in the war effort. Until now, we had agreed to assist when opportunities came our way, but this was a truly concrete contribution. Our house would be in contact with someone, somewhere across the Channel, sending information of strategic importance! Although I had no part to play in the exercise, I felt a degree of satisfaction I had not known for a long time.

44

High Risk Activity

To share in such a secret did not affect my everyday life but it gave it an extra dimension. Now that we were in touch with participants, the great battle that was taking place overseas and on our shores became more real.

For the present our only contribution was to discuss who to approach amongst my parents' acquaintances and mine in order to find other locations. It was all very delicate; if the objectives were admirable, the consequences could be grave for those enouraged to take part. Of the people we knew we had first to select those we trusted one hundred per cent, then eliminate those we would not wish to take risks, like families with young children. It was a heavy responsibility to involve any person, and we concluded that the proper approach would be a confidential conversation where the offer of help could come spontaneously, where it would be the person's own decision, rather than an outright request. And so we drew up our short list.

We were soon to hear from Jacques Bailly who gave my father a date; then it was suddenly cancelled, God knows why. Was it going to be like the RAF fugitives we were willing to shelter, but who were never turning up? No, it had only been postponed and would take place the following Saturday – in the lunch hour.

We received our instructions, which were clear and precise. My mother and I would go out while the operation was in progress, but Marie would remain at home so as not to awake her suspicions, she would simply be told that lunch was required later than usual because my father had some visitors coming to discuss business. The wireless transmitter woud be delivered to our house the day before.

Behind these orders could be sensed a timing and organization that were highly professional. Information was of course the most important contribution that could be made to the Allied Command from our side of the Channel, and wireless operators who had been trained in England and parachuted into occupied Europe had great expertise. They also showed complete coolness, living as they did under the ever present threat of detection. We were told that the Germans possessed very sophisticated devices and moved with speed when alerted, so transmissions had to be brief.

Jacques Bailly had urged my father to disappear, at least for a time, if he or other members of the 'line' were caught.

'If they get you, they'll make you talk' had been his words.

So the least we all knew, the better. An escape route had been worked out from the window of the laboratory on the first floor if an emergency occurred. It meant a small jump on to the side of the glass roof of the workshop, and a leap into some neighbouring garden or courtyard, and then, the best of luck!

Once it had been delivered, I gazed with awe at the innocuous-looking leather case that was the transmitter – just a shabby little piece of luggage! The next day, at the appointed time, I went out with my mother and we came across Esther Bailly on her way to take her post as a watcher in our street. We pretended not to know her. It was not easy to take our mind off what was happening and to persuade ourselves that we were unaware of it.

Back at home, we found Jacques still there, having an aperitif with my father, and Marie impatient to serve lunch, because it was her afternoon off. Everything had gone well. They were now discussing another location my father had found, luckily in a more isolated part of the town.

My father's job had been to watch the street from behind the net curtains. Not long after the start of the transmission, he had spotted a small army lorry parked some fifty yards away on the other side of the road. He informed the others but Louis – the radio operator by his nom de guerre – went on tapping his message undisturbed. Only a raid on the house would have prevented him from completing his job – such were his orders.

I did not like the idea of that army lorry as the little leather case was still under our roof, but it was collected the next morning without mishap.

The same evening as the transmission, amongst the BBC *'messages personnels'* was a particular one we had been asked to listen for; a little nonsensical phrase which confirmed that the coded information sent from our house had been received. There was no harm in our knowing the words, since they did not mean anything to us, but it was a gratifying experience.

In the days that followed I reflected on the courage of people who undertook such risky work. My eloquent praise of Esther Bailly led to a misunderstanding with my mother, who read in my words – quite mistakenly – an aspiration to emulate her. With all the passion of a hen defending her brood, she voiced her opposition to such an adventure. She implored and remonstrated, all a wasted effort, because I did not wish to live my life in the shadow of torture and death. As a family, we were all agreed to lend our support to the struggle for our liberation, but that was quite different from being a commando-style agent.

45

The Dawn of Hope

Another transmission at the friend's house, where my father acted as a watcher went well too. I had now discussed the subject with an old school friend, who was very enthusiastic and was debating with his parents the possibility of using their apartment. Although the matter was present in my mind, it was no more a novelty. The time was not yet ripe for another transmission from our house, and life was very much like before: a mixture of work, recreation and fear.

My young friends from the camping days in the Ardennes had taken to the new craze and were dancing 'le swing', any excuse for a party or a get together where they would bring their records. I was invited to join in this lively dancing, itself a form of protest, because jazz music was American and not played in public places. Their most popular record was Glenn Miller's 'In the Mood' and I feel I ought to have been more curious at the time about the origin of the records.

One morning after starting work, I was called downstairs, where the postman wanted me to sign something. That was it – the registered letter from the *Werbestelle*, the one I could not throw into the fire. I had never signed a paper with so much reluctance.

I had about ten days to return the questionnaire, and it would be several more days before I was called for a medical examination – time to breathe. One choice opened to me was to hide at the Clary's, a kindly couple in their late fifties, who, having no children of their own, were longing to have someone to pamper. It was a safe place to hide as M. Clary was managing director of a French Industrial concern that was regrettably compelled to allocate much of its production to the Germans. I would have been thoroughly spoilt in their household, and I believe they were quite disappointed when I chose another solution that was preferable to being confined for weeks on end in an apartment, however select and full of *objets d'art*.

Help came from a man who was himself asking my father a favour at the time I received the letter. He was seeking a position for a young French girl whose family had just suffered a tragedy and who was desperate to earn a living. We could not employ her, but by pure coincidence, my father found her a job in M. Clary's office, and by a later coincidence, the shy, blonde young lady was to become my sister in law. The gentleman in question was also facing a problem with the *Werbestelle* who wanted to hive off the small staff he employed into the STO. Now he had been put in touch with a Belgian employee of the *Werbestelle* who would – for a fee – put aside the files of his staff for a duration of three months, when they would have to be reviewed again. For an extra fee, he was willing to include me in the manoeuvre.

Three months from the 16th May 1944, the date of my reply to the *Werbestelle*, which I inscribed on the threatening slip of paper that came with the questionnaire.

It sounded like an eternity and put my mind at rest. But only because my father could afford to bribe the clerk, and we had some well-off friends willing to hide me. This was a time when the unfairness of life weighed more than ever on the impecunious.

The 6th of June was a day like many others, a sunny day in spring when it would have been more pleasant to play tennis than to breathe the acids of the laboratory. But work comes before play and it promised to be a pretty busy day. By late morning, I was still drilling, weighing and preparing new assays when I heard someone run upstairs with such haste that I feared something terrible had happened. Whoever it was pushed open the door of my room, shouting:

'*Les Alliés ont débarqué! Ils ont débarqué en Normandie!*'

My delicate balances suddenly suffered a storm and were left to their own devices as I ran downstairs with the bearer of good tidings. 'How do you know?' was my question to the elated crowd in the office. A neighbour had just brought the news, someone had heard it on the BBC! I ran upstairs to our apartment to tune in to the English language wavelength – it was true, absolutely true.

Oh the rapturous feeling, the fulfilment of a hope that had not been in vain. It was obvious from what I heard on the radio that this was the real thing, a large scale operation, unlike the experimental raid on Dieppe.

Feeling excited as never before, I returned to the office to confirm the news. It was lunchtime now, and before we closed the premises, I went out into the street.

The news must have travelled like wildfire because some passers-by were smiling broadly and knowingly. Only the knowledge that the Germans were still about stopped people from cheering aloud. We spent our lunch hour with our ears glued to the wireless and when the firm reopened, we had brought glasses downstairs and we celebrated.

We were entering a new phase, a great moment of history. From now on, listening to the news would take on a new significance. That evening my father dug out some old Michelin maps of Normandy and we prepared to monitor the operations with big red and blue pencils.

When news of an event, like the gunning of the Gestapo, had been suppressed, it travelled by word of mouth and was quickly widespread. Now, only the day after the landings, we heard of the tragic death of a dental surgeon who was a customer of our firm. On the afternoon of the 6th of June, he had been a passenger in a tram where people could hardly contain their pleasure at the latest news. A young man was expressing his feelings rather too strongly for the taste of a German officer who angrily kicked him off the tram. As the young man lay motionless on the pavement, the dental surgeon jumped off the tram to attend to him, followed by the German officer, who drew out his pistol and shot him dead.

There were enough bystanders to witness this brutal act and give details to the dentist's wife. The obituary in the national press was brief: '. . . regret to annouce the sudden death of Dr X, a dental surgeon.' My father paid the widow a visit, distressed that the 6th of June – our new hope – had turned out to be so tragic for that family.

In the general euphoria, it had been difficult to visualize that the 6th of June was about war, about battles on our shores, that would bring destruction and death in their wake.

46

Bad News

While the war raged in the lanes of Normandy, we leaned over our Michelin maps at news time, trying to pinpoint the advance of the allied armies and the retreat of the Germans. The lack of progress showed that the invasion was no walkover. The pessimists and the collaborators soon concluded that the operation was a failure and that the Anglo-American landing force would be thrown back into the sea. Maybe it was an unequal fight, with the Germans entrenched on our soil since 1939, but if nothing seemed to go well, nothing seemed to go too badly either; and I passionately wanted to believe that it could not fail.

Normandy, the tranquil land that I remembered from our camping holiday in 1937; how could it be a theatre of war? With its farmhouses nestling amongst the apple trees, its gentle cows grazing in lush pastures. I remembered the cream, the cheese, the butter and the cider we bought in farms; I remembered gathering mussels at low tide and preparing them on our camp fire. We bathed on the little beach below the cliffs and we went to Bayeux to see the tapestry and to shop on the square on market days. Sometimes my parents took us to Port-en-Bessin, a little harbour where we watched the arrival of the fishing boats.

War did not belong to the scene in my memory, yet it was there, necessary, because of the madman who had overrun Europe. The area around Bayeux was now a British sector. Perhaps some of the boys I had known in London had landed there for they were now the right age to be in the armed forces.

All over France, Resistance movements had been called into action to support the invasion. Their role was to disrupt communications, sabotage the railway and generally delay enemy reinforcements on their way to Normandy. Unfortunately, the forces of occupation reacted in some French regions by creating a reign of terror, their wrath falling on the 'guilty' and the innocent alike.

I cannot recall how soon after the event the BBC broadcast the news of the martyrdom of Oradour-sur-Glane. The massacre took place a few days after the landings, the climax of German anger, an atrocity difficult for a normal mind to grasp. Only a monster could have ordered the slaughter of completely innocent villagers, the burning alive of mothers and children in a church, the total wiping out of a peaceful village. But the soldiers who carried out the orders? What kind of human beings were they? We pictured this village, so similar to those we knew in my father's native region, which was not all that far away from Oradour, and we shivered at the thought.

The myth that Pétain's collaboration with the Nazis was to save France from destruction and ruin was now exposed as the aberration that it was. Other countries whose government had refused to collaborate and gone into exile were not paying such a price.

For my father, the shock of discovering that the rule of the jackboot did not spare his own village nor his own family came with a letter from his eldest sister. A letter too old to be fresh news yet explicit enough. It simply stated that her husband had been arrested.

'He had opened the door in person, knowing that he had nothing with which to reproach himself, and he had been taken away on the spot.'

By whom, the letter did not say. We knew, of course, but as far as the censor was concerned, it might have been the local Gendarmerie. My aunt believed that he would soon be returned to her, but my father didn't.

'You shouldn't open the door to them, whether you have done something wrong or not; when they come to your front door, you skip away through the back.'

Other names were mentioned in the letter, that of the local postmaster and M. Dubois and his son Alain, who had been arrested in the same swoop. I remembered Alain Dubois, I played tennis with him in the summer of 1941 and we both got sunstroke for playing in the midday heat; he was the boy who swore in English every time he hit a ball into the net.

My aunt's optimism would be to no purpose, all four men were to perish in Dachau concentration camp. The reason for their arrest will for ever remain a mystery since there was no charge, no trial, no judgement.

We have often speculated in later years about our own fate as a family if we had remained in our small French town, instead of returning to Brussels and sending my brothers to Switzerland. In 1944, when the landings had raised my hopes of an imminent liberation, and I was still working at my job in relative security, the situation in the south of France was sombre in the extreme; my schoolfriend Bobette Duteil was enduring in Ravensbrück concentration camp the nightmare that would lead to her death; my other schoolfriend, Marianne Delambre, was running a hospital in the Maquis with other medical students; and the principal of the *Collège de Garçons* which my brothers had attended – the man who had forced on the boys a large poster of the Maréchal – was denouncing his own pupils to the Germans; the inhabitants of a nearby village were compelled to watch it go up in flame as a punishment for resistance activities in the area; the blacksmith of my father's native village, walking through the countryside, came across the remains of a group of young maquisards who had been caught and massacred in an unmentionable way.

That was the climate down south, of which we only had a vague notion. Surely our departure had been timely.

After the 6th of June, the jamming of the BBC in French increased greatly, so I listened more often to the broadcasts in English where news items such as 'Cherbourg has fallen' could be heard with more clarity! When spring turned into summer, only a parcel of Normandy had been liberated in spite of the mightiest operation ever mounted from the sea.

The long summer evenings attracted people onto their balconies to watch the huge formations of bombers on their way to Germany. When the aircraft reached a certain point in the sky, the flak started up, and every day, it scored a hit or two.

Ignorant as we were of the tactics of aviation, we could not understand why they kept to such rigid formations instead of dispersing to avoid the flak. If a plane was hit, we saw the parachutes open and slowly float downwards. Occasionally one would become a brief burst of flame, then cease to be visible – tragic evidence, right under our eyes, of the reality of war.

In the French FFI group, where I had been allowed to act as a messenger, things were livening up a little. I soon knew where the members lived, as I cycled to their homes to inform them of impending meetings. More significant was the talk of another wireless transmission from our house.

But it never took place. A messenger brought instead the news of the arrests of 'Louis' and of our friend Jacques Bailly. These two arrests had not been simultaneous. Louis had been trailed and caught by the Gestapo, while Jacques was in the hands of another German security force. Esther had disappeared and was known to be in a safe hideout.

Confronted with such worrying information, we realized that my father's own safety was at stake and that he had better make a business trip to Paris – this, at least, would be the official version. At the same time we were stunned by the news of the arrest of such a good friend and fearful of his predicament. 'Paris', in the present case, would be only a few tram stops away, in the home of Carlos Bonar. He had agreed to shelter my father if he were ever in danger. It was now four years since we had sheltered the Bonar family, during the débâcle. Those four years had seemed like a lifetime. The fact that Carlos was Spanish, made him less vulnerable to the attention of the Germans and it afforded a greater sense of security to someone on the run.

47

Early Morning Call

The Bonars lived, like us, in a flat above their business premises. But they also owned a villa easily accessible by tram, where town meets country, and where Fernande took the household during the summer months. That was to be my father's temporary retreat.

Maman and I, now alone at mealtimes and in the evenings, had to persuade ourselves that Papa had really gone to Paris and we concocted all the details. We had access to my father through a go-between who passed messages about work. After a while, my mother and I went to Sunday lunch at the villa, being extra careful when we left our house.

My father decided to return after three weeks. He had done plenty of reading, plenty of gardening, and an awful lot of washing up! With this latter activity, Fernande had succeeded where everyone else had failed. My father had been the second of six children in a household where at lunchtime there were many mouths to feed. As well as the family and the grandparents, there were the seamstresses my grandmother employed in her dressmaking workshop, and sometimes a guest or two. The one maid they employed could not cope with all the washing up and the two eldest children had to do it with her. So he had often declared that never again would he wipe a plate – he would help with anything else, but not the washing up. Well done Fernande!

My father returned home looking healthy and a little fatter. He must have drunk plenty of good wine, for Carlos always reserved the best of his merchandise for his own consumption.

The day after his return, an amiable lady paid us a visit.

She was Esther Bailly's mother, a dignified person, tall, elegant in her navy blue suit, who combined social graces and a certain heartiness – maybe a trait from her native State of Virginia. Nothing in her attitude gave the impression that this was not a social call.

'Monsieur Rey' – she went straight to the point – 'they have arrested my son in law, it is intolerable! Esther seems to have gone into hiding out of fear, I don't even know where she is. I wonder if, as a friend of Jacques, you can possibly help us? I know where he is being held, so I went to see the German authorities of that prison and told them that it was ludicrous to arrest a Swiss citizen whose country has nothing to do with their war. I assured them they were making a terrible mistake . . . '

The strong Anglo-Saxon accent in an otherwise impeccable French was even more pronounced when she was excited. How did she have the nerve to confront the Germans with such an intonation in her voice? Was it courage or blissful innocence? Our pretence at knowing nothing of Jacques's arrest seemed convincing to her, and she urged my father, as his friend, to join in her efforts to have him freed.

Our connection with Jacques Bailly was the very last thing we wanted to flaunt in front of the Germans. Sadly we had to persuade her that it was not a safe approach and that patience would be preferable until the Germans realized their mistake. We gathered a few facts from this conversation, mainly the confirmation that it was not the Gestapo who had arrested Jacques. The security police that held him might be less cruel.

Every week that had elapsed made the situation less risky for my father, yet caution was still the order of the day. We had made plans for his escape, should the Germans pay us a visit, that included a small leather bag ready for him to grab, containing money, his false identity card and a gold ingot that could finance a prolonged stay away.

My sleep must be deeper in the small hours of the morning because at first the sounds did not wake me up, I thought I was hearing them in my dreams. At the instant I discovered what they were – the door bells on each floor ringing simultaneously – I saw my mother appear at the door of my room, meaning business:

'Come on, they are here, you know what to do! Hide your father's pyjamas and any other trace of his presence while I help him dress and escape.'

Her voice, her manner, spurred me into action. There was no time to think, only to get on with the job as fast as possible. I folded my father's pyjamas neatly and put them away with the clean washing in the cupboard. Then I pulled the clothes back from the double bed in order to cool his place and I rearranged the bed as if only one person had slept in it. He was now ready to leave, carrying his little bag.

My mother's capacity to be herself whatever the circumstances brought a shade of relief to an unbearably tense situation:

'Oui, ça va!' (yes, all right!) she shouted irritated towards the door bells as if they were being rung by any old impatient visitor.

My parents then went down to the laboratory where my father would leave by the rear window; the concert of door bells was now accompanied by loud banging on the front door. I watched the escape from the wide open window of my bedroom, and I saw my father jump onto the side of the workshop roof; I saw how the heavy bag he carried hit one of the glass panes of the roof, breaking it in bits and making a terrible fracas as the pieces fell to the ground. And I gasped in anguish.

He dropped the bag in the next door garden, then let himself down from the wall. The laboratory window was shut now and my mother must have been opening the front door to them; so I went back to bed as though nothing had happened.

There were steps and voices in the landing, and I heard them next in my parents' bedroom. The door between our rooms was closed, but the voices sounded angry and my mother was protesting saying that her husband was in Paris. I feared they might be ill-treating her, so I caused a diversion by calling 'Maman, what's happening?' Immediately three uniformed men rushed into my room with torchlights and guns. They looked at me for a while and must have decided that I was harmless because they moved to the window where they exchanged words between themselves. One of the men in uniform was a Belgian who interpreted for the Germans and he indicated to my mother that they wanted to go on searching the rest of the house.

At first she had been led at gunpoint, but now she was allowed to walk unfettered. It was then that my mother's capacity to be herself in all circumstances caused me terrible anguish, because she was such a pessimist. As she followed the men out of my room, she leaned over my bed and whispered:

'They have seen something!'

I was thunderstruck by those words – they could only have meant that my father had been spotted. Now we were all doomed, finished, and I was as good as dead. It was like descending into eternal night. My mind was not totally blank for I remembered that 'I knew nothing of my father's activities'. I swore I would never betray him, whatever they did to me.

This oath was my life-raft; it gave me strength and helped me to regain an awareness of my surroundings. The house was silent now. I crept out of bed and tiptoed to the landing. Not a sound. Had they taken my mother away?

Then the staircase echoed again with voices and a banging noise that was the closing of our heavy front door. I heard someone coming up the stairs – no doubt about it, they were my mother's steps.

'They have gone,' she said, 'for good I hope. They were the Gestapo all right, but thank heavens their raid was quite unconnected with what we had in mind!'

With a sensation of well-being slowly returning to my body and soul, I heard how they had searched the house from loft to cellar without speaking a word about who or what they were after; how in the bedroom they had not believed in her story that her husband was in Paris and that she lived alone with her daughter in the huge house; how they had insisted that two people had slept in the double bed. This angry argument was the commotion I heard, but they had not touched her.

Once in the workshop they had demanded an explanation about the broken roof pane.

'I don't know, it was not there last evening. It must be a cat that jumped on the roof; and it would not be the first time.'

As the reply appeared to satisfy them, my mother experienced a great sense of relief. She felt sufficiently emboldened to appeal to them to disclose the purpose of their visit:

'I may be of some help to you if I knew what you are looking for.'

There were people in hiding in this street, had she heard of anything?

'No, but we have received one or two letters addressed to strangers and we returned them to the post office.'

Now she was a pal! They showed her the list of names. She did not recognize any. Then they were off.

Why had my mother been so alarmist and whispered in my ear the words that had plunged me into despair? It was the way the Gestapo men had peered from the rear windows on every floor level at the courtyards and gardens below, commenting and pointing, that had caused her to panic. She had thought it better to warn me; it was also a way of sharing the strain to which she was subjected.

It was still the early hours of the morning and the curfew had not yet been lifted. Wherever my father was hiding, he had no way of knowing that the raid had not been 'in his honour'. Since there was nothing more we could do for the moment, we took breakfast to help us recover.

48

The Crime of Carlos Bonar

By mid-morning we had traced my father to the Bonars. He reacted with absolute caution to my mother's telephone conversation with Carlos. She explained in covered words that all was in order and that he could return home. He would not come to the phone for fear that she might be speaking under some kind of duress. In the end I went there myself to reassure him that the alarming episode had not really concerned us.

One is always wise after the event. In this particular instance, it would have been safer for my father to have opened the door to 'them' rather than risk being caught escaping – an escape that had been relatively easy, but for the incident of the broken glass. He had been able to let himself into the house next door by reaching for the key through a missing pane in the back door that had been temporarily replaced by a piece of cardboard. He had crept inside like a thief, unsuspected by the occupants, a doctor and his family, who were still fast asleep. From the street door slightly ajar – after unbolting it with the utmost care – he had been able to see the German car parked outside our house and the soldier on guard pacing up and down. He reckoned he could cover a few yards unseen every time the man had his back turned, then hide in a doorway. Shutting the heavy street door silently had not proved easy.

At that rate he had soon reached the next street corner. Now he walked cautiously along the walls to the first tram halt, where there was still some time to wait until curfew was lifted, so he chose a deep porch to hide in. After boarding the first tram, that carried the early morning workers, he was soon at the front door of an astonished Carlos.

My parents were the closest beings in my life during those war years, and I would have been beyond despair, had something tragic happened to my father. Yet danger was at everybody's door. Only a few days after our own traumatic incident, Fernande Bonar came to see us in distress because Carlos had not returned the night before. She had no clue as to his whereabouts, and he was not the sort of man to go on an escapade and abandon his family without a word. It was with the help of the Spanish Consulate that Fernande eventually found out that her husband had been arrested by the Gestapo. She was dumbfounded at the news that 'he had insulted a representative of the Reich.' Neither we nor Fernande believed that he would do anything so foolish, yet he remained in custody a fortnight before the efforts of the Spanish Consul succeeded in setting him free. He could think himself lucky that his country was on the side of the Axis! What is called an insult by a Belgian member of the Gestapo does not necessarily agree with the views of a law-abiding citizen. On that Wednesday, like every Wednesday, Carlos had met with other wine merchants at the stock exchange to trade in his own field of business, after which they had eaten a well washed down lunch at a nearby café-restaurant. Suddenly there was a raid on the premises as they were finishing their meal. The shifty fellows in their black trenchcoats and black hats burst in, ordering all outside doors to be locked and proceeded to check the identity papers of every diner.

With the confidence of someone who has just had sufficient to drink, Carlos asked the man what authority he had to demand to see his papers.

'Gestapo!'

'Can you prove it?'

The man took a card from his pocket and waved it fleetingly. Carlos was not satisfied because he had not properly seen it. Before the man had time to replace the card, Carlos grabbed his wrist firmly and proceeded to read out aloud in a clear voice:

>Achille van de Put
>such and such a number
>so and so road
>Brussels

Carlos was immediately arrested and handcuffed to Achille van de Put. He was dragged round this restaurant as the Gestapo man inspected the papers of other customers, then had to follow him in other establishments that the men in black were raiding. It lasted a long time, and the two men, locked together in this intimate manner, had plenty of time to converse. Carlos wanted to know the reason for his arrest. The reply was simple:

'You announced my name and address to all and sundry, and when the war is over, me bang bang!' said the man, pointing an imaginary gun to his own forehead. Carlos was encouraged by the fact that the man had no illusion about the issue of the war, nor about the despicable task he was performing. Eventually he was put into a van with other unfortunates, although he had invoked in vain his Spanish nationality. He was thrown into jail, but never forgot the name of Achille van de Put, nor his address.

On his release from prison, Carlos was greeted with emotion by his three children, who did not really know what had happened, yet sensed it was something nasty. The youngest, a cuddly dark-haired, dark-eyed little girl, not quite three years old, would not let go of him for fear he should go away again.

49

While We Wait

Now we knew that our friends from non-belligerent countries were no safer from arrest than we were. In the case of Carlos Bonar, he would never have been freed without the help of his own consular authorities.

There was no doubt any more that our liberation was in sight because of the sustained progress on the Normandy front. The essential now was to survive the coming weeks, and the Germans were not the only danger; rail travel offered plenty of hazards too. A journey I made to visit customers of our firm in a provincial town reminded me of the trip from Paris with *mein Onkel*. We were compelled to travel in the portion of the train just behind the engine, and this time it was not us, but the train in front that was attacked by the allied air force, causing havoc on the line and interminable delay. Air raids on railway installations and other targets were frequent in the outer suburbs and did not always spare Brussels itself.

The disruption of communications and the general tension caused a considerable reduction in commercial and business activities. I remember August 1944 as a month when we discussed and chatted rather than worked. We were often gathered together in the main office, cosy but rather sombre with its walls covered by mock tapestries, exchanging news, speculating on the outcome of battles, daring to talk about a future in freedom.

The star amongst us was definitely Theo, the smelter, who with the mimicry and sparkle of a genuine comedian, entertained us with numerous stories from his colourful district of the *Marolles*; they were usually about the way people behaved towards the Germans there. We did not believe half of his stories, but they were the sort one enjoyed listening to. And all the things Theo was going to do when war was over! He would need two life-times to accomplish them. Unfortunately Theo was not always well – he had serious problems with his appendix – and when his verve ran dry, the place was all the duller for it. He had a real terror of surgery; they would not catch him on an operating table! So he went on suffering.

With business so slack and the weather so fine, playing tennis was an agreeable way of relieving the tension of those grim days. We belonged to a tennis club that had a small membership and a friendly atmosphere. The President of the club could speak English as well as he spoke French, having been a child refugee in England during the First World War, and that set the tone for any of us who were keen on practising that language.

One thing I treasured was my tennis racket, of a model called 'Hurricane' which had been purchased in England during my holiday of 1939. We played with 'remploy'[1] balls, that were not altogether satisfactory, but better ones were available for the diverting tournaments the President organized at weekends. The *Tournoi des Ménages* was the one with the most unpredictable result. Although the lack of suitable male company was frustrating to a girl of my age, this *Tournoi des Ménages* nearly put me off marriage for the rest of my life. When the matches were over, my parents were bitterly reproachful of one another's mistakes, Mr and Mrs X were having a serious argument, Mrs Y was crying in the ladies' cloakroom, and Mr and Mrs Z were looking very angry and left in a huff. It was all right for the President, his wife did not play tennis, and he, himself, had only acted as an umpire.

In peacetime, a tennis club would be a place where boy meets girl. Now, many young men were in hiding, in the resistance, or simply did not show themselves in public; the masculine element in the club consisted mainly of older men, usually married, a couple of misogynist students from Louvain university who kept aloof from girls, and boys in their last years at school. I had just turned twenty-two and

---

[1]Reconditioned

saw myself as a mature person, who tended to be indifferent to the schoolboys' attentions. I enjoyed their company all the same since they made me think of my brothers.

What were Gilbert and Georges like now? I so longed to see them. From a photograph, I gathered that Georges had changed out of all recognition. The little boy I had said goodbye to would be a man when he returned to his family. Alas the exchange of mail with Switzerland was a casualty of the intensification of war, for we received hardly any letters and ours probably did not reach them. What was there to write about anyway since most of the events that affected our lives – the tensions, the fears, the excitement of our approaching liberation – could not be mentioned?

The mail from Paris was still working, albeit in an erratic way, and I received some letters that caused me great pain. They were from my uncle and aunt, explaining that Grand'mère was in hospital, following a fall in her house. She had multiple fractures, yet had been able after falling, to crawl to an armchair where she remained, undiscovered, for forty-eight hours. Eventually, a neighbour had worried that she had not been seen; he looked through the window, and discovering her predicament, had forced his way in.

The letters had arrived in a jumbled up order, then the telegram announcing her death. It was so painfully sad that owing to incessant bombing of railway lines in the Paris region, my uncle had to walk sixteen miles to visit his poor mother who was dying of gangrene in a hospital ward; yet her ultimate wish had been to die at home, with dignity, as was customary with her generation. My aunt's dramatic letters reduced me to floods of tears; I also felt some guilt about those Sundays – when Grand'mère had no doubt expected my visit – which I had chosen to spend with Frédéric. But it was this dreadful war that made the end of my grandmother's life such a heart-break. She could have lived to be a hundred for she was in good health and had never broken a bone in her life; I was convinced that her fractures were caused by weakness due to privations. In normal times news of her accident would have reached me quickly, and I could have been with her in a few hours. Grand'mère had had a sad life, it was so unfair that she should have such a wretched death. Now I was left with the memory of her warm affection and the wonderful stories she had told me over the years.

While we were mourning my grandmother's death, Theo's appendicitis turned to peritonitis, and there was nothing the doctors could do for him. He who had cheered everybody up and had sometimes made the occupation sound like a joke would not see his town free of the Germans. Theo was a great loss to my father, who had known him since his early days in Brussels. In 1939, when my father had been called up, Theo had made an emotional scene, convinced that he would be killed in the war. Now my father sat by him during his last hours, promising to take his son Gustave into the firm and train him as a smelter – Gustave who, right through the war, had limped ostentatiously every day of the week but had played rugby on Sundays, leaving his walking sticks in the dressing-room. My father gave Theo a nice funeral and we all regretted that he had not held out a little longer, for we were sure that our liberation was imminent.

After two-and-a-half months of fighting, the allied armies were at last forging ahead. They had advanced beyond the confines of Normandy and the Germans were retreating fast. It was not just through the BBC broadcasts that we knew that the Germans were sustaining heavy losses: we had tangible proofs of it. The little railway line that ran alongside our tennis club suddenly burst with activity. It had been until now a sleepy branch line where the occasional train carried a few passengers to nearby villages. Now train after train of wounded or exhausted soldiers, damaged war material still under its camouflage of branches, passed under our astonished eyes – a retreating German army who did not like the sight of people playing tennis. There were shouts and threatening gestures, and I felt safer in the clubhouse when one of those trains was passing by.

Not that all my spare time was occupied with tennis. In mid-August, when it was clear that the liberating armies were advancing towards Paris, the head of the FFI group set me a task.

Black Citroen cars with French registration numbers had been noticed parked outside the main hotels in town. They had come from Paris and their occupants were the French traitors who now felt their days were numbered and were fleeing towards Germany, the only safe place for them. They were the torturers of the French Gestapo, the paid informers, the persecutors of the Jews, the Nazi thugs who had run the press during their country's darkest years. Their cars were known to the Resistance, and my job was to note the registration numbers to establish who was trying to escape.

Standing by the cars with note-pad and pencil was out of the question. I had to remember the numbers and go elsewhere to write them down. As I have always had a poor memory for figures and the cars increased daily, I enlisted the help of one of my schoolboy friends from the tennis club, who was thrilled to assist me. We sat at a café terrace, strategically located, noting the numbers we had remembered on our wrists. The cars only remained in Brussels overnight, but the next day there were more, because the Second Armoured Division, commanded by Général Leclerc, was at the gates of Paris.

On 25 August, the intoxicating news came over the radio: Paris had been freed! The next day, a Saturday, there was great rejoicing and a celebration at our little tennis club. My parents and I were toasted because we were French, it was as though we had liberated Paris ourselves! This was wonderful news, and with Paris free, there was hope for the rest of the occupied world. But it had not happened without a fight, and the siege had lasted several days. In Brussels also, we had better brace ourselves for a difficult time ahead. That was the general mood in the population, for there was a run on provisions; even the *smokkeleers* had nothing more to sell. In spite of the excitement and tension of the moment, housewives still had to feed their families, and that was no mean problem. In my own family, we were certainly not prepared for a siege.

50

The Third of September . . .

For the first time since June 1940, the news was consistently good and improving all the time. Not so in the pro-German official press and radio, which continued to claim victories on land, sea and air and to affirm that the invading Allies would be thrown back into the sea.

Extensive sectors of France had now been freed including Paris, its centre of gravity, and American and French columns were advancing up the Rhone valley after having captured Marseilles and Toulon. My country was being reborn. In spite of Vichy having abolished the Republic and democracy, enough French people were fighting to restore them, within the ranks of the allied armies or in the underground, to ensure a liberation in dignity, a liberation in which we as a nation would have taken part.

Glued to our BBC wavelengths, we monitored the progress of the British army that had crossed the Seine and was advancing at speed towards the North. Here in Brussels there was evidence of troops leaving the capital and of German offices closing down after loading tons of documents into lorries. Every sign that the oppressors were taking their leave was greeted with jubilation.

In my father's FFI group, there was a sudden surge of activity. I reported daily to the officer in command in case my services as a messenger were required, and on 3 September I received my instructions to deliver safe-conducts to the members, as well as arm-bands in the French colours on which the letters FFI and a Cross of Lorraine were embroidered in bright red. The passes, which bore the members' photos, were signed by the legitimate 'Bourgmestre' of Brussels, now in hiding, but ready to take over the moment we were freed. This signature, which was also on my own pass, delighted me, for I saw it as a token of our impending freedom.

The BBC news did not report details about the advance of the British army into Belgium, probably for strategic reasons. At this time, we did not know how far they were nor how fast they were moving, but we knew they were on their way.

My documents did not have to be delivered until the afternoon. That gave me the chance to have lunch with everybody else at the Bonars who had invited us to the villa for the day. Brussels being a large city, I would have to cycle many miles to reach all the members; my father therefore offered to share the task with me, when he would cover the North half of the town and I the South. We set out on our bicycles for the villa, while Maman went by tram, and we rather gobbled up our food, so keen were we to go on our mission.

The ride back into town was pleasant enough, in the sunshine, and not a sign of traffic on the road. After a while, something rather extraordinary caught our eyes: all the road signs on that main road into Brussels had been turned round to face in the wrong direction. Undoubtedly the work of the Resistance and a sure sign that the battle was imminent. We pedalled faster.

When we reached our house, we could see clouds of black smoke in the distance. My father picked up his parcel of documents and armbands and was off in a tick, but it took me a little longer to conceal my own things inside my clothes. I heard an explosion in the distance and opened the window to survey the street scene from the balcony. The cloud of smoke was now thicker and blacker and appeared to emanate from the Boulevard du Midi, the very direction in which I had to go. When another explosion resounded in the air, and I saw down below two men carrying someone looking very dead on a stretcher, my martial enthusiasm suddenly vanished. How could I find the will to leave the security of my house for what, from here, appeared like a battle-ground? Trying to reason with myself did not help much until my eyes met the cupboard where my parents kept the drinks. I poured myself a large glass of rum, which a few moments later, began to have the desired effect. Fortunately the warm feeling of insouciance that engulfed me did not blur my memory to the point of forgetting what I had to do!

Cycling towards the cloud of smoke was no more a problem. 'The town must be on fire' I said to myself, rather unperturbed. The Boulevard du Midi, source of the offending smoke, was an amazing sight: a number of German tanks, aligned one behind the other on the central reservation had been set on fire and were smouldering or still burning. The acrid smoke and the fumes from the fuel made the air almost unbreathable. A few German soldiers seemed to be in charge of this scene of desolation and pollution from which I sped away in search of a cleaner atmosphere. Had my mind been more alert, I might have wondered why the Germans were destroying their own tanks. Reflecting later about this point, I concluded that they must have run out of fuel or ammunition.

Before turning off this main thoroughfare, I saw a vast building on fire in the distance. The flames that were leaping into the sky could only come from the dome of the Law Courts, a huge edifice that towered above its surroundings. Once I had turned into the tree-lined avenue that led me to my first call, I felt safer and more relaxed. On the way I witnessed a strange scene: a German soldier, grey-haired, bow-legged, a real veteran, was walking in the company of a Belgian tram conductor who helped him carry his luggage! Until now, I had only seen tram crews trying to aggravate the Germans; this act of pity was amazing. Maybe the soldier's young companions had departed, leaving the old man to fend for himself.

Thanks to the rum, I was in a happy frame of mind when I called at the houses of my 'contacts', where we chatted about the things I had just seen and usually concluded that 'it can't be long now'. By late afternoon I had completed my duty, and I set out for home via the Gare du Midi. Several main roads converged on the square outside that station. While crossing one of these roads I became aware of a clamour coming from my left and I perceived a glow of colour in the distance. I did not even have time to interpct this image, for a burst of machine-gun fire erupted from that very direction, causing me to dismount in haste and throw myself flat on the ground. It was followed by a burst from the other direction, and this cross-fire continued for a while as I lay petrified in the middle of the road. Lifting my head a little, I saw that the second salvo had come from some German armour, speeding away in the opposite direction to the clamour and the colour.

How long would I have to stay prostrate on the road, while the battle went on about me? It must have been a matter of seconds, perhaps half a minute, before I succeeded to crawl to the other side of the road, dragging my bike behind me, but it seemed like an eternity. When there was a lull, I stood up, close to a wall, and pedalled away to the safety of the next boulevard.

There I paused, recovering my breath and gathering my thoughts: 'What I have just seen were khaki coloured tanks, British tanks somewhat blurred in the distance; the spots of bright colours on the walls of houses were flags; the clamour was the cheering crowd; and the fugitives in the opposite direction were the decamping Germans!'

I had just lived a magic moment, yet been robbed of its spell by the fear and the danger. Now I had to rush home and break the news to everyone, for the column was not advancing towards my part of town. Propelled by my intense elation, I whizzed home like the wind.

The house was empty for my father had not yet returned from his own expedition. The fright, the excitement, and the rum, had been rather too much for one afternoon; I sat on the stairs, restless, incapable of deciding what to do next. When I became less confused, I ran to the loft to find the flags, but I could not think where we had hidden them. This bout of amnesia lasted a few minutes, until I calmed down and could go straight to the cache.

With the French windows of the dining room wide open, to let in the air of freedom, I hung the flags of France, Belgium, Great Britain, the United States and the Soviet Union to the railings of our balconies. The reaction was immediate: people appeared at their windows, and as far as my voice could carry, I proclaimed the wonderful news, and assured them that I had seen the real thing! Shyly, another set of flags was unfurled, then another, and another, until our end of the street was ablaze with colour. When my father returned, he could not believe his eyes, and when I told him I was the cause of all the decking out, he hoped 'I knew what I was doing'. His expedition had been quite uneventful until he had seen the façade of a house smashed by gunfire; the occupants of the building, guessing that the British army was entering the town, had displayed their flags too early, to the displeasure of a lone German tank on its way out. There had been a brisk trade in flags and dyestuff during the summer, many people had made their own out of old sheets resulting in some peculiar Stars and Stripes or Hammer and Sickles.

The heartening news I had spread was soon confirmed by a rumbling noise and cheering voices coming from an adjacent street. From our balcony, we could see armoured vehicles crossing the road and advancing towards the centre of town. My joy knew no bounds and with my father I hurried to join the crowds that were cheering with unrestrained enthusiasm.

If too much excitement has blurred in my memory the minor events of that day, the moments that made it glorious have remained clear in all their details. I don't recall for example when we first saw my mother walking along the column of army vehicles on her way back from the Bonars. It had been a long march, yet she was smiling broadly, having witnessed the moment of liberation in a less dramatic way than me when the British troops had passed through the rural district where the Bonars lived, attracting a spontaneous crowd along their route. She had been reminded later that it was war, not just a military parade, when some German motorcyclists had run straight into the advancing column, fooled by the reversed road-signs. Nor do I recall where my parents were later that night, maybe with our neighbours, the Denans, whose daughter Armande still cherished the vain hope of her husband's return.

What I do remember is the smell of petrol and hot metal, a smell sweeter than any I had experienced before, and the first soldier I addressed in English. He was standing on a passing tank, and when I called to him, he jumped down onto the road and we hugged each other like long lost friends.

'Here is my last one' he said, as he pulled a button from his greatcoat and presented it to me[1]. In their triumphal advance, the soldiers had been stripped of their badges by delirious crowds. He was amazed at my fluent English when I told him what the moment meant for me and for all of us cheering in this street. But he had to hurry back to his tank.

When vehicles stopped an instant, I talked to their passengers, still wondering if all this was really true. There were these strange looking 'cars', that reminded me of model T Fords I had seen in Laurel and Hardy films, and I later learnt were called 'jeeps'. As they were completely open, it was easy to speak to the occupants.

Sometime after dusk, the column came to a halt, a wonderful excuse for the bystanders to surround the soldiers and express their gratitude. People in my proximity soon realized that I could speak English and wanted to use me as an interpreter:

'Tell him that my husband is a prisoner of war in Germany; tell him that my son is in the Resistance; tell him ... tell him ... '

The soldiers of the Guards' Brigade who had liberated Brussels responded cheerfully to the demonstrations of friendship, but they had paused in order to take a rest. Since crossing the Seine, they had only had a few hours' sleep and they were very tired men indeed. 'Arthur' with whom I was in conversations asked me to be their spokesman:

'Explain to the people that it is wonderful to be honoured like this, but the chaps must have some sleep, for the battle is not over.'

My listeners responded immediately. Everybody became quiet and the tank crew shut itself inside; it was Arthur's turn to be on guard so we went on chatting in a low voice. The tank struck me as a very uncomfortable place in which to sleep.

I would have liked to show my gratitude to the 'tommies' by showering them with presents, but what does one give a fighting soldier? After rushing home for a few minutes, I returned with my father's cigars and bottles of wine from

---

[1] I still have it!

the cellar which I gave to Arthur to share with the rest of the tank crew. It was for me a thrilling experience to discover that after years of occupation, I could still converse in English with ease.

Eventually the column received orders to move on and my conversation had to come to an end. The sleeping soldiers were woken up and came out to stretch their legs; I kissed them all good-bye, but Arthur demanded more than a sisterly hug.

I saw them leave with a heavy heart. Others would follow, but these had been the first amongst our liberators, the front-line men who were going on to fight the hated Nazi enemy.

My parents were back at home and, tired as we were, we recounted our adventures of the day. I pointed out to my father, that although the FFI unit did not accept girls in its ranks, I was probably the only person in the group who had seen fire today. The short bursts of firing that had gone on above my head must have been all there was to the battle of Brussels. No siege, no fighting in our streets, just a sudden change over from tyranny to freedom.

51

. . . And the Days That Followed

Waking and remembering was an experience unequalled in my life. My father had already left to take up his new duties, for the 'Group L' (named after its leader) of the *Forces Françaises de l'Interieur*, attached to the Belgian Secret Army, was now temporarily in charge of French affairs in Belgium. A vacuum had to be filled between the restoration of normal government, with its international relations, and the past years of ruthless military rule. Fortunately, behind the scenes, all had been made ready for this very day and for ensuring a smooth take over that would avert chaos, always a possibility with such a swift change in the situation.

The group had no more need of a girl messenger. With my turn of duty completed, I could thus wallow in the euphoria that had taken over the town.

An old school friend called and we embraced as everybody seemed to do when they met acquaintances that day. We went along to share in the joy of the multitude. Everything seemed to be happening in the town centre, on the main arteries, where one met people one knew with cheerful, laughing faces.

It must be said that the scene in the streets of Brussels was not one of unmitigated glory. Only a few houses down my street we had come upon a neat bonfire on the pavement, a smouldering pile of furniture, ornaments and household objects that appeared to have been flung out of a first floor balcony where the windows were still wide open – the first of several ignited heaps we would meet in our wanderings. Everywhere the same pattern under a wide open window; although the burning items were sometimes good or valuable there was no sign of looting, just a 'rough justice' against collaborators that had been swift, premeditated and organized.

I felt neither compassion nor revengefulness. My thoughts were on another plane, still trying to adjust to the overnight change in our lives. We met my camping friends and went on roaming with them in the streets teeming with people, where army lorries rumbled by every few minutes, where we saw tanks of terrific size give rides to members of the public, dispatch riders, soldiers on duty directing convoys, a procession of armoured cars, all things that were beautiful to our liberated eyes.

Never had I led such a disorganized life as I did during the few days that followed the liberation of Brussels. I went on wandering in the exuberant town with one friend or another, with my mother, or in a group, staying the night on some friend's floor, or bringing people to sleep in my house. We did not bother much about food, which was just as well, as my mother had failed to stock up in time; in the end all she had been able to acquire was some kind of smoked tongue, which was as hard as wood and practically impossible to slice, yet it had to satisfy our appetite for a few days.

Soon rations were restored, and *smokkeleers* back in force, while a certain section of the population did well for itself by pillaging the foodstores of the German Army that had been left unattended. The Germans certainly had plenty of provisions and men were seen carrying tremendous loads, perhaps a side of beef or a pig's carcass on their backs.

The joy of being liberated had been intense, yet it reached new heights when in the afternoon of the 4th of September, I spotted a tall silhouette I knew well amongst the cheering crowds: that of Jacques Bailly, blissfully looking at some passing tanks. He looked well, if somewhat slimmer, and I ran to him at the same time as I called to my mother who was only a few yards away. After the first moments of emotion that followed that fortuitous meeting, we heard the extraordinary story of Jacques' release from captivity.

When the Germans decided to evacuate Brussels, they planned to take their prisoners with them. They therefore drove them from the jails to a waiting train bound for Germany, a train that had come from France already loaded with French captives.

That was in the evening of the 2nd of September, when there was evidence that a British column was advancing on Brussels. The Belgian driver and his fireman suddenly found that the locomotive was giving trouble: it failed to gain speed, it kept on stopping and by midday on the 3rd of September it had only reached the town of Malines, a few miles from Brussels. That was when the miracle happened. Those in charge of the prisoners and the other Germans in the train, no doubt aware that the British were on their heels suddenly abandoned the train to its fate and decided to find their own way home. As if by magic, the engine was cured of its troubles and raced back to Brussels where the prisoners found themselves free and at large in a town practically empty of German troops. Jacques had just walked home! The next day he came to our house to celebrate with Esther and Esther's mother – who now understood why her son-in-law had been arrested and Esther had been in hiding! The young wireless operator had been in the same train and freed with the rest of the prisoners, we were relieved to hear. He needed a few days to rest and recover because he had been tortured by the Gestapo, but the Baillys assured us that he would be all right, being the tough fellow that he was, and they promised to arrange a reunion with him in the near future. Jacques had not been ill-treated as his captors were not the Gestapo itself. In fact the rivalry between the different German forces of repression had probably saved us from being discovered; when one considers that my parents' name and address was in Jacques' diary, and that the Gestapo had named our street to Louis as a location for one of his transmissions, we were lucky that the two organizations were not on speaking terms and did not put two and two together. It seemed clear now that the lorry spotted from the dining-room window by my father on the day of the transmission had been a detection vehicle. But that was all in the sombre past!

Now the French prisoners who had been freed in the famous 'last train' became the responsibility of the FFI group and my father had the task of caring for their welfare and seeing to their repatriation. There was no want of support from the members of the French colony for their unfortunate compatriots, the most lavish coming from a man who had been a great admirer of Vichy in the early days of the occupation, but had changed his views with the changing fortunes of the war, and was now displaying the biggest flags in his road.

On the Tuesday evening, a restaurant was found that could improvise a dinner in the heroes' honour – for they were heroes, gallant fighters in the Resistance, who for the most part had been condemned to death and were awaiting execution.

The host brought his family, and my mother and I were also invited. It was a moving experience to spend an evening amongst these reprieved men, who only two days before had been living their darkest hours: a catholic priest who had been at the head of an underground network, a leader in the communist Resistance, undercover agents who had signed-on as workers on the sites of the V2 launching pads, men from different parts of France, walks of life and political persuasions, who for the moment at least were united Frenchmen, having suffered the same fate in fighting for the same cause.

So much was happening in the aftermath of Brussels' liberation, so much that was happy. I was enjoying the daily experience of chatting with members of the passing British forces, the enthusiasm of the people did not dwindle, and the soldiers were visibly thrilled by their welcome, knowing they had not been fighting in vain.

For weeks we had been unable to write to my brothers in Switzerland but now that there was hope of normality returning to the life of the town, my mother composed the first letter in freedom to the sons she was missing so much describing in her lucid style the moments we had just lived:

Mes chéris,   *Le 8 Septembre 1944*

> *Comment vous décrire les heures inoubliables que nous avons vécues depuis dimanche soir. Les mots sont impuissants à exprimer la joie, la folie qui souleva la foule lorsque les premiers tanks anglais entrèrent dans la ville. Et cela*

presque sans combat. Les allemands qui, depuis le mercredi, fuyaient en colonnes serrées nous faisaient pressentir que notre libération était proche. Mais on aurait jamais osé espérer une libération aussi rapide. Les trams ont marché jusqu'a midi, rien n'a manqué. L'eau, l'électricité n'ont pas été coupés, les ponts n'ont pas eu le temps de sautger et tout s'est fait pour Bruxelles même avec un minimum de victimes.

Maintenant, après plusieurs jours de fête dont les anglais se rapelleront nous revenons à la réalité. La guerre n'est pas finie et il faudra peut-être encore souffrir, mais c'est avec le sourire que nous le ferons.

Papa est parti depuis jeudi a Paris pour conduire des voitures de français qui avaient été condamnés à mort et qui ont été libérés dimanche à midi. C'est un convoi qui n'a pas eu le temps de partir pour l'Allemagne, grâce au mécanicien du train qui a mis 16 heures pour aller jusqu' à Malines (et seulement 3/4 d'heure pour revenir sur Bruxelles). Jacques Bailly faisait partie de ce train et de ce fait a été libéré avec ses camarades. Quelle joie nous avons eu de le revoir et de l'avoir à dîner avec sa femme at sa belle-mère mardi. Pour lui comme pour tant d'autres, la libération de Bruxelles leur aura sauvé la vie.

J'ignore si cette lettre parviendra vite car le courrier est toujours arrêté, mais on l'accepte, c'est dèjà quelque chose. Dès que cela reprendra, je vous écrirai plus longuement.

Je vous embrasse mes chéris, bien tendrement, ainsi que Gisèle. J'espère que Papa rentrera au début de la semaine. A bientôt.

Votre Maman.

Note

In the following translation 'les anglais' is rendered by 'the British'. The continental people tend to refer to them as 'les anglais'.

My darlings,
How can I describe the unforgettable hours we have lived through since Sunday night? Words are inadequate to express the joy, the ecstasy which

seized the crowd when the first British tanks entered the town. And that almost without a fight. The Germans who, since Wednesday, had been retreating in close order, made us sense that our liberation was approaching. But we would never have dared to hope for such a rapid deliverance. The trams ran until midday, there were no shortages. Neither water nor electricity were turned off, the bridges were not destroyed and Brussels itself suffered a minimum of casualties.

Now, after several days of rejoicing which the British will never forget, we are returning to reality. The war is not over and we may yet have to suffer, but we shall do so with a smile.

Papa left for Paris on Thursday with a convoy of cars taking home some Frenchmen who had been condemned to death and were liberated Sunday at midday. They had been on a train that was never to reach Germany, thanks to the driver, who took sixteen hours to get to Malines (and only three quarters of an hour to return to Brussels). Jacques Bailly was himself on that train and was thereby freed with his companions. How happy we were to see him again and to invite him to dinner on Tuesday with his wife and mother in law. For him, as for many others, it was the liberation of Brussels that saved his life.

I cannot say whether this letter will reach you soon, for the mail is still at a standstill, but it is accepted by the post office, which is at least something. When it is resumed, I shall write you a longer letter.

With much love my darlings and also from Gisèle. I am hoping that Papa will be back at the beginning of next week.

See you again soon.

Your mother.

PART THREE

... AND BEYOND

52

The Town and the Tommies

The people's elation did not wane. It was like a new era, this transformation in the scene. At last the moment had come that we had longed for yet wondered if it would ever materialize, but I had not imagined it like that. There were always joyous crowds in the streets and the barriers between people seemed to have evaporated: between young and old, between rich and poor. Those who had wished for an allied victory – and they were the great majority – really loved each other at that time. If only the world could always have been like that!

I went to church with my parents on the first liberated Sunday. The sermon was an expression of the beatitude that overwhelmed the town; it ran something like this: 'Now my Brethren, you know the difference between Hell and Heaven! Only yesterday, demons dressed in green roamed our streets and today they have been replaced by those angels in khaki, bearers of our freedom and our new hopes . . . '

We bought our first edition of *Le Soir* published in freedom. It was clear that the Germans were still at our door and far from being beaten. But as far as the population of Brussels was concerned, they might have been on another planet. We listened to the news every day but we were no more glued to our sets as we had been in the dark days of the occupation. And we were too engrossed in the tumultuous rejoicing to spend time pin-pointing the position of armies on a map. For a while it required a mental effort to remember that the war was still on. It was difficult to imagine that the non-stop armour, the lorry loads of soldiers arriving and departing from Brussels were about to be engaged in the fierce battle still raging around Antwerp and the Scheld. For the population these vehicles were an omen of returning peace and freedom. One did not see them as objects of war.

In the main arteries the people cheered and talked to the soldiers who were as bemused by their welcome as we were by our lightning liberation.

The huge tanks were teeming with civilians who had clambered onto them but there was not much the soldiers could do to resist this assault from a loving crowd. Soon fatal accidents were reported in our now liberated press. Because I was able to communicate in English, I was favoured with rides in a variety of military transport. I sometimes landed in a remote part of the town, which meant a long walk back but the chat with my liberators had been worth the exertion.

My father had been involved from the first day in the affairs of the French community. He acted as a kind of temporary *chargé d'affaires*, dealing with the tasks that had been envisaged when the group was still an underground organization. He carried out his functions with total enthusiasm and dedication, but my role as a messenger was over. Since girls were not allowed in the unit, I had never been an official member.

The first duty of the French Group had been the welfare and repatriation of their compatriots condemned to death by the Germans and freed in the notorious 'Last Train'. Painstakingly a fleet of cars was assembled and my father led the convoy on the road to Paris. I know that the chance to drive a motor car again delighted him.

While he was away on his mission which took several days, my mother and I got together with the wife and daughter of another FFI member, also in Paris. We knew each other well because the girl was one of my friends from the camping adventure and we decided it was time to approach some of our liberators in order to invite them to tea.

The weather was nice, so in the evening we made our way to a crowded boulevard, two mothers and two daughters in search of some boys in uniform. In spite of the relaxed, unrestricted mood brought about by the liberation, one had to show some tact and also some judgement in the matter. There was no lack of servicemen strolling up the boulevard, how should we approach them? We passed many before making up our mind.

'What about him? No this one looks nicer.'

In the end we asked two young RAF boys if we could invite them for a drink. Their response was utterly cautious. You could see hesitation, even mistrust on their faces; they must have been told to beware of continental women!

It took an enthusiastic speech about the liberation to persuade them that we were harmless and to agree to sit with us at a café terrace. We clinked glasses with the milkman from Newcastle and the baker boy from London and asked them questions about themselves and their families. We arranged a tea-party at our house for the very next day, for they might not stay long in Brussels. We were not even sure they would turn up, but they did, complete with sten guns and gifts for us all: soap, tins of corned beef, tea, all very welcome. Our own tea was very stale, obtained a long time before in the black market, and would have been hardly adequate to receive our first British guests. We had concocted a cake, produced some sandwiches and it was a very jolly party. My understanding of the Geordie and the Cockney was limited but Bill and Ken made an effort to speak slowly. We gathered that they were engaged in guarding aerodromes and their unit soon moved away as the forces advanced. But they had our address and we would see them again whenever they were on short leave in Brussels.

Brussels was becoming a British town. Inscriptions in English appeared everywhere; orchestras in public places, organs in cinemas, played interminably 'It's a long way to Tipperary . . . ', and would strike up 'God save the King' at the end of a performance when all present would jump to their feet. Most entertainments finished with a flurry of national anthems from allied countries, some of which we were hearing for the first time. Numerous families strove to strike a friendship with individual members of the forces and welcomed them into their homes. 'The Tommies' could do no wrong.

Even Marie, our home help, enthused about the newcomers. Disenchanted with all men since her divorce, she had listened absent-minded to my forecast of a changed world once we were liberated. She did not really believe me when I insisted that it would not be another occupation, that the allied armies would free us, that they came from decent democratic nations and that it would in no way resemble the German oppression. Marie had listened politely but I could see she was not convinced. I was therefore delightfully surprised when I saw her again a couple of days after the liberation and she declared with great enthusiasm:

'Oh Mademoiselle, you were so right, they are wonderful! And friendly, and so polite. I got a ride on the back of a motorbike and I went all around town. Then I had a drink with one who wants to see me again.'

I had no doubt that Marie's discreet beauty, her ability to look smart in the most ordinary clothes, was to the taste of the English boys. Subsequently I became her translator for she received much mail from admirers.

It is of course natural that a liberating army, eagerly acclaimed by the town, should be more fun for the girls than for the boys. When the president of our tennis club who was a great anglophile let it be known that he was organizing a liberation dance, the theme was: 'Chacun amène son Anglais.'

It was not difficult to oblige, the town was swarming with them. On the Saturday of the dance, the little club house was bulging with boys in uniform, as well as members, everybody was doing the hokey-cokey, and as it was the first time the members had met again, there was great rejoicing. Not for everyone though. A small group was sitting gloomily in the dark on a bench near the entrance. Curious to see who they were, I found the older schoolboys who had been our male company during the last phase of the occupation when young men had been a rare commodity.

'What's the matter with you sitting miserably in the dark when everybody else is enjoying themselves?'

The boy who had helped me record the number plates of the Gestapo cars fleeing from Paris answered, dispirited,

'*C'est gai tu sais, la libération!*' Nobody was taking any notice of them now. The girls only had eyes for the chaps in uniform.

Our firm had remained closed for several days, until some kind of normality returned to the town. It was very quiet when we reopened and my father was dividing his time between the office and his other duties. Our chemist had emerged from hiding and returned to claim his job; there would hardly be enough work for both of us in the circumstances and that gave me the chance to accept, with my father's blessing, a voluntary job which required some knowledge of English.

Our friend, Esther Bailly, was now free from her war service and she had joined the Belgian Red Cross who, in connection with the British WVS, was launching a service that would further the welfare of the forces stationed in the capital. I could work there until I was needed again in the firm.

One objective was to encourage meetings between servicemen and local families willing to invite them, and later a gift shop was opened that offered a variety of things obtainable in Belgium. At first I was employed as a kind of filing clerk, making notes on index cards about people offering hospitality to soldiers, and others seeking employment with the British Army. On one of the index cards, I found the particulars of my first English master who was hoping for a job. He was quite old now, but I was very pleased to see his name because he was a Jew, one the Germans had not caught. Of course nothing ever happened to the job seekers, the organization was not really appropriate to arrange employment; but many servicemen on short leaves found places with families.

One late afternoon, I was about to go home, a colleague came to me from the adjacent office looking embarrassed, and said that two soldiers had just come to her desk seeking a family to contact –

'But the way they look! I dare not send them to anyone. You would not take them, would you?'

I took one look at them and whispered a categorical NO in her ear. It was not only their appearance, scruffy uniforms, unshaven, dirty, but if in those days I still believed that there was a 'criminal type', they fitted it perfectly.

I must go home. After all, it was her problem, they had

come to her desk.

When I arrived at home, I found my mother a little flustered because some lady from the 'Welfare' had telephoned, asking her to take two soldiers for a few days' leave.

'It is a bit difficult at such short notice,' said my mother, 'I am rather short of food, but I did not have the heart to refuse. They should be here in a quarter of an hour.'

'My goodness,' I exclaimed, 'you don't know what you have let yourself in for!'

I thought my colleague had a nerve, after I told her I did not want them.

I gave a succinct description of the two men in khaki I had had a glance at, and we wondered how we would occupy them for several days, let alone feed them. My father was in Paris again, which did not help matters. We decided we had enough ingredients to make pancakes and were getting them together when the bell rang. Going downstairs, I tried to stir up in me all the anglophilia I could muster, then I opened the front door.

'Hello,' said two pleasant fellows in RAF uniforms, 'we are Ron and Andy. The Welfare Centre said you would take us for a few days' leave.'

Two nice boys, well mannered. I was dumbfounded and repentant; I rushed them upstairs and managed to whisper to my mother, 'They are not the ones', before I introduced them. We immediately got on well together and after showing them their room, we chatted in the kitchen while my mother was making the pancakes. I had forgotten the English for pancake and said 'We are having frying pans for tea,' which prompted immediate laughter and my mistake was corrected.

My father returned from Paris and approved of Ron and Andy. It was difficult for my parents to communicate with the servicemen we received in our house; most had an elementary education and my parents' English was basic and rusty; I had to do an awful lot of translating. Ron was a Londoner, a tall, fair, good looking boy with a cockney accent, who did some amateur boxing and was able to talk a bit about sport with my father. Andy, a sombre looking, dark-haired Scot would forever tell us tales and legends from his native country. They loved being with us and would come back on further short leaves.

The boys who were fighting to liberate Europe found the doors of Brussels opened to them. They were welcomed in all sorts of households, some of a background and lifestyle completely different to their own. And in these early days, there were comments about the social attitudes 'totally different to England.' There were remarks like: 'Now, at home, people like you would not take people like us to that smart patisserie for a treat!'

Perhaps some of these young boys did not grasp what they meant to us, the uniqueness of a moment never lived before, ever to be repeated. Things were just the same here, but not in the days that followed the liberation.

At the 'Welfare' my duty changed. From a filing clerk, I became a sales girl in the gift shop. The universal demand was for silk stockings, which I realized must have been in short supply in Britain. We, the girls at the counters, were puzzled by the expression 'fully fashioned', which recurred with every enquiry about the stockings. Eventually the technicality was explained to us and voices were heard at the counters, repeatedly stating: 'ALL Belgian stockings are fully fashioned' – there is not even a word in French to say it. All the time I was hoping that the precious stockings would get to the wives and sweethearts for whom they were purchased, for we were only taking orders, addresses and money – the goods were to be dispatched later – and in the actual state of postal communications, it was a bit worrying.

This job involved a lot of chatting with the visitors to the gift shop, enjoyed by both sides. I was once asking a little chap in khaki how he liked being in Brussels and he answered cynically: 'I expect you girls went out with Jerry as you goes out with us!'

What do you say to such an imbecile? I thought of the time it took all my courage to insult the German *Feldwebel* who had sat opposite me in a tram. Maybe these 'angels in khaki' were just humans after all.

53

Not Such A Happy New Year

Six weeks after our liberation, troops were still pouring in; Americans and Canadians as well as British. There was no change in the military situation nor in the euphoric mood. Holland and part of Belgium were still occupied. Those first contingents who had liberated Brussels, whom we had hugged and cheered, where were they now? Perhaps engaged in fierce battles.

After the jackboots and the green, very military uniforms, the khaki battle-dress looked so casual, so unwarlike; these men were civilians in army clothing and there was nothing intimidating about an allied soldier. The worst feature of the German uniform had been the helmet. It made the men look like robots, whilst the tin-hat of the Tommies was a cheerful head-gear. You could see their faces. We were full of admiration for the quality of American uniforms, such high-grade cloth! All offices and buildings previously occupied by Germans were taken over by the newcomers, from where they directed the military operations and organized the logistics, but we were no more occupied. We now had our own legitimate government.

We were about to celebrate my mother's birthday, but the only present she really wanted was the return of her sons. There was no hope of that yet, and they certainly would not be home for Christmas.

Work at the gift shop was not particularly inspiring. It seemed to me a bit of a commercial venture and I made arrangements to return to my own work a few weeks later. But at least it had offered me a chance to practise the English language and to hear it spoken in a variety of accents.

On the eve of my mother's birthday, the 23rd of October, I returned home a bit tired from having been on my feet all day and from my linguistic exertions, to find her on the phone to someone who was inviting me to a party for the evening. The reason was that they had English guests and they wanted me to help with the language.

I hinted to my mother that I was tired and that I had spoken enough English for the day, I would rather not go. But they were insistent and succeeded in persuading my mother that I should join the party where amongst their guests were two English officers. I had no choice but to gobble up my dinner and go.

The Granier family who were inviting me that night, I had only met once, on the 6th of September, when they had organized a dinner for the French prisoners just freed from the notorious 'last train'. They had also brought as guests two members of the liberating army they had welcomed in their home and this is how they knew I could converse in English. I shall never forget that dinner with the men rescued from impending death; at one point the heroic priest in their midst reproached me for talking so much English and neglecting my own compatriots. One of the soldiers was a Canadian student and the other was an Irishman from Dublin. That surprised me since his country was not at war with Germany, yet he told me that a fair number of them were volunteers in the British Forces to join in the fight against Hitler. He gave me a little medallion of the Virgin Mary he had found in the ruins of a church in Caen. The devastation of that beautiful town had been a great shock to him.

The Graniers' house was also in the centre of the town, a few tram stops from us. They lived, as was often the custom in Brussels for people who owned a business, in a flat above their working premises, a building dating from the turn of the century. I was received into a vast room with correspondingly high ceiling, a room full of people, cluttered with furniture that seemed to have the function of dining-room, drawing-room, study, and even spare bedroom all in one. It made me think of a stage where lots of furniture had been arranged to provide sets for the different scenes of a play.

After having been introduced to some of the guests, I was

taken to the two young men in uniform to whom I said a few friendly words in English. They responded with a look of great amazement, they had obviously expected to hear one more girl try her school English with a strong French accent. The young captains, Ian and Peter, told me I was the first person they had met in Brussels who could converse in fluent English. Ian looked the most surprised; then it was his natural look anyway, his blue porcelain eyes seemed to stare in constant astonishment. Peter looked too young to be in his position, he must have grown that moustache to add years to his appearance.

Party games were organized, we drank wine and chatted. The two young officers knew some French, in contrast to the other servicemen we received in our home. In fact Ian's French was good but Peter's was rather like the other guests' English, a few words remembered from school of a language never used and never quite understood.

Ian and Peter wanted to know where I had learnt my English, so I explained how I had stayed in England through my father's rugby connections. They were surprised that the game was played in Belgium at all. They thought one of their fellow officers who captained the unit's team would be interested to meet my father, if they were going to be in Brussels for any length of time. I gave them my father's address before we all rushed to catch the last tram. As we chatted on the way to the tram halt I found out that Ian had been here for several weeks but Peter had only just arrived. He had not even seen the town yet, so I offered to show him the sights when he had some free time.

It was only two days later, while we were having lunch, that the front door bell rang. My mother, leaning over the balcony said:

'Gisèle, c'est un anglais', and suggested that I should answer the door.

The caller was a tall, smart major who asked if he could see my father about arranging some rugby. As we were walking up the stairs, the major who was following me and had introduced himself as Neil erupted into boisterous laugh – ha ha ha! Ha ha ha!

'Something funny?' I asked.

'I think you ought to play in our team, ha ha ha! Ha ha ha!'

A little taken aback by this familiarity, I wondered if he thought I had the figure of a rugby player – I did not think I had. I soon realized that he was just a hearty fellow. When we entered the drawing room he exclaimed with the same exultation about some roses we had given my mother for her birthday. We hurried to finish our lunch and joined him to drink some coffee. His French was sufficient to make himself understood, but on the important points, I acted as interpreter. He would however, address my parents in French in his lovely, noisy, English school boy accent which to us was attractive.

Rugby was discussed and the possibility of a match floated, circumstances permitting. My father was quite excited at the idea. It was ironic that not so long before he had feared an approach from the German Army and the clubs had to be wound up and changed into an 'Ecole Belge de Rugby'. Now, to be invited to play a British military team was indeed an honour.

Before Neil left, my parents invited him to spend an evening with us and asked him to bring the other two officers who had passed on the message to him. It is said that when he saw Ian and Peter in the mess, he boasted:

'I have been invited by the Rey family,' and after a silence, straight-faced, in a despondent voice, he added: 'and you two as well.'

To make the evening more convivial and facilitate the conversation my parents had also invited a couple who were old acquaintances; the wife spoke fluent English, or should I say fluent American, having lived in Detroit as a child. The evening was a fraternizing success between liberators and liberated who had much to learn about each other. Ian impressed us all with his good French whilst Neil's ha ha ha was contagious and in harmony with his 'la plume de ma tante' French. Peter was the quietest, maybe because he found French so difficult. He got teased by the others about his enthusiasm for steam engines and made to relate an adventure that had happened to him the day before.

Whilst others were discovering the city they had just liberated, Peter in his free time tended to haunt railway stations. He would try to enter into conversation with engine drivers until one of them invited him to climb into his locomotive. More than that, he let him drive it! I must explain that Peter was a trainee railway engineer in civilian life and knew about regulators and other gadgets. All the same, this engine was different from the ones at home and when the moment came to slow down and stop, Peter could not find the brake valve nor express himself in French. There was a short moment of panic before the Belgian driver rescued the situation.

Peter had related the story half in French, half in English, aided by the others when he could not find the words. Our American-speaking friend and myself had of course done our share of interpreting. When I saw her next and we recalled the evening, she said to me:

'Did you notice how that Peter never took his eyes off you?'

I had not noticed, too busy being sociable and translating when it was required.

As promised I showed Peter the town of Brussels – minus the stations which he had already seen. After having walked a good deal, I realized that he was limping badly. I thought perhaps he had been wounded, but the cause was a motorcycle accident in Normandy.

Although he was somewhat hesitant to tell me how the accident happened, I eventually found out that he and Neil had had a motorcycle race in an overgrown field near Bayeux. Peter had won the race, but failed to see the large stone in the long grass at the end of the course, with disastrous consequences for his leg. A bad fracture that had kept him in hospital in Bayeux, whilst his comrades had travelled to Brussels immediately after it was liberated and shared in the tumultuous atmosphere.

We resumed the sight-seeing at a later date; we did not walk so much, took trams, and I even found myself having to ask technical questions to the drivers about their vehicles, then translating the answers. I had never met someone quite like Peter. Taking him round a town was certainly a different experience.

I asked my mother if I could invite him to dinner one evening and quite unexpectedly another guest turned up the same day, the first of the boys I had known during my pre-war holidays in England. I remembered Don very well.

In fact I had first met him in 1936 when his school had visited Brussels and my father and the French master in charge had organized a rugby match between the sixth formers and our club. So we asked him to join us for dinner with his driver Jock and I had fresh news from friends and that corner of London I had known in happier days. I was to see Don whenever he passed through Brussels and other old boys of the school for he wrote home about our reunion, which was mentioned in his local paper with our address. It would bring us a number of visitors, some I had known in England, some I was meeting for the first time.

When I wrote to my brothers, I had so much to tell them, so many happy events to relate, and without fear of the censor. The prevailing theme of their letters was their longing to return home.

Winter was coming and as we were enjoying our new freedom, there seemed to be stalemate at the front. After the excitement of D-Day and the triumphal advance from the beaches to the Siegfried line, the war appeared to have stalled.

Peter now chose to spend all his free time with me and was a constant visitor to our house. At the Graniers, where we were regularly invited, nobody noticed our mutual penchant. We kept it quiet, partly because it was not done to pinch each other's 'Anglais'. I have known friends fall out on this point of etiquette.

I knew that if the front advanced, Peter's headquarters would move with them and the thought upset me. But at that time there was no hint of it.

Actually the news was bad. In mid December we heard that the Germans whom we had presumed were on the run, had launched an offensive and were advancing towards the Meuse. We soon realized that this attack was significant and fear began to mount in the population. Oh, the horrible thought that they might come back! Rumours were rife, they had reached the Meuse! They were taking revenge on the population who had acclaimed the liberating armies! The American sector had collapsed!

One thing that had nothing to do with rumour was the awful weather. A blanket of fog had engulfed the country which prevented air power from operating. We never heard the sound of an aircraft.

I was spending my last days at the 'welfare' before returning to my work in our firm. One of the perks of our job was the right to buy cups of tea and light snacks at the 'Café Blighty', run by the Naafi. There we mixed and chatted with servicemen. They were concerned but their mood was not as pessimistic as ours. Repeatedly we heard:

'Wait until there is a change in the weather and we can send up the air-force, then the situation will change.'

Also a tone of impatience from the British about the Americans:

'Why don't they put Monty in charge?' One day near Christmas, the fog lifted, the sky became clear. A soldier with whom we had been drinking tea left and came in again, urging us to follow him outside.

'Look, a Spitfire,' he said, pointing at the sky, 'everything will be all right now.'

Soon the roaring of aircraft returned above our heads, bringing reassurance to those on the ground.

Someone my father knew, who was perhaps a victim of insidious German propaganda behind the lines, advanced the theory that this was a massive German offensive, backed by many divisions, that would recapture the Meuse bridges, cut off the allied forces from each other and push them back to the sea; it would be Dunkirk all over again, only worse.

We were fortunate to know Peter who had access to the map room in the Headquarters and although for obvious military reasons he could not give us any details, he assured us that the front had stabilized and that we were not in danger. We knew of the heroic stand of the Americans in Bastogne and by Christmas we knew that von Rundsedt's offensive had been stopped.

Many Belgian families were preparing to celebrate their first liberated Christmas with the soldiers they had welcomed in their homes if they were free. There was no chance of the ones we knew turning up on short leave because of the military situation. Only those stationed in Brussels were available, so Ian, Peter and Neil were our guests for the 'réveillon', as well as the Bonars who had been such reliable friends in time of danger. For Neil and

Ian who were married and had children it was not quite a family Christmas; nor for us without the boys. But it was as near as we could make it with a Christmas tree, candles and a nice dinner.

One feast followed another. For our first liberated new year we were invited to spend the réveillon at the Bonars.

Early in the afternoon of the 31st of December, my old friend from the London days, Don, turned up with another artillery officer. They could only stay until the next morning, but we phoned the Bonars, saying we were bringing two more guests and they were delighted. Peter was on duty that night and could not join us.

No more curfews! We could come back in the middle of the night if we wished. At the dinner, I sat between Don and his friend and we chatted happily in English enjoying the good fare and the wine. I became conscious of a distant pounding which seemed to become louder as time went on. I questioned my two companions.

'Yes, guns,' they said. They were firing continuously.

There was another army guest at the table, but he and the other people who knew English were sitting far from us, they could not hear what we were saying. My two table neighbours were talking to each other across me, calmly, knowingly.

'These guns can't be more than thirty miles, maybe forty, from Brussels.'

They both thought so, not conscious of the fear it was causing me. I said to Don:

'What you say is dreadful, it sounds as though they are coming back!'

To make matters worse, he asked if we would hide him if he were caught behind the lines. I lost my appetite. All these cheerful people, chatting, laughing around the table, they had no idea.

At midnight the telephone rang. I knew it was Peter, for he had promised to phone me. We exchanged greetings and regrets at being apart at such a festive time, then I reported the conversation between my two table neighbours. Peter said he too could hear the guns, he did not know what kind or where they were, but he assured me that the Germans were nowhere near Brussels. He had a look at the operational map and insisted that the situation was under control. I passed on his comments to the artillery experts who were reassured but still puzzled by the guns. But we did not worry any more about it and we went on drinking and dancing for part of the night.

We had to walk home because there were no more trams, quite a trot but it did us good. There was no time for Don and his friend to sleep, they would soon have to be off.

While we were having breakfast, the noise of an aircraft engine, just above the roof made us rush to the balcony. There, with our English guests, we witnessed pandemonium in the blue morning sky. German fighters with their black crosses and Spitfires were engaged in an air battle. Several dog-fights were taking place simultaneously, above our heads, and the Germans had the upper hand. Spitfires were falling down in flames, it was heartbreaking to watch.

The air battle above Brussels was intense but of short duration. From the subsequent news bulletins we learnt about this massive attack on Belgian airfields which resulted in great losses for the allied air force. At the time so many amongst the personnel had been feasting with Belgian families; what a time to strike! The guns we had heard through the night must have been anti-aircraft guns defending the airfields around the capital, that's why they sounded so near.

After that New Year's Day scare, we heard no more bad news of a German advance. The inhabitants of Brussels, and elsewhere in Belgium and in Northern France, had lived two weeks of great anxiety. But from then on, even though the front moved only slowly eastwards, they did not envisage the return of the Germans.

54

Happy Moments

In spite of the blue sky and the sunshine, the 15th of March was a cold day. It was fortunate that Don had turned up unexpectedly that afternoon for a couple of days' leave in Brussels for Maman and I could hardly bear the wait. Don was good company and he helped us to forget our impatience. We took him out to tea at the 'Directoire', a smart restaurant on the Grand' Place where we knew one of the musicians in the jazz trio, and where I sometimes went with Peter. I remember hurrying home afterwards because it was so cold.

We had no idea when they would arrive. Trains were running between France and Switzerland and between France and Belgium, but not with the time keeping of pre-war days. Europe was still at war, but the Swiss frontier was opened and it had been a lot easier for my father to obtain the necessary visas to recover his sons than it had been years before to send them to Switzerland. As soon as the situation had appeared stable after the Ardennes counter-attack, documents had been applied for on both sides and the boys had obtained their *visa de retour à domicile*, their *autorisation* to travel through France, without delay.

We arrived home with Don and we were on our way upstairs to the flat when suddenly the bells rang – all the bells, of all the floors. A somewhat dissonant, but joyous jingle that could have but one meaning.

Then they were in the entrance hall, all three of them. Immediately there were embraces mixed with tears of joy, we were going from one to the other, kissing, exclaiming, cherishing the moment of reunion for which we had had so long to wait.

Poor old Don did not know where to put himself, what countenance to have, in the face of this unbridled display of French emotion. Eventually we rescued him from the corner where he was shyly waiting and introduced him to my brothers.

Gilbert was somewhat taller but looked the same; as for Georges, I did not recognize him, he was another person. The young boy we had said goodbye to in 1942 was a man, I was quite upset to find him so changed. But my mother was so happy, it must have been one of the happiest days of her life.

What a wonderful evening. Peter joined us for dinner and met his future brothers in law. They had some idea of each other for in my letters, I had prepared my brothers for this new encounter. And Peter had seen photographs of them – older ones where Georges did not look so different – yet the introductions offered no surprises.

Georges had been learning English with a very good and fluent teacher and he was able to converse in that language, but Gilbert was doing German for the Baccalauréat. However he had made the effort of learning for a few weeks with a self-teaching method and the result was amazing. Now both were equipped for living in a town where the English language was so prevalent.

My parents had insisted that we wait for the return of my brothers to celebrate our engagement. Now hopefully we could fix a date for it, keeping our fingers crossed in case Peter moved to Germany before the projected party. As for dreams of marriage, they would have to wait a long time, until the war was really over and demobilization in sight for Peter.

Now the family was complete again. Although we three children were adults and had grown in our different ways, we were once more enjoying the togetherness we had known in former days, above all in the early part of the war. We never stopped talking for we had so much to tell in spite of the assiduous correspondence we had kept since our parting. One day I would leave for England. Now was the time to enjoy each other's company.

There was the future to be considered. Gilbert, nineteen, went straight back to our former lycée for he was taking his

Bac de Philo in July, having passed the first part in Switzerland. But Georges had never been devoted to studies. At seventeen, he was longing to start an adult life, to work, to earn money. Since the boys were destined to enter the firm, he did not wait and started training straight away, beginning with Gustave in the workshop. That meant I could see him in the day time because I worked in the laboratory and also in the office and at the counter.

France was in the throes of reorganizing its administration and its army, but my brothers had not yet reached the age of military service – surely, when they did, the war would be over. It could not possibly last much longer.

We prepared the list of guests for the engagement party, young friends, friends of my parents, the family where we had met, and Peter proposed to invite several of his fellow officers; Neil could not come because he would be on leave. With my mother I planned a big buffet and on the morning of the great day, friends came to help.

There was however great cause for concern. The main participant, the betrothed himself, had been unexpectedly sent on a mission to London. He was confident that he would return to Brussels in time, but the night before the party, I had no communication from him. At lunch-time on the day, there was still no Peter. Understandably, the war effort was not concerned with our engagement party.

A friend who was helping me and trying to keep me cheerful said:

'Hear that plane? I bet he is in it!'

Whether in that one or another one, he arrived early in the afternoon, when I was beginning to despair. You could nearly hear the relief amongst those present.

Whilst in London Peter had been able to see his parents, and his mother, in spite of the problems of rationing, had made an elaborate cake for our engagement. Unfortunately it had been very hot in the transport plane and when the cake was removed from the box it offered a very sad sight. All the intricate decorations made of icing sugar had melted and it was just not presentable. There was consternation all around because of the wasted effort. A cake brought from England, from Peter's family, still unknown to me, had been such a nice idea. Now, my mother was always one to know how to deal with a disaster. She phoned a well-known *patissier*, explained the sad story and he collected it in no time at all. It was returned in time for the party, decorated in a somewhat different manner to the original intention, but very presentable.

55

Legacy of the Occupation

It had been too good to be true. Six months after I had met Peter at a party where I had gone reluctantly, he was still in Brussels. But we owed our good fortune to a stalemate at the front. It could not last for ever.

Now at last the operations were going well and in a massive assault the allied armies had crossed the Rhine and established many bridgeheads along its course. We had the feeling that the German war-machine would soon collapse.

Without much warning Peter was sent to Germany. His assignment was to test the performance of the new Centurion Tank in field conditions. We had time to say good-bye, but it was the beginning of a long separation, much longer than the time we had had together. From then on, we would only see each other during short leaves or if he could find an excuse for a mission in Brussels. The rest of the HQ was to leave soon afterwards and they gave a farewell party in their mess for the friends who had welcomed them in Brussels.

At last the war in Europe came to an end. On the 7th of May 1945 the German High Command surrendered on all fronts, bringing joy and relief to the nations who had fought the Nazis and those who had been occupied by them. It was wonderful, but it did not compare with the rapture I had experienced at the moment of liberation. That feeling was unique and could never be matched. This was a more tempered joy, the realization that so much suffering was coming to an end.

We had taken our neighbour Armande to the farewell party given by Peter's colleagues. We did our best to include her into our social life, to comfort her in her loneliness and the now certain knowledge that her husband would not return. The liberation had brought her no news and she had lost hope. Her little daughter Nadine had now accepted that she would never see again the father she hardly remembered.

For Armande, there was no sudden shock, the realization had come gradually. Yet she was eager to know what had happened to her husband. In vain she tried the Red Cross and other organizations, but it was not until my first trip to England, in the autumn of 1945 that things got moving. I had been told to contact a certain Canadian gentleman who had an office on the top floor of the Savoy hotel and who made it his business to trace missing combatants. I provided him with the necessary particulars and before the end of the year, Armande received a letter confirming the death of her husband and his brother. It originated from someone who actually helped men escape from Marseille in 1940 and recognized the two Belgian captains from photographs.

A sad story of bad luck and impatience. Eight men, British, Belgian and French, had bought a ten ton fishing boat with an auxiliary engine in the hope of reaching Gibraltar. Soon after they left, the magneto developed trouble and they had to turn back. The fugitives, who included two officers of the British Merchant Marine, were not prepared to wait the few days necessary to repair the magneto and decided to leave with only sails. That is, all but one captain in the Royal Artillery who would not take the risk and lived. Later he confirmed the facts and the names of the men on board. Sadly, two days after the departure of the fishing boat called 'The Resurrection' there was a terrible storm which must have caused her to sink. She was never traced and nothing was ever heard of the members of her crew. For Armande the letter was an epitaph. She felt better for it.

The end of the hostilities also brought news of a grim discovery: the concentration camps. What we read in the press, what we saw on the news reels was beyond belief. We had known about Gestapo torture chambers, about prison camps in our own lands, but the sheer enormity of horrors found in Dachau, Buchenwald, Belsen, Auschwitz, where countless millions died, sent shivers down our spines.

This discovery rekindled the hatred we had felt for our invaders. In this climate it was impossible to feel pity for the sufferings the German nation was now enduring. Not only had they started the war but we held them responsible for these outrages, for following Hitler. Families would now learn that their loved ones who had disappeared had perhaps met their death in a gas chamber.

A few came back. Roger Timmermans, the gendarme and husband of our *couturiére* came back, skin and bones. Yet he had been fortunate enough to be imprisoned for a long time in a civilian jail. Only the last few months had he been in a concentration camp, terrible months. But there was still enough life in him and with his wife's loving care, he would pull through.

As the inmates were slowly being repatriated, it was not unusual to meet in our streets people with emaciated faces walking about in their striped prison suits. They were the survivors, the ones strong enough to enjoy the air of freedom and probably on the first stage of their journey home. Seeing one old man so attired passing near our house, my brother Georges approached him; he turned out to be French from our own region. Georges brought him home. We found it difficult to make conversation with him because he was so incoherent. What we did find out was that he was not an old man, he just looked like one.

The French inmates who were repatriated via Brussels were first given medical attention and a rest at the *Hôpital Français* before leaving for their destinations. With my father I paid a visit to those not strong enough to continue their journey, wondering what I could bring them to cheer them up. But when I saw them, I knew that nothing could cheer them up. Some were lying in their beds, motionless, their eyes void of all feelings; others were sitting, skeletal, in armchairs. They had been so starved, they could not be fed in the normal way; they needed special medical care to restore their digestion. I wondered whether their families would recognise them when they reached home.

With rail communications working more or less normally, my father was able to visit his native village and the town where we had spent the early part of the war. The news and the distressing stories he brought back confirmed that we were lucky to have left when we did and to have dispatched my brothers to Switzerland.

In our life in Brussels we had run some risks but the anonymity of a big town offered protection. In a village or a small provincial town everybody knows everybody else, their activities, their opinions, and one is therefore more vulnerable to denunciation.

Amongst the news my father brought back the saddest for me was the death of my school friend Bobette Duteil. It was so tragic that she survived the death camp only to die soon after her return home.

My brothers too were to learn the fate of some of their ex-school friends at the hands of the Germans, sometimes denounced by a classmate. Worst of all, the Principal of the collège had become an informer. We had always known his pro-Vichy views, but how could a man in his position descend to such depth of baseness? He had been arrested and was now being judged for his crimes.

A list of names found in his possession, the pupils he considered Gaullists, Anglophile, or whatever he saw as subversive, contained the names of my brothers. Fortunately they were well away when the Germans invaded the 'Zone Libre'.

The village where my father's family lived suffered terribly. As everywhere in France, many young men chose to join the Maquis, rather than be used as slave labour by the Germans. For those who were caught, it meant death, brutal reprisals.

The present day visitor to France may wonder at those crosses of Lorraine, bearing a few names and found by the roadside at some isolated spot or on the edge of a forest. They are memorials to young martyrs slaughtered there. For those who were caught by the Germans or their French friends in the *Milice* received no quarter. They were simply regarded as terrorists although many had joined the Maquis to avoid deportation.

It was natural for some people in the local communities to support these young patriots secretly by supplying them with food and in other ways; after all they were their sons, relatives, friends. The Germans knew that and responded with arrests, executions of hostages, even burning a village as a punishment.

My father found his own village counting the cost of several years of occupation and his eldest sister mourning a husband who had been deported and had not returned.

Other people deported with him did not return either: his friend and neighbour the post-master; Alain Dubois with whom I played tennis in 1941 and his father and a number of villagers whose names were unknown to me. The bad news brought back by my father from his first trip down south contained few details. One thing was certain, my uncle died in a gas chamber as did the others.

Years after the event, I spent some time with my cousin Marcelle, his daughter. We had an emotive conversation about the arrest of her father and the bleak days of the occupation. The time that had elapsed had in no way dimmed the vividness of her memories. As she was relating the painful story in its minutest details I knew she was reliving it and that it would be with her for the rest of her life.

In our childhood, my brothers and I used to spend part of the long summer holidays in the village with our paternal grandmother. My cousin Marcelle, (her pet name was Nénette then) was my playmate. I used to go to her house, or she would come with her little brother Pierrot to play with us at our grandmother's house. Our grandmother herself had died in 1940, aware that two of her sons – my father and her last born – had been taken prisoner and that France had capitulated.

She had had a strange premonition in 1939, during the time of the 'phoney' war, when the hostilities had not even started. She had predicted that it would end in a rout far worse than that of 1870. This defeatism I took to be the anguish of an old woman who had two sons on active service. Yet how right she was proved to be. The village, so calm, where few cars ever passed, where nothing ever changed, where nothing ever seemed to happen except in the gossip of the washerwomen at the public *lavoir*, where I played with Nénette during hot summer days, where the only event was the annual fête, lost its peaceful visage during the dark days of the occupation.

My cousin Marcelle and I grew up hundreds of miles apart. Our lives followed different paths; as adults we did not meet often, yet the day she unfolded the story of her father's arrest I recognized in the grown up woman the earnest little girl, serious, dutiful, conscientious in life as she had been in our games.

'The day they came for my father, he had gone to bed early because he was very tired. I can still see him, hurrying downstairs, adjusting his clothes, and having to sit on the last step to do up his shoes.'

Then Marcelle described how they took away her young brother Pierrot, in his pyjamas, and marched him to the village square. Their next job was to go next door to arrest the post-master. As it was a nice light evening he had gone fishing, yet his wife told them where to find him. Hearing that, I expressed my surprise to Marcelle. She said the lady thought they would catch him anyway when he returned home. The truth is that neither my uncle nor his neighbour thought they ran the risk of being arrested or they would probably have acted differently.

After a long time Pierrot returned home, so hysterical they could hardly make sense of what he said. The whole evening he sobbed and shivered. For three quarters of an hour he had been stood against a wall with some young men from the village, faced by what he thought was an execution squad. At fourteen, he was still very much a child, small for his age, and all that time he thought his last moment had come. Whilst the others were taken away in a lorry, he was left there alone, so he ran home to be hugged and comforted by his mother.

The men arrested that night were taken to the jail of the nearest town. Marcelle and her mother cycled the nine kilometres to try and visit their prisoner. Eventually access was granted.

'He had been put in a cell where a man had just been executed. There was blood on the wall, on the floor, everywhere. But my greatest shock was the way he looked. If anybody had told me that a man in his forties could turn into an old man overnight I would not have believed it. But I saw it with my own eyes. He was not the same man as the day before. He was old, he was already finished.'

The visits from the family, the parcels of food, could do nothing for his morale; it had sunk too low. One day my aunt Margot and my cousin Marcelle arrived to be told that the prisoners had been moved to a fortress in Bordeaux. They felt desperate; sixty miles from home at a time when travel was near impossible.

Right through that crisis Marcelle would stand by her mother, be at her side wherever she went. They would go to Bordeaux, they would try to visit her father, leaving Pierrot and his eight year old sister with relations.

It was a hazardous journey.

'A journey I shall never forget,' said Marcelle. They cycled for miles to a station where they could catch a train travelling in the right direction. Railway traffic was repeatedly disrupted by attacks from the resistance. Their train stopped miles short of Bordeaux and could not go any further. In a frantic effort to reach their destination they hired at great cost a gas-fuelled taxi.

My aunt was prepared to go to great lengths to have her husband freed. Near Bordeaux they had some relations whom they knew to be unashamed collaborators and who socialized with Germans, including the commandant of the Fort. She begged these people to arrange an interview with the commandant and it was granted.

'He received us in his palatial office. When we told him my father's name, he looked in some file and laughed. A cynical laugh that went right through me. Oh him, he said, Maquis! And went on laughing. We insisted that my father was a perfectly respectable village trader who had nothing to do with the Maquis, but he dismissed us still laughing.'

Marcelle's father was the village butcher. He certainly was not in the Maquis. Whether he supplied people connected with the resistance, or someone had suspected him of doing so, and denounced him will remain a conjecture since he was never accused of anything; nor were the other people arrested with him. Malicious denunciation remains the likely cause of their fate.

My cousin went on to describe the visiting day at the fortress. The official time was between eight and ten am. Although they went early they found a crowd of relatives of the detainees already waiting at the gate, wives, mothers and children. The Germans imposed a quota of twelve people at a time; there were so many waiting, they could not possibly be cleared by ten o'clock. When the turn of my aunt came a commotion suddenly broke out inside. A German guard who was counting the 'entrants' suddenly discovered that one of the women was carrying a baby – a very small baby – that made thirteen people, that was against the rules. The turmoil was taking time away from the visitors; one woman was forced to leave and to be in the next batch.

Eventually Margot and Marcelle got to a desk where the German in charge told them they would not be allowed to see the prisoner but he accepted the food parcel. Also the one Marcelle was bringing for their neighbour whose wife could not leave home because of her young children. Amongst the visitors my aunt met other women from the village. Their parcels were taken in but it transpired soon after that their men had already been shot at the time.

My aunt and my cousin returned home. After that there never was any more news.

When they arrived back at the village the place was teeming with heavily armed soldiers and armoured vehicles. The inhabitants were soon to learn what was at stake. A feeling of panic and terror overwhelmed them when they were told that the village was going to be set on fire and razed to the ground.

For hours they waited in fear while the mayor, who was also a doctor, tried to negotiate a reprieve. As a doctor, he had given medical attention to one of the Germans and apparently saved his life. As he pleaded, the oppressors took that into consideration. He persuaded them to leave without carrying out the order.

One village, twelve miles away, was not so lucky. On the grounds that it was helping the local resistance, all the houses were burnt down and the young men found in the village were shot. That is all the houses but one, for on the piano of that house was found the score of a Beethoven sonata. A piece of Teutonic sentimentality not really appreciated by the poor villagers who were rounded up and forced to watch their homes go up in flames.

The war ended. People found out about the camps.

I had always thought Marcelle's father had died in Dachau. She told me that he was there for a time but later transferred to Mathausen, a place even more hellish; he was sent to the gas chamber, then to the gas oven. The news had come gradually via the Red Cross. One man from the region who had been with Marcelle's father came back alive, only just. He was able to say a few words about him, mainly that he was so dispirited, he had given up the will to live. But they did not let Marcelle talk to this man who died a few days later; his cadaverous, lice infested body was not a sight for a young lady, it would be better if she did not have that image of her father in his last moments.

There is a little postscript to this sad story. Before the war our firm had the franchise of high quality dental alloys manufactured by a well known bullion concern in Frankfurt. Some of their representatives who knew my father were in uniform during the war and called to pay a courtesy visit to our firm where they got a very cold reception from the personnel. My father had not yet returned to Brussels at the time.

In May 1946 a card arrived from a certain 'Sonderführer L.' prisoner of war somewhere in central France, identifying himself as an ex-representative from the firm in Frankfurt. Remembering that my father had relations in the country in the south of France he asked with elaborate politeness '*Auriez-vous l' extrême obligeance*' to ask them to send him parcels of unrationed food!

My father's reply was short and to the point.

'The only person amongst my relations who would have been able to fulfil your request ended up in the gas oven of the terrible camp of Dachau in February 1945.'

A silence of several months. Then a long letter from the Sonderführer in impeccable French:

' . . . your letter which made me so sad! I have been profoundly moved by the fate your relative had to endure. But I cannot understand why you did not get in touch with me or someone else in the firm at the time of the arrest, so that we could intervene with the German authorities . . . '
Was it delusion, humbug, remorse, naivety, to suggest that the German authorities would concern themselves with the fate of a French village yokel in one of Himmler's death camps?

56

The Railway Bride

The news from Peter was that his tank trials were very successful and all was going well. For his personal transport he had a little Bedford truck on which he had my Christian name painted in large white letters. He sent me a photo. The grave accent on the e was slanting the wrong way.

He would not return to Brussels. His H.Q. was now permanently based somewhere in Germany. For many months to come letters would be our bond.

The liberation, in its wake, had brought me freedom, and more, but my case was not unique. The widespread fraternisation had caused many romances to flourish but some were to prove fragile. In the somewhat artificial mood created by the general euphoria, it was easy to forget the stark realities of life. The British military authorities had quickly organized social clubs where a soldier could bring a civilian guest whom he entertained with refreshments and dancing. The officers' clubs were glamorous, either splendid private houses or smart hotels previously occupied by the Germans. To dine and dance there to the rhythm of a band in uniform was romantic.

My loved one, a realist, had wanted me to know that if he took me back to England life would be very different. Back home he had no job to go to because he had not completed his engineering studies, no money, no home to take me to in the railway town where we would have to reside. Had he painted the sombre picture even blacker, it would have made no difference to me. Why worry about material conditions when there would never be any more Gestapo?

But it is a fact that some of the liberation marriages were to prove short-lived. The young brides who later returned to Belgium could not bear to live with their in-laws, they complained about the food, the shortages in the shops, the dullness of English Sundays.

Peter's letters made me conscious of the devastation of German cities; Hamburg reduced to rubble and ashes – the bombers we had cheered on their eastward flights! Hitler in the end had made us into heartless human beings.

I gathered that Peter now spent his free time in search of steam locomotives, some pulling trains or in depots, some lying destroyed in sidings. He looked for German ones, but also those that had been pillaged from occupied countries. With an old camera I had lent him, he made some spectacular pictures of those shattered machines, twisted masses of iron, wounded monsters, disembowelled, shedding their insides of tubing on distorted track. Some of these photos were later published.

But there was more than letters. There were short visits and also leave that he chose to spend in Brussels during the many months of separation. He took every chance he had of coming to Brussels, either in the little truck that bore my name or on a motorbike. That could be a strenuous journey for perhaps a few hours we could spend together. If it was official leave, he would travel by special leave trains. In the cold winter of 1945, his train had no heating, which made the long journey unpleasant.

On another occasion, all went well when the leave-train was hauled by a German locomotive as far as the frontier. Then a British austerity locomotive took over. Peter realized that the brakes of the coach in which he was travelling were not released; that caused the wheels to slide on the track and sparks to illuminate the countryside in the night.

The train was going too slowly for his taste. In order to put matters right, he alighted at the many stops and pulled a rod under his coach that released the brakes, a frequently repeated operation. An ironic sequel to this story was a military notice on the platform at Gare du Nord in Brussels, saying:

'Hurry off the train and away from the station because it's your own time you are wasting!'

With rumours of demobilisation on the horizon, we could

start to plan our wedding. Peter would have to obtain permission from his commanding officer and my parents decided to sound out the local priest about the feasibility of my marriage to an Anglican.

'You must break the engagement, you must not let your daughter marry a heretic!' was the answer.

And when another bigoted member of the Belgian clergy was told I would not break my engagement and would ask the Anglican church to bless our union if he wouldn't, he said coldly:

'Well, she will be a concubine.'

In the end it was agreed that I would be a concubine and at Peter's next leave we went to speak to the Padre of Brussels' Garrison Church. There would be no problems there.

Brussels was gradually recovering its pre-war visage, commercially active, with few official restrictions, and goods in short supply returning slowly onto the market. My father thought it was time to renew his relations with a firm in England where in pre-war days he used to send his refining work. He would send me as a representative – visa permitting – and I could on the same occasion meet Peter's family. He would try to arrange his leave in England at the same time.

Armed with commercial documents, letters from the firm in Sheffield, and papers to prove my status in our firm, I encountered my first obstacle, the British Consulate. The obstacle was in the shape of a woman sitting at a desk. A woman with straight dark hair, parted in the middle and pulled tight into a bun at the back of her neck, a white, cold face, eyes that looked as though they hated me the moment I sat opposite her. There can't ever have been a smile on that face.

She took my documents, asked me a number of questions, and dismissed me, saying I would hear from her. I had to return several times to see her, answer her questions, answer the same ones as if she was trying to trip me. A kind of Gestapo interrogation without the torture. No doubt because my trip had to do with trade for Britain – I kept quiet about my other reasons – my visa was granted.

The dark haired woman would soon become a legend for

those who applied for visas. When the niece of some friend of ours, engaged to a British serviceman, openly explained that she wanted to go to England to meet her future in-laws, she was told on her next visit that the man was already married! It was a complete lie, but a worthwhile bid to keep these foreign women away from England. It was many months hence, when I was already married and Peter stationed for a few weeks at a new post in Brussels, that she made her biggest blunder.

Instead of me, my brother Georges was going to Sheffield to arrange the next transaction and had to face the same woman who welcomed him with the same cold stare. He was asked why he was going this time instead of his sister.

'Ah,' said Georges, hoping to please her. 'My sister is married, she is married to a British Officer!'

'You will hear from me.'

A few days later my father received an insulting letter from the British Consulate saying that he had lied to His Majesty's Consul, pretending that his daughter was going to England on business when in fact she had gone there to get married. The visa was refused.

This was quite a shock for the anglophile family that we were, and quite a shock for Peter. He showed the letter to his new Commanding Officer who was outraged and went to see the Consul forthwith. Having seen proofs that we were married in Brussels, the Consul was forced to write a letter of apology to my father. Rather a cold letter, from a man who had to swallow his pride.

Going back to the granting of my own visa, it fulfilled my dream, so long denied, of seeing England again. The dream was too much for me as the ferry approached Dover. Seeing again the white cliffs, so close, so majestic, I could not suppress my tears. That was not my country, yet they stirred a multitude of emotions – years of hope, years of fear, sad memories, new happiness.

The ferry went on to dock at Folkestone. Just as the train was due to leave, a silhouette in uniform appeared on the wrong side of the train, climbed up and entered my compartment. Peter! More emotion. And we travelled together to London where his father was waiting for us at Victoria Station.

My arrival at the comfortable flat in Hampstead was eagerly awaited. Mother who had learnt a little French poem to welcome me with forgot the words in the excitement of the moment. Young brother David, only fourteen, smiling and wide-eyed because he had no idea what a French girl looked like, also tried a little sentence in French. The family made me feel at home and introduced me to friends and relations.

I left them to accomplish my mission in Sheffield and on my return I paid a visit to our old friend in London, the schoolmaster whose letter I had kept and reread so many times during the long war years and which had sustained my hope. I found that he had aged and lost some of his vitality. The family where I had been a boarder had moved to another town. But I was taken to the Old Boys Club which had been the centre of my English social life in 1939. The dividing line on the floor of the bar beyond which women were not supposed to go was still there; I had once crossed it unwittingly when I was sixteen and been brought back forthwith to my quarters; such customs were so totally alien to me.

I saw a young man I had known in 1939. His face was damaged, altered; he had difficulty in expressing himself. He had been shot up in a tank, he was shell-shocked. The whole place looked sad, I searched in vain for the atmosphere of my former holidays.

I thought London looked sad, the people seemed exhausted by the war. I was shown the ruins of the city.

The local bank manager was unpleasant when I tried to change money into pounds Sterling with an authorized document. He scrutinised it, accusing foreigners of coming over here to try and take advantage. I found this feeling elsewhere, this exasperation with foreigners who were the cause of all the recent ills. The England I remembered was not like that.

Peter drove me to the town where we were going to live in his Austin 10. Back in London I went on a shopping expedition with his mother and bought presents for my family; then it was time to return. Peter's family would now have to apply for passports in order to come to the wedding which was fixed for the 26th of March.

Sometime before the great day, I travelled to Paris with my mother to buy different accessories for our wedding garments but above all to visit relatives and friends we had not seen for several years. There was a wonderful new train on this line *'le Train–Autorail Rapide'* and the journey was a lot more pleasant than my last trip during the war.

I had a great reunion with Odile and Lucile who were going to be my bridesmaids, but I was particularly pleased to see Marianne again because she was now studying in Paris. We had so much to talk about: the hospital she had helped to run in the Maquis and also the old days at the collège. She would not come to the wedding; she did not see herself in a long dress and social events were not really her thing. Our lives would follow different courses.

My father wanted to give me a great send-off. Weddings were very important family occasions where he was brought up, in the country, and my marrying one of our liberators was worth celebrating. Relatives from his village were invited, close friends, and among them the Bonars and our neighbour Armande. Her daughter Nadine would also be a bridesmaid. We could not put up the people who had come from afar but they joined us the evening before when Odile and Lucile gave a musical entertainment on the grand piano we had hired for the occasion. We had chosen my friend Don as a best man and by chance, an old school friend of Peter, also serving in Germany, was able to come.

My country aunts approved of an Anglican ceremony. 'Anglicans are not protestants, just a separated church'. They were more tolerant than our local priests.

In real French tradition, the wedding took a full day. After the church ceremony, there was a *'vin d'honneur'* for many of our Brussels friends and when they departed, the conventional luncheon just for the family and close friends. Rooms had been hired at the 'Cercle Français' for the occasion and we had found caterers that produced a good meal since restrictions in Brussels were not severe.

There was a quiet moment when my friends from the conservatoire played more music, then, in the evening, there was a dance. One must dance at a French wedding. My young friends and my brothers' friends were invited. The bride with father-in-law and the bridegroom with mother-in-law opened the ball. My brothers were in charge of the gramophone and there was a light buffet. I think my new in-laws, used to the quiet formality of an English wedding, found it a bit overpowering.

So did the bride and bridegroom whom my brother Georges discreetly helped to escape. On the way down the stairs to the car he had arranged for us, he read me a poem he had written about parting from his sister and it made me cry.

Where do you go on honeymoon when everywhere still shows the scars of war and feels its aftermath? The army had given Peter a fortnight. I wanted to spend a few days in Paris to show him my beautiful native city and some friends had suggested Amboise, a lovely small town on the Loire where they had a house. They wrote to the local hotel and asked them to open for us!

We travelled to Paris in the *'Train Autorail Rapide'* that I had praised so much. We soon became conscious that people were looking at us, people who were reading the newspaper *Le Soir*. Now, the president of our Tennis Club was a sports journalist at *Le Soir* and he had sent some photographers who took pictures when we left the church. To my amazement, he had managed to put our photo on the front page. I say to my amazement because we were not well-known people – but as journalists do he had found a caption to have the picture accepted.

Then our wonderful autorail stopped in the middle of nowhere. We waited and waited. Engine noises were heard on a line and I lost my bridegroom of one day who could not contain his curiosity. Then he returned, smiling, to tell me that the pride of the French Railway was being hauled by an old Belgian steam engine. Eventually we stopped at a depot where the defect was corrected and from there onwards we progressed at high speed under our own power.

A few days in Paris. Peter agreed it was a wonderful city. Then another journey by train to our destination, this time in a long train hauled by a powerful electric locomotive.

There were many stops on the way. At each one I was hurried along the train to act as an interpreter between my husband and the driver, although his French was getting better by now. By the time we arrived at Amboise we had got to know Monsieur Poupon. He was so nice and very flattered that the Englishman in uniform showed so much interest in his machine. He let Peter climb up into the cab several times. Strict timing was not quite so important in those days! We exchanged addresses, he was going to send Peter some books on French locomotives.

Amboise was romantic with its ancient chateau perched on a rock above the town, the bridges on the Loire, the old streets. But it was very quiet. The hotel did its best, because food was not easy. We went on a couple of excursions in a gas-fuelled taxi. The uniform of a British officer became a sensation. Everywhere we went we could not help being noticed. Every man whose clothes resembled at all a uniform saluted Peter, the postman, the station master, even the news vendor.

The weather was beautiful for the time of year and we walked in the countryside. In a field half a dozen German prisoners were working under the surveillance of a man with an FFI armband. As he caught sight of us, the French guard blew his whistle, lined up his men on the side of the road and made them salute smartly. Had I seen this scene in a dream when the Nazis were our masters, it would have warmed my heart. Now it made me feel embarrassed.

57

Dénouements

Back in Germany Peter was waiting for his demobilization papers and clearing his desk in anticipation of his return to civilian life – after nearly seven years in the army! How long would we still be apart? – A matter of weeks perhaps, as I was myself applying for the documents that would allow me to join my new husband in England.

Meanwhile an opportunity arose that, although it would prolong Peter's time in the army, would enable us to live in Brussels until the end of August. He had been offered a posting with a unit involved in the repair and overhaul of army vehicles prior to their being sold to the Belgians. The job turned out to be enjoyable and his colleagues an interesting and amiable bunch. It was a happy summer.

The officers were lodged and had their mess in a comfortable house which must once have been a smart private residence, taken over by the Germans during the occupation. But Peter and I had been offered the Bonar's flat as that family always moved to their out of town villa in the summer months.

On occasions, I was invited to lunch at the mess, which was a rather daunting experience as I was the only female amongst a dozen men in uniform, all older, some very much older than me. The Belgian housekeeper, who seemed to have remained attached to the house through its various occupancies, had a grand way of calling *'Ces messieurs sont servis'* when lunch was ready and all made their way in due form to the impeccably laid table in the spacious dining-room. In spite of this ritual, lunch was a very informal affair.

Then there was the occasional cocktail party at the mess,

and, because there were still troops stationed in Brussels, the army organized dances where soldiers happily mixed with people of the town. It was expected of the officers that they should show up on such occasions. And I have a vivid recollection of returning from one of these dances confined to the floor of a rather crowded staff car, wearing an army cap for better camouflage. The reason for my being ferried back to town like a stowaway was an announcement by the band leader than the last tram was due to leave soon and there would be no army transport for civilians.

As Peter and I prepared to leave at that rather early hour in the midst of general enjoyment, a chorus at our table said, 'Not you! we'll give you a lift.'

Ever since the liberation, servicemen had flouted the army rule of not giving rides to civilians in military vehicles. I had often travelled in the back of Peter's van.

The thing was not to be caught. Once Peter had suffered pangs of conscience when he had found himself prosecuting officer in the case of a soldier who had done just that. As providence would have it, a mix-up of the dates ensured that the fellow was acquitted.

In the end my transport problems were eased by a little document given me and signed by Peter's CO to the effect that I was acting as an interpreter for the unit and allowed to travel in W.D. transport – I did on occasions interpret for them. That was the same major who demanded that the British Consul write a letter of apology to my father after the arrogant blunder of the visa woman at the consulate.

These final days in Brussels were indeed a happy ending to the war years for me. But those who had endured deportation or long separations had sometimes found it too difficult to come to terms with the sudden return to freedom and normal life. Some of them could not cope emotionally and their marriages went dreadfully wrong. In our own circle, we witnessed the drama of the Timmermans whom we had always regarded as a devoted couple. After years in a German prison and many months in a concentration camp, Roger Timmermans had not been able to settle down to life at home. He was moody, touchy, bad tempered, and the company of his wife became an irritation to him. That patient wife who had longed for his return, who had suffered the terrible bombings that destroyed the Gendarmerie flats! One day he left her to set up home with a woman of 'easy virtue'.

A tearful Madame Timmermans came to pour her heart out to us. In her anxiety she showed selfless concern for the health of her husband; she thought the woman quite incapable of caring for her Roger, of providing the diet he needed for his recovery.

Sure enough the paramour soon got tired of him and a repentant Roger Timmermans returned, knocking at his wife's door. The prodigal husband was allowed in.

That was months before our wedding. The marriage having been repaired, the couple were present at the reception we gave for our many acquaintances, Roger Timmermans wearing his ceremonial Gendarme uniform and his decorations with pride.

More surprising perhaps was what happened to our friend Armande who for years had borne with fortitude the wait for the return of her husband. Even after the liberation, which brought no news, and it became abundantly clear that neither he nor his brother had ever reached England, she remained the same. Although she had had the certainty from the end of 1944 that he would not return, it was the official news, in black and white, that seemed to act as a trigger for the release of her frustration and her pent up emotions. She was now legally, officially, a widow. Armande was good-looking, sociable, not averse to a man's compliment, yet she had never shown herself flirtatious and it was not the lack of opportunities. She had joined wholeheartedly in the festive mood of the liberation, met some of the liberators at our house or at parties, but formed no attachment.

Now the volte-face in her behaviour, her eagerness to live again, caused the break-up of a marriage. A young couple with a child where the husband, a resistance fighter who had been caught and sent to Buchenwald, was still emotionally unsettled many months after his return. To Armande, the affair proved to be just a passing fancy. She later remarried, someone of her own age, in her own circle; but the young couple remained parted. It was particularly upsetting to my parents because the two families had met in our house. The Timmermans, Armande, were people we knew well but we heard too of other broken relationships, of irrational behaviour, of private lives shattered amongst the survivors of concentration camps or of some other war-time ordeal.

One of my school contemporaries was so changed when I met him again after the end of the hostilities that I found it difficult to believe he was the same person. Jacques had been in my year and was spending a holiday in England at the same time as me in 1939. He had charmed the family who were my hosts with his old fashioned French politeness, his sociability, his humour, when I had invited him there. Now there was nothing left of these personable qualities; he returned from his war in the resistance more like a hunted beast. He had fought in the maquis of the Vercors, lucky to survive, and having witnessed the evidence of the bloody reprisals inflicted by the Germans on those who were caught. He would not talk about old times, just the terrible things he had seen. Not all these young men had suffered such a traumatic experience, but for many the only choice had been to serve the Germans or fight in the Resistance. Before leaving Belgium for good, I met another of my old school friends who had lived and fought in a forest of central France. He was in a maquis run by a famous cavalry regiment which had gone underground after the total occupation of France in 1942. The actions in which he was involved were more like skirmishes compared to the heavy fighting of the Vercors.

'We even took a German prisoner,' he told me. 'But he was so much older than us, we treated him with respect.'

News of the old pupils of our school were now filtering through. Some of the boys, like those just mentioned, had fought in the Maquis. One I knew well had escaped to England and been parachuted into France as a special agent. Alas, one had joined the *Milice* and been killed fighting the Resistance, and another, an Alsatian, had been enrolled in the S.S., willingly, and gone to the Russian front. Such was the tragic division the war had brought amongst young people who until 1940 had been school friends.

After the liberation had come the day of reckoning for

collaborators and traitors. Our friend Carlos Bonar had never forgotten 'Achille van de Put' whose misdeeds were obviously well known because he was already under arrest when Carlos reported him. But he was a witness at his trial. The activities of the Gestapo man had sent people to their death and he, as he had himself predicted when he was handcuffed to Carlos on the day of the raid, finished in front of a firing squad. As for the Gestapo informers we had mistaken for spectators at the rugby match they were also tracked down and proved to be no better than Achille van de Put. I was interested to learn that the black Citroëns fleeing Paris with their sinister occupants, whose numbers I had secretly noted and passed on to our FFI group, had been traced as they sought safety in Germany.

There were inevitably some unfortunate arrests, like the Rumanian lady who had traded in *'Ausweisse'* with the Germans. My father pleaded in her favour, naming a number of people she had helped, albeit for money, which resulted in her acquittal.

Some of the people who had openly collaborated had escaped arrest, but it was now their turn to live in hiding. During a trip to Paris, my father came across such a fugitive, a man dressed no better than a tramp whom he thought he recognized. Indeed he turned out to be a close pre-war friend in the world of sport. Our two families used to see a lot of each other, although my parents did not agree with his politics which tended towards the extreme right. As a fluent speaker of German and admirer of German culture, he saw his chance during the occupation and collaborated wholeheatedly. He had been a portly man before the war; now, he was thin and hungry. He was so pitiful, my father bought him a meal during which, crushed in spirit, he showed himself completely penitent.

When my brother Gilbert, who was now a student in Paris, had a similar encounter, he was not so generous. Recognizing on a metro platform one of his school contemporaries, who, like the principal of their collège had been an informer responsible for deportation and death, he could not contain himself.

'Hello Mahonnier,' he called out at the top of his voice, 'what are you doing here, I thought you had been shot as a traitor!'

As the crowd stared, Mahonnier did not hang about but hurried towards the next exit instead of waiting for his train.

The success of the landings in the summer of 1944 had made it evident that the Allies were winning the war. Frenchmen who had supported the New Order or been sitting on the fence could now see which way the wind was blowing. Just in time some of them became Gaullists and decided to help the winning side by passing on information or in some other useful way. Then they emerged after the liberation, full of confidence, sometimes claiming the same position of influence in the new Provisional Government of the restored Republic as they had held under Vichy. There was much correspondence from the FFI group in Brussels to the authorities in Paris when the administrative posts of their movement were offered to such individuals. Their main contention was that the newly found heroes issued testimonials to their friends and relations as though they had been active in the Resistance. Eventually, in 1946, the head of a famous underground network came to Brussels to sort things out, invalidating and removing the testimonials of people who had not been properly registered in the network under his personal authority. The return of political life, the sudden change after the Nazi occupation, were bound to bring difficulties of this kind in their wake.

I had already been shocked, back in September 1945, when the group of French prisoners, liberated in the famous last train, had returned to Brussels to celebrate the anniversary of their release. My father invited them for an aperitif and they had hardly been in our house a short time when a major political row developed. The men who had been so united and subdued after the Belgian driver saved them from certain death were now engaged in accusations and counter accusations. It seemed to be about the amount of influence their Resistance movements, based on different political organizations, could exert in the newly restored Republic, and about political manoeuvring. As far as de Gaulle and his government were concerned, the Resistance organizations had outlived their usefulness and were being absorbed into the body-politic. It caused bitterness, particularly amongst the Communist Resistants. The argument revolved around that. I was really upset and embarrassed to hear them shout and quarrel in that way, especially as I had an English guest that day to whom I wanted to introduce these men and tell their story. He was an artillery sergeant, an old boy of the London school where I had friends. But the behaviour of my compatriots prompted me to take him to see the sights of Brussels instead.

Yes, things were returning to normal, but the legacy of the war was being felt in so many different ways, not least on the economic front when the Belgian Government had tried to stabilize the currency. Much money had been printed under the Nazi regime and was now floating about, partly in the coffers of the black marketeers. In his endeavour to restore sound finances, the Minister of Finance, M. Gutt, decided to call in the current banknotes and issue new ones on a certain date. Yet the Government acknowledged that the black market had been inevitable in the circumstances of the occupation and people were asked to make an honest estimate of their earnings during those years, after which they would be allowed to retain a sizeable amount in the newly issued currency. But there was panic. In the days that preceded the change over, the shops were literally emptied of consumer goods; fur coats, clothes, works of art, furniture. People would purchase anything in order to get rid of surplus notes. But some colossal fortunes were going to be lost overnight. Suicides were reported in the press. After the turmoil, though, the currency was stabilized.

Now, I was leaving all this behind. As I packed my things, I made sure to take with me souvenirs of an unforgettable time: the famous letter sent from England in 1941, my summons from the *'Werbestelle'*, my pass issued by the Underground on the eve of the liberation, and also a testimonial, a genuine one, given me by the head of the FFI group, certifying that he had recruited me in November 1943. Since girls were not officially allowed in the group, it was nice to be recognized.

Peter had to go back to Germany to be demobbed via Bremerhaven, and in Hull he received his allocation of civilian clothing. His 'demob' suit was of a gaudy blue and a bit shapeless.

My parents and my brothers were on the quayside at Ostend to wave me good-bye. We were all a bit tearful.

At the other end, everybody was allowed off the ship except me and two other young women, emigrating wives, like myself. We had to sit with the purser of the Belgian ferry in a small room for what seemed an eternity. He was very rude too, would not answer our questions, and treated us like naughty school girls. Eventually the word came that all was in order with our documents and we were allowed to step ashore. Peter and his father were waiting for me and we were going to drive to the Welsh border where the family were spending their holiday.

It was a wonderful late summer day. There must have been some festivity in Dover because the town was full of bunting.

'It's for you,' said my father-in-law!

It was more than six years since that day in June 1940 when I thought my world had come to an end.

POSTSCRIPT

In the foreword to this memoir I state that I have preferred to give people fictitious names although the people themselves were real enough. If I do not reveal the identity of the people mentioned, it is because the book is merely an attempt to portray the atmosphere of a period. I do not want to use my recollections to expose people I knew, their conduct or their attitude.

However I have no reason to conceal the real names of friends and acquaintances who helped or supported the struggle against the Nazis. There is no need to conceal the names of those who were their victims, or of people who add interest to the story. To name but a few – the letter in the chapter 'Thoughts of England', from which the book draws its title, was sent to me by Norris Ellison, French master at Rutlish School, Merton Park, London. The real names of my school friends Marianne Delambre and Bobette Duteil in the book are respectively: France Dehorne, who helped to run a hospital in the Maquis, and Poupée Dubreuil who was to die of ill–treatment in a concentration camp.

The Parisian family I call the Mosalskys were the Shlutskys, the daughters names – Odile and Lucile in the story – Josette and Yvette. They adopted their father's christian name as a surname when they went to live in Los Angeles after the war and called themselves Josette and Yvette Roman in their concert activities.

A variety of interesting people resided in the bohemian pension in the latin quarter. The 'young girl with striking black eyes', Juliette Gréco, became a well-known singer and the 'aspiring actress', Hélène Duc, made a name for herself on the stage.

We owe our involvement with wireless transmissions to our Swiss friend Jean Bille and his wife Eleanor Bille de Mot who are the Baillys in the story.

Salvador Ricart was the real name of Carlos Bonar, our friend who was not afraid to shelter my father when he was in danger and who had his own problems with the Gestapo. The French 'FFI' group attached to the Belgian Secret Army of which my father was a member and where I was allowed to act as a messenger was the 'Groupe Lacomme', named after its Commanding Officer, André Lacomme.

Amongst British Servicemen mentioned in the book, Don who appears in the chapter 'Not such a Happy New Year' is my Old Rutlishian Friend Ronnie Holden, and my husband's last C.O. in Brussels who demanded that the British Consul send a letter of apology to my father was Major W.R. Haywood, in civilian life the Chief Engineer of the RAC.

L'Abbé Froidure, a well-known Belgian Churchman – whom I call Father Fraissait – was involved in the welfare of poor children and arrested for his Resistance activities. He also deserves his real name.